Swiss Legal History

René Pahud de Mortanges

Swiss Legal History

PETER LANG

Bibliographic Information published by the Deutsche Nationalbibliothek
The Deutsche Nationalbibliothek lists this publication in the Deutsche Nationalbibliografie; detailed bibliographic data is available online at http://dnb.d-nb.de.

Cover image: © René Pahud de Mortanges

Edited by Eveline Spicher-Bürgy

ISSN 0344-290X
978-3-631-79209-4 (Print)
978-3-631-80779-8 (E-PDF)
978-3-631-80780-4 (EPUB)
978-3-631-80781-1 (MOBI)
DOI 10.3726/b16386

Peter Lang – Berlin · Bern · Bruxelles · New York · Oxford · Warszawa · Wien

This publication has been peer reviewed.

www.peterlang.com

Preface

This book is based on the 2nd edition of the German-language work *"Schweizerische Rechtsgeschichte. Ein Grundriss"* (2017). It aims to give a concise overview of the complex development of law in Switzerland. A common legal history does not really exist until 1798, perhaps even until 1848. Previously, the Swiss Confederation consisted of a conglomerate of around 50 territories with different constitutional systems. The total number of legislative jurisdictions was even greater. Before 1798, when the French invaded Switzerland, each territory, however small, had its own legal system, which consisted of statutes, unwritten customary law and court decisions. The influence of Roman law varied according to region and epoch. It was not until the 19th century that modern laws were passed under foreign influence, first in the cantons and then at the national level. It is therefore hardly possible to present all aspects of legal development before 1789 in one single publication. This book, therefore, lays emphasis on constitutional development, legal sources, court organisation and jurisprudence. It also aims to illustrate their political, economic and social background. A fact-oriented presentation and "conventional" epoch classification were deliberately chosen. Footnotes were omitted, but not a bibliography of the most relevant literature.

Without the help and enthusiasm of others, this book would not have been possible. Andreas Kunz had the idea and created a first English-language translation in an admirably short time and pro bono. That this book exists is primarily due to him. Barnaby Leitz (MLaw) polished the text with a lot of patience and care. Together with Andrea Rotzetter he edited the tables and graphics and obtained the image rights. Dr Kurt Wallat, editor-in-chief of the renowned Peter Lang Verlag, agreed without hesitation to publish the manuscript. Sincere thanks to them all. With their help, it is now possible to retrace in the *lingua franca* of science the legal history of this small country in the heart of Europe.

Contents

List of the most important abbreviations

Switzerland

aBV/aFC	alte Bundesverfassung vom 29. Mai 1874 (*Old Federal Constitution of 29 May 1874*)
AHVG	Bundesgesetz vom 20. Dezember 1946 über die Alters- und Hinterlassenenversicherung (*Swiss Federal Law of 20 December 1946 on Old-age and Survivors' Insurance*)
BV/FC	Bundesverfassung der Schweizerischen Eidgenossenschaft vom 18. April 1999 (*Federal Constitution of the Swiss Confederation of 18 April 1999*)
BVG	Bundesgesetz vom 25. Juni 1982 über die berufliche Alters-, Hinterlassenen und Invalidenvorsorge (*Swiss Federal Law of 25 June 1982 on Occupational Retirement, Survivors' and Disability Pension Plans*)
IVG	Bundesgesetz über die Invalidenversicherung (1959) (*Swiss Federal Law on Invalidity Insurance*)
KUVG	Bundesgesetz über die Kranken- und Unfallversicherung (1914–1918) (*Swiss Federal law on health and accident insurance*)
KVG	Bundesgesetz vom 18. März 1994 über die Krankenversicherung (*Swiss Federal Law of 18 March 1994 on Health Insurance*)
MStGB	Militärstrafgesetz vom 13. Juni 1927 (*Military Penal Code of 13 June 1927*)
OR	Bundesgesetz vom 30. März 1911 betreffend die Ergänzung des Schweizerischen Zivilgesetzbuches, Fünfter Teil: Obligationenrecht (*Swiss Federal Law of 30 March 1911 on the Supplement to the Swiss Civil Code, Part Five: Code of Obligations*)
PGB	Zürcherisches privatrechtliches Gesetzbuch (*Zurich Private Law Code*)
StGB	Schweizerisches Strafgesetzbuch vom 21. Dezember 1937 (*Swiss Penal Code of 21 December 1937*)
USG	Bundesgesetz vom 7. Oktober 1983 über den Umweltschutz (*Swiss Federal Law of 7 October 1983 on the Protection of the Environment*)
ZGB	Schweizerisches Zivilgesetzbuch vom 10. Dezember 1907 (*Swiss Civil Code of 10 December 1907*)

International

ABGB	Allgemeines Bürgerliches Gesetzbuch für Österreich vom 1. Juni 1811 (*General Civil Code for Austria of 1 June 1811*)
ADHGB	Allgemeines Deutsches Handelsgesetzbuch (Draft 1861, in force 1869) (*General German Commercial Code*)
ALR	Allgemeines Landrecht für die Preussischen Staaten vom 5. Februar 1794 (*General Land Law for the Prussian States of 5 February 1794*)
BGB	Bürgerliches Gesetzbuch für das Deutsche Reich vom 18. August 1896 (*Civil Code for the German Empire of 18 August 1896*)
CC	Code civil des français von 1804 (*French Civil Code of 1804*)

Part 1: The Roman and Frankish Period

1 Celts and Romans

1.1 The different tribes

Celts, Rhaetians and Lepontians

Just before the Christian era, the territory of today's Switzerland was integrated into the Roman Empire. It was inhabited at this time by different tribes: the Celts, the Rhaetians, and the Lepontians. The Lepontians settled mostly south of the Alps, in the Ticino and the Rhaetians in the Grisons valleys. The rest of the various Celtic tribes lived in other parts of today's Switzerland: the tribes of the Uberi, the Seduni, the Veragri, and the Nantuates settled in the Valais; on the western tip of Lake Geneva the Allobroges and the Rauraci in the Basel region. The largest Celtic tribe, the Helvetii settled in the Swiss plateau (Mittelland). These Celtic tribes had no common political organisation but lived as largely autonomous communities.

Historical research only has a fragmentary knowledge of these different tribes, especially of the smaller ones. This is mainly related to the lack of records. The Celts, whose culture dates back to the 5th century BC, were not completely illiterate and knew a script. However, they left few written documents and in particular no historiography of their own. Historical knowledge about them originates from historically not quite reliable reports of Roman and Greek authors, as well as from archaeological findings, from inscriptions and linguistic research. In particular, the law of the Celtic tribes is mostly unknown. Only for the Helvetii, some significant statements are possible in this respect, which is why they are focussed on separately.

1.2 The Helvetii

De bello gallico

The main source of historical knowledge about the Helvetii is the work "Commentarii de bello gallico" – Comments on the War in Gaul. It was a kind of accountability report to the Senate in Rome, in which Julius Caesar reported on his successful subjugation of the Celts as a Roman proconsul in the years 58 to 52 BC. Caesar, like other Roman authors, identified the Celts as Gauls. In the first book, he reported on his military campaign against the Helvetii, whose settlements he described as follows: "on the one side is the Rhine river, on the other the Jura heights, and on the third the "Lemannic lake" (today's Lake Geneva) and the Rhone river". He did not mention the southern border, the alpine ridge, which he presumed to be well known. Caesar pointed to the natural boundaries, which much later became political boundaries. Even though the concept of modern Switzerland cannot be applied to the days of Ancient Rome, there was some continuity in the geographic demarcation of the territory.

Reconstruction of the defensive wall of a Helvetian settlement on the Mont Vully in the canton of Freiburg. Photo: Author

Clans

The Helvetii lived in clans, that is, in large family units. The nobles and the druids occupied the leadership functions in these clans. The nobles owed their political influence to their social standing, which was based on the number of subjects and slaves dependent on them. The Helvetii were not egalitarian people, but adhered, like other Celtic tribes, to a sort of aristocracy based on allegiances. The druids performed religious functions but were also involved in public and private dispute settlements. They settled boundary- and inheritance-disputes and passed verdicts on criminals. Their reputation as religious leaders also gave them the authority to decide on legal issues, a phenomenon that can be found in other early cultures.

Oppida

In his work, Caesar reports on the 12 oppida (fortified towns) and the 400 villages of the Helvetii. The oppida were larger settlements, fortified by protective ramparts; they were the political, economic, and religious centres of the clan. The interior area of the oppida was only to a small extent permanently populated, because their real purpose was to enable the population living in the surrounding area to retreat behind these fortifications in times of war. Today only a few oppida can be archaeologically identified beyond doubt; like the ones on the Enge peninsula near Berne, at the loop of the Rhine near Altenburg-Rheinau and on Mount Vully between Lake Morat and Lake Neuchâtel.

The Battle of Bibracte

In 58 BC a large part of the Helvetii decided to leave their settlement area and to move westwards in search for better new livelihoods. It is also possible that their ancestral habitat between the Jura heights and the Alps might have turned out to be too small due to the influx of Germanic tribes. Before their exodus, they destroyed their settlements and part of their supplies. Since Caesar was anxious to prevent this exodus and negotiations failed, the battle of Bibracte (probably near today's Montmort in the French department of Saône-et-Loire) was fought from which the Romans emerged victoriously. Caesar forced the Helvetians to return, whereby today's Swiss Plateau (Mittelland) fell under Roman rule, and in the subsequent period belonged to the province of Gallia in the Roman Empire.

1.3 Political Integration and Romanisation

Province of Gallia

The integration of the territory of today's Switzerland into the larger structure of the Roman Empire had already begun before the Battle of Bibracte. In the second century BC, the regions of the south Ticino and Lake Geneva had been integrated into the province of Gallia. With the establishment of two colonies (Colonia Iulia Equestris near today 's Nyon in 45/44 BC and Augusta Raurica near today's Augst in 44 BC) and with the final conquest of the Alps by Augustus (25 to 13 BC), the integration was completed. In the time around the Birth of Christ, the territory of today's Switzerland was completely under Roman rule.

The territory of today's Switzerland under Roman rule. Picture: Peter Dürrenmatt, Schweizer Geschichte, Vol. 1, 3rd ed., Zurich 1976, p. 31.

Acculturation

Acculturation (social and cultural integration) by the Romans took place during the first three centuries AC, and not only by military means but also in the political and cultural realm. The Celtics along with the immigrating Romans formed the majority of the population and became later the "Gallo-Roman". Increasingly more people lived according to Roman law, were involved in the Roman state and administrative structures, paid homage to the Roman gods, traded with Rome, calculated with the Roman numerical system and spoke beside the Celtic colloquial language also Latin and learned to write. In the countryside, large estates (villae) based on the Roman model were introduced as a new operational way of farming, hitherto unknown crops were cultivated and new livestock bred. So as a new form of settlement, especially in the west of today's Switzerland, the city became more and more important. In historical research, Romanisation is often referred to as a process of urbanisation. However, the intensity of Romanisation needs to be differentiated: It was deeper for urban residents than for rural residents. In many places, the Celtic culture survived not only in religion, art, and architecture but also in names of persons and places. In many realms, the Celtic culture also influenced Roman culture.

The "Stork's Column." Remains of a Roman temple in Avenches. Until 1978, the column served as a nesting site for storks. Photo: Author

Administrative units

In the year 22 AC, Augustus enforced a territorial reform of the Roman province of Gallia, which also affected the territory of today's Switzerland. The Swiss Plateau, where the returned Helvetii had settled, became a part of the province Gallia Belgica. The northern valleys of Grisons and Ticino became part of the province of Rhaetia. The southern valleys were added to the province of Italia. From a Roman point of view, the territory of today's Switzerland was a border and buffer zone, which should protect Rome against the Teutons. Based on this view, military fortifications were erected and retired mercenaries resettled, and the political and cultural integration of the Celtic tribes was accelerated. Representatives of the Celtic nobility were given privileges, administrative tasks, and Roman citizenship. As a territorial administrative unit, the Romans formed civitates instead of the old tribal areas. The civitas of the Helvetii included large parts of the Swiss Plateau. In addition to the existing Roman settlements (Kolonien) and military camps, the main town Aventicum (Avenches) was established as the principal administrative point of contact for Rome. Several smaller urban centres were also set up, such as Eborudurum (Yverdon-Les-Bains) and Aquae Helveticae (Baden). The main town of the civitas Vallensium for the tribes in the Valais became Octodurum (Martigny). The former Roman mercenaries, as well as the Celtic aristocracy, established large estates and farms for the management of land and property.

1.4 Administrative structures and law

The organisation of the civitates

The territory of today's Italy was administered from Rome. In the provinces outside of Italy, the administration, due to the vast distances, was delegated to imperial legates of Rome. The imperial legate of the province Gallia Belgica resided in Trier, far away from the Swiss civitas. As a consequence, he restricted himself to the preservation of Roman domination and providing military security and left the day-to-day administration to the individual civitates.

The main towns of the civitates, as well as the towns founded as Roman colonies, used a political organisation similar to that of the city of Rome. Although there were some differences between one town and another, it followed roughly this form: As in Rome, there existed a senate, which elected the top officials: the Duoviri, the Aediles, and the Quaestors. The two Duoviri acted as city leaders and judges, and so had both administrative and judicial power; they were not only responsible for the townspeople, but also the rural population. The Aediles were entrusted with the maintenance of public order, the Quaestors with the financial administration. This form of political organisation is well documented for the places of western Switzerland, the Swiss Plateau, and the Valais; but details on the situation in today's Eastern Switzerland are less clear.

Citizenship rights

What kind of legal status did inhabitants of the Roman province enjoy? Roman law knew three levels of citizenship rights: Apart from the Peregrines - the non-citizens - there were citizens under Latin law (ius Latii) and then the actual Roman citizens. A citizenship right conferred to the latter apart from being able of political participation, the right to an entirely valid marriage, the right to establish a will, and legal and contractual capacity. Citizens under Latin law were initially excluded from the Roman ius civile. Over time it was also extended to them. Now they had, like Roman citizens, the commercium, and the connubium, and could according to Roman law conclude significant legal transactions and enter into a completely valid marriage. From the point of view of civil law, but not politically, they were equal to Roman citizens.

The members of the conquered Celtic tribes either had the status of Peregrines or were citizens under Latin law. Thereon individual citizens were gradually given full citizenship. First to be admitted, were municipal officials, then members of the Celtic nobility, and later also other groups of the population. With this system of conveying Roman citizenship as a distinction and reward, increasingly larger groups of the population were politically and culturally linked to the Roman Empire. In 212 AD, Emperor Caracalla granted Roman citizenship to all freedmen in the empire. This was, of course, less due to magnanimity than to a lack of financial resources, since citizens were subject to an inheritance tax.

Roman law

For Roman citizens and citizens under Latin law, the Roman law was applied as mentioned before. According to the customary era classification of Roman legal history, the classical Roman law had existed since the middle of the 1st century BC and the post-classical Roman law from the middle of the 3rd century AD. Classical Roman law was the result of a long development process, in which a series of legal principles of the civil law, which are still important today, were created: Such as the principle of legal capacity, capacity to act and contractual capability; marriage, paternal power, and kinship; property, ownership, easements and lien rights; legal succession, will and legacy; obligation and crime

- just to name a few notable examples. As culturally high-minded people, which traded intensively, the Romans had created through their private, family, obligation and property law a civil law system that was exceptionally sophisticated for their epoch.

The Classical Roman law was a jurisprudential law, in contrast to a statutory law established by the state. It was mainly developed by the jurisprudence of the Praetors and the expert opinions of jurists. The Praetor, an official on the Forum before which a trial was initiated, decided with which action could be sued and which judge had to decide. As there were initially only a limited number of lawsuits, the suing party had to convince the Praetor, usually by way of an expert opinion, to determine a specific action. If an applicant succeeded, it meant already a half win, for the judge endorsed the claimant as being right in the subsequent procedure of taking evidence if the opponent could not make a convincing plea. For the jurists the question: "What applies (by law)?" was less important than the question "How to enforce a claim?" In other words, the substantive and formal law was less divided than today. However, the development of the law progressed further by admitting new complaints to the Praetors because the limited number of actions often led to unsatisfactory results.

The jurists did not only influence the legal development with their private legal opinions. Since Augustus, the most distinguished among them were bestowed with the ius respondendi ex auctoritate principis (Right to answer with imperial authority), which gave their legal opinions the same authority as if the Emperor himself had given the expert legal opinion. Usually, the parties handed over the expert opinions of the responding jurists to the judge. Since he was not legally literate, he scarcely deviated from the content of the expert opinion. The expert opinions, therefore, became an authorised form of rulemaking. The jurists also exercised influence on legislation and jurisprudence as members of the imperial council (consilium) and as holders of senior positions within the Roman state organisation.

Most researchers see the time of the post-classical Roman law as an epoch of decline of jurisprudence. Several economic crises, military rebellions, and emerging Teutonic invasions led to a change in the Roman constitutional system. The Principate (princeps - the first), established by Augustus in 27 BC was superseded by the Dominate (dominus – master). The Roman emperor was no longer the first citizen of Rome but ruled as a dictator with rescripts. These individual case decisions left no room for free legal development through the responsa of jurists, which had so far been the stimulation of jurisprudence. The Roman private law had been built on the liberal constitutional principles of the Principate; these were now obsolete and with them the whole previous legal system. Collections of previous expert opinions and opinions of famous jurists, such as Ulpian, Papinian, and Paul, were still studied, but they could no longer be applied under the changed conditions of state politics. The traditional classical texts of jurists and imperial decrees were re-edited simplistically. For legal education and practice, short excerpts from classical legal material were prepared. Several legal figures were developed further but in a distorted form. In the west of the Roman Empire, the level of jurisprudence declined rapidly. Roman law continued now in a – as earlier research called it - *vulgarised* form.

End of the Roman rule

The third and fourth century AD became an epoch of crisis for the Roman Empire and its provinces. In 260, Gallienus, the son of Emperor Valerian, was forced to withdraw the Roman troops from the imperial border at the Rhine river, which led to invasions by the Teutons. Towns, villages, and estates were plundered and destroyed. In the civitas of Helvetii, the main town of Aventicum was severely damaged. The turmoil forced Emperor Diocletian around 300 AD to make drastic reforms. The frontier to the Teutons in the north was taken back to the line Danube-Iller-Rhine and was now where the northern border of Switzerland still runs today. New forts and fortifications were built, the design for the reconstruction of destroyed cities was narrower and directed towards defence. The lifestyle of the people also became more modest. The administration of the whole region was reorganised, a large part of the Swiss Plateau was integrated into the province Maxima Sequanorum and the remaining regions of today's Switzerland were added to other provinces. Despite great military efforts, Roman troops were unable to restore security permanently in Helvetii. Urban centres became partly abandoned. Whoever had the right of Roman citizenship and was wealthy went to Italy; others sought safety in the countryside. After the capture of Rome by the Visigoth king Alaric in 410 AD, the Roman troops were withdrawn from Helvetii. This did not mean an abrupt end to Roman administrative structures and Roman culture, just as the decline of the Roman Empire in the West was hardly noticeable to contemporaries. In 476 AD, Odoacer, the leader of the Herul tribe, invaded Italy and established the last legitimate West Roman Emperor Romulus Augustulus. He sent the imperial insignia to Constantinople, the metropolis of the Eastern Roman Empire, with the remark that one emperor was entirely sufficient for the whole empire. It was not until the 6th century AD that Germanic invaders settled permanently in the Swiss Plateau of today's Switzerland.

1.5 First traces of Christianity

After Christianity had first been persecuted in the Roman Empire, it became a legitimate religion under Emperor Constantine the Great in 313 AD, and the state religion under Emperor Theodosius in 381 AD. The toleration and later promotion of Christianity led to the first wave of Christianisation in the region of today's Switzerland. It covered city dwellers predominantly, while the rural population continued to pay homage to their ancient Celtic gods. The legends of Beatus on Lake Thun, the Thebaean Legion in the Valais, Felix, and Regula in Zurich tell of an early, but historically hardly verifiable presence of Christianity. Early archaeological traces of Christianity were found only for the first half of the fourth century; for the second half, the construction of baptismal and burial churches as well as bishop's seats has been verified. These were built with preference at the same places, as previous Celtic and Roman cult sites were located.

The ecclesiastical organisation adapted the late Roman administrative structures: Bishop's seats were established in the main towns of the civitates (Avenches, Martigny) and other cities (Sion, Geneva, Augusta Raurica, Chur). The boundaries of the bishoprics partly coincided with those of the dioceses into which the provinces had been divided since Emperor Diocletian. The divisional structure of the late Roman Empire constituted the basis for the diocesan integration of the church and continued to exist after the fall of the West Roman Empire. The depopulation of cities, which had started due to the invasions of the Teutons, did not lead to a withdrawal of a bishop's seat. So Christianity survived the age of mass migration of peoples in the cities.

2 Germans, Franks, and their Law

2.1 Germanic tribes

Mutual Assimilation

In the 2nd century AD, Huns from the steppes of Central Asia penetrated Europe, which led to a mass migration of various tribes living there. Most of these tribes moved in the Early Middle Ages to the West and South. In the course of this mass migration, new ethnic groups entered the region of today's Switzerland. This movement did not lead to an abrupt end of the Roman-Celtic culture. On the contrary, what followed was a mutual cultural assimilation process, which varied according to each tribe. Newly emerging administrative structures were also partly built on the already existing ones. Also, the sources of law that have survived from this period are often compilations of older legal norms.

The Roman emperors and military leaders of the 5th century tried to protect the northern borders of the Roman Empire by entering into alliances with the Germanic tribes and placing them within the frontiers of the empire. The settled tribes should keep newly advancing populations away from the Roman Empire. Soldiers from friendly tribes were added to the Roman legions, and Germanic army leaders were integrated into the Roman imperial administration. This kind of pacification policy was not new. The Roman Empire had always been a "multi-ethnic state", in which both the infantry and the elites had been harnessed for the Roman city-state.

Burgundians, Alemanni, Langobards

In 443 AD, Burgundians, originally from northern Germany, were settled in the area of today's western Switzerland. Their number was not very large; the Burgundians made less than a third of the total population in the new settlement area. As a result, their culture blended with that of the Romans.

In the region of today's German-speaking Switzerland, the Alemanni settled permanently from the 6th century onward, after they had already attacked several times since the 3rd century. The Alemanni, unlike the Burgundians, were not an autonomous old tribe, but a union of different tribes, which had formed during the mass migration. The Greek and Roman historians described them pejoratively as a "scrambled mob". Since the Alemanni had been pushed to the West by the Franks and then to the East by the Bavarians, they settled in the sparsely populated South, first in southern Germany and later also in today's German-speaking Switzerland.

The Langobards, a third Germanic group, occupied northern Italy in 568 AD and from 588 AD the Ticino and the southern valleys of Raetia, while the rest of today's Grisons remained mostly independent.

Both the Burgundians and the Langobards adapted rapidly to the social and cultural environment of the existing Romanised population. With the Germanic peoples it was different. Since they penetrated relatively late into the territory dominated and defined by the Romans, they missed a close connection to the ancient world. Mutual assimilation consequently progressed at a slower pace. For a long time, Christian-Roman cities formed a kind of cultural islands in a pagan environment hostile towards cities. As a result, a linguistic and cultural wedge was thrust into the territory of today's Switzerland, which led to a trisection: the East and the South, influenced by the Rhaetian and the Langobards, the West shaped by the Burgundians and in the centre the Alemanni. This division formed the basis for today's popular linguistic areas in Switzerland, with some zones remaining mixed for a more extended period. The linguistic boundary between German and French is today located in the western part of the Swiss Plateau and was only set definitely between 800 and 900 AD.

2.2 Political empires

New political empires arose in the Early Middle Ages on the foundations of the Western Roman Empire. Their rulers sought to increase their legitimacy by emphasising the continuity to Western Rome by using their symbols of power and political concepts.

In the Early Middle Ages, the Burgundians formed a separate empire for a short time in the area of today's Burgundy and today's Western part of Switzerland. The most famous king was Gundobad (480–516). The centre of this Empire was first Geneva, later Lyon. From there it stretched to the south and north, and also included the Valais and the civitas of the Helvetians in the East.

The Frankish Empire

The Burgundians were defeated by another Germanic tribe in 534 AD, the Franks. This tribe was formed around the middle of the 3rd century from various small tribes and gained in importance after the break-up of Western Rome. Thus Western Switzerland became part of the Frankish empire. Like the Burgundians, the Alemanni were also defeated by the Franks in 749 AD, and in the early stage loosely integrated into their realm. They were subordinated to Frankish officials, but they retained their tribe name, their law, and their territory.

The Frankish Empire expanded over Western Europe until the 9th century. It reached its most significant extent under Charlemagne (768–814) and covered today's France, Germany, Austria, Switzerland, the Netherlands and Northern Italy. Due to tensions between the three grandsons of Charlemagne, the Empire was divided in 843 with the Treaty of Verdun into the Western Frank Kingdom (from which later emerged France), the Eastern Frank Kingdom and the centre, Lotharingia. The latter formed a long narrow strip from the coast of the North Sea down south to Central Italy. The territory of today's Switzerland belonged in the west of the river Aare to Lotharingia and the east of the river Aare to the Eastern Frank Kingdom.

The individual parts of the Frankish empire further disintegrated, namely into independent duke- and earldoms. The territory of Switzerland became on the one side part of the Kingdom of Hochburgund and the other side the dukedom of Swabia.

The kings of the Eastern Frank Kingdom, which increasingly merged with Lotharingia, were able to preserve the constitutional unity through smart negotiations with the dukes and earls. This integration formed the basis for the emergence of the Holy Roman Empire at the beginning of the 10th century. It established a constitutional framework for the various, politically mostly autonomous rulers who had emerged after the disintegration of the Frankish central power. In addition to the duke- and earldoms, which had initially developed from Frankish administrative structures, monastic- and episcopal domains, as well as cities, belonged to it. The subsequent period of the High and Late Middle Ages was characterized by a multitude of higher and smaller rulers of different importance. In the area of today's Switzerland a whole series of ruling dynasties appeared, but many of them only for a short time.

2.3 Social strata, administrative structures, aristocracy

King and subjects

Germanic tribes were led by those men, who had distinguished themselves by particular courage in previous fights against enemies. The leader had actual or natural authority. Apart from that, the relationship between men was probably egalitarian from a legal point of view. Also, the position of the Frankish king was mainly the result of his military and political success. The King and his subjects were affiliated with a duty of allegiance. The king's reign was based on this mutual relationship with his people. He called himself *rex Francorum* and not *rex Franciae*, which meant that he was primarily the ruler of a people and not of a territory.

In the Frankish society, various social and legal strata existed. Besides the *free*, there were also *un-free people* who stood at a legally and socially lower position. On the lowest level were the slaves; these were often mercenaries of enemies captured during military expeditions. Their legal status varied according to the different laws of a tribe. At the other end of the social ladder was the nobility. It had developed from the circle of the *Free*, mainly through the acquisition of rural land, the increase of the family awareness, garments and the inheritance of offices in the Frankish imperial administration (*Earls* and *Dukes*).

Second Wave of Christianisation

In this period, the Church played an important cultural and political role. A broader Christianisation of the population took place under the Frankish influence. Apart from bishops' seats, which had survived the mass migration period, monasteries were added, established partly through the leadership of Irish friars in the 6th century. This movement occurred first in the western part of Switzerland (e.g., St. Maurice, Baulmes, and Romainmôtier) and from the early 8th century on in the Alemannic and Rhaetian regions (e.g., Reichenau, St. Gallen, Disentis, and Mustair). To ensure the spiritual care of the population in the countryside, bishops and even wealthy landowners had parish churches built. These church founders financed not only the construction and maintenance of their *family churches* ("*ecclesia propria*"), but also the livelihood of the priests working there. In return, they enjoyed the right to participate, for example, in the appointments at the parish. The population also had to contribute to the alimentation of the priest; the faithful owed a tenth of their income to the church (*tithe*).

Administration

The administration, which kept the empire of the Frankish kings together, was not a trained apparatus of public officials with dense structures like today. At that time domination was porous and fragile. It was exercised more over certain persons than over a specific territory. At the centre of the administration was the royal court, which had no fixed seat, but was moved from one Palatine to the next. The Palatines were castles belonging to the king. The king and his administration continually changed places within his empire, to assure himself on the spot of the loyalty of his subjects. Therefore his rule was unstable. It had to be secured continuously and renewed by his commitment. Reliability of the subjects was generated by the donation, later by the grant of land. In this time, the property was the material basis of existence for the people; those who possessed a great deal of ground were rich and as a consequence powerful.

Earldom and Dukedom

The administrative units in the provinces of the Frankish empire, which partly corresponded to the late Roman administrative structures (especially the civitates), were now designated as *comitates* (earldoms), headed by a *comes* (Earl), or *pagus* respectively *ducatus* (dukedom) headed by a *dux* (Duke). Western Switzerland belonged to the *ducatus ultraioranus*, whose boundaries roughly coincided with those of the old civitas of the Helvetii that represents an impressive continuity from today's point of view. A *ducatus alamannorum* existed west of the river Aare from the 7th century onwards.

The dukedoms and their subordinated earldoms were as administrative units the traditional form of royal domination. *Duke* was initially a military position. The Duke raised squadrons in the tribal community and led them in military campaigns. Especially in the Eastern Franks Kingdom, the Duke enjoyed a particular authority over his tribe. He exercised sovereign rights, which initially belonged to the king, and thereby attained a dominant position. In general, the power of the king and those of the duke were reciprocally inverse; the weaker the king, the stronger the duke - and vice versa. There were often conflicts between the central power of the king and the regional influence of the dukes. As mentioned before, some dukedoms later became in the High Middle Ages independent bearers of political rule.

The institution of the *Earl* has its roots in Late Antiquity. During the late Roman period, the Earl was a high court official and imperial commissioner in the provinces. In the Frankish time, he was employed by the king in a specific region to maintain peace, and so, in modern terms, exercised police and judicial functions. At his tribunal, justice was dispensed. The Earl, by order of the King, also raised duties and mobilised the men for compulsory labour (corvée). He also set the boundaries of agricultural estates donated by the king and entrusted the entitled persons with their property.

Until the High Middle Ages, many of the earldoms became like the dukedoms de facto politically independent and thus autonomous rulers. Thus emerged an aristocracy, which in the High Middle Ages became famous for the territory of present-day Switzerland: the Earls of Savoy, the Kyburgians, the Zähringers, and Habsburgs, as well as various others. De iure they remained constitutionally integrated into the Holy Roman Empire, even though they were de facto wholly independent.

2.4 Feudal System (Fiefdom)

Vassalage and Beneficium

How did the Frankish kings exercise power? At the beginning was the military conquest of individual territories and the tribes living there. The kings possessed their most important property: the land. Then, as per description, they appointed local bearers of the royal administration, the dukes, and earls, who exercised power on their behalf. They bound them through fiefdoms, and so secured their fealty.

The feudal system in the 6th and 7th century emerged from late Roman and Germanic roots and consisted of two elements: one personal, the *vassalage* and one tangible, the *Beneficium*:

- The *vassalage* was an individual, reciprocal relationship of fealty between the king and his immediate subjects. The latter could be dukes or earls, but also ecclesiastical rulers such as bishops or abbots. The relationship of fealty, on the one hand, obliged the subjects to lifelong service, to fidelity, and to obedience, the Lord, on the other hand, had an obligation to protect and provide. The service to be rendered by the vassal was initially military, but over time became connected with an administrative position. The bearer of high rank was bound through the vassalage to the crown. Charles the Great had around 2,000 direct vassals and 30,000 sub-vassals.
- The *Beneficium* consisted of lending, later donating of property, income in kind, or money rent from royal assets to the vassal. His fealty and services were "purchased". The property belonged to the king through military conquests; in a later phase, he would also secularise some of the fortunes of the Church to pay off his vassals.

The fiefdom, formed from these two elements, was very personal and ended in principle with the death of one of the two parties. At the death of the king, the vassals had to beg his successor within a year for renewal of the fiefdom. When the vassal died, his heirs had to appeal to the king for renewal. Usually, the sons or grandsons of the vassal were the heirs. If male descendants were missing, female descendants could also enter into the feudal relationship. Over time, the fiefdoms and the positions connected with the feudal relationship became hereditary and were passed on within a family. Only in the case of breach of fealty (Felony), the king could seize the fiefdom.

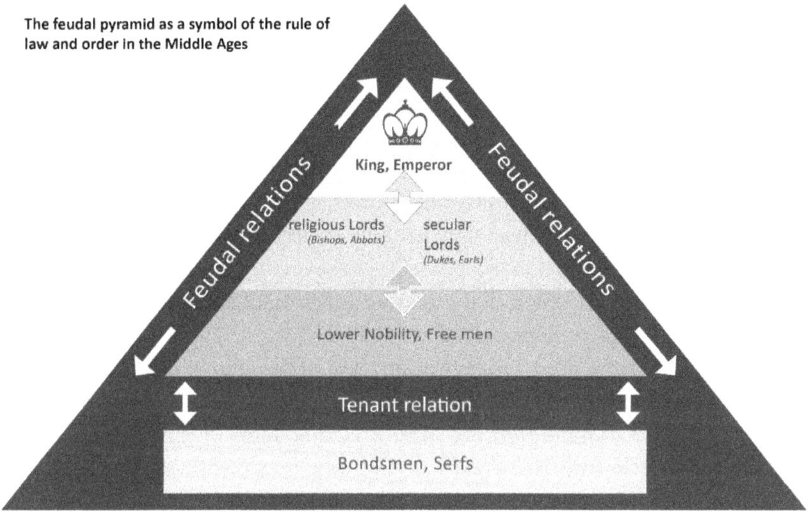

The feudal system bound the highest nobility to the monarchy. On the other hand, the nobility often extended their fiefdoms to sub-vassals. In consequence, a feudal pyramid developed, at the top of which stood the king, whose political rule was secured downwards. The local ruling dynasties, such as the Savoy and Habsburgs, kept the duties and rights of their sub-vassals in charters. With the disintegration of the royal power, the personal ties underlying this form of rule took a backseat. The dukedoms became now purely territorial defined feudal principalities. This situation created the prerequisite for the establishment of regional, provincial Lords since the Late Middle Ages

2.5 Tenant or Manorial System

Closely linked with the feudal system was the tenant or manorial system. This was a legal figure that regulated the cultivation of agricultural land. The vassals were given landed property for their services by their feudal lord, but they did not cultivate it themselves but lent it to non-free peasants. The tenant in the manorial system formed the lowest level of the feudal pyramid. Unlike today's lease, it was not a legal relationship purely based on private law. The tenants also had sovereign rights over the people who cultivated their fiefs. They were not only allowed to demand levies from them, but they also exercised police authority and jurisdiction over them. The tenant in the manorial system exercised both the domination of the landed property and the domination of the people who had been given this land for cultivation and economic use. The tenant, in modern terms, had power based both on the private and public law.

Duties and Rights

The peasants, who cultivated a fief, were called *owned men* (Eigenleute) or bondsmen. They were not slaves without power, for the manorial system included mutual rights and duties. These were broadly speaking as follows:

The crop yield belonged to the peasant. However, he was obliged to deliver an annual *ground rent*. It constituted a regular income for the landlord and thus a material basis for his existence.

If a bonded peasant died, his utilisation right of the landed property, his home and yard passed to his heirs. The landlord was, however, entitled to the *(death-) toll*: the heirs had to hand him the most precious items of the chattels, i.e., the best piece of cattle (the *Best Head*) or the best dress, with which he secured another portion of the labour income of his bondsmen. If the bondsman died childlessly, his entire chattels often passed to the landlord.

The bonded peasants constituted a cooperative under the jurisdiction of the landlord. The *manorial court* appointed by the landlord ruled over disputes within this collective. It was held several times a year, at fixed dates in the church calendar, chaired by the landlord or his deputy (Bailiff, Steward, Mayor) and observed by distinguished men from the manorial system.

Bondsmen were often not free to choose their spouses but restricted to members of the cooperative. There existed a *prohibition of an un-cooperative marriage*. Therefore, the landlord secured his right of inheritance to the assets of the deceased bondsmen in the case of inheritance. If somebody violated this prohibition, the landlord could confiscate the whole estate of the deceased bondsman.

The bondsmen utilisation right to the landed property was usually inheritable, often even for a certain number of generations. The property title of the landlord was as a result severely restricted. As long as the bondsmen were fulfilling their duties, the landlord had hardly any chance to get the property back.

The landlord was furthermore obliged to offer protection and shield to the bondsmen. He had to protect them against predatory and warlike attacks, to represent them before superior courts, and to waive the ground rent in times of need.

Religious and secular landlords

Since the 8th century smaller and larger land ownership groups had existed in the region of present-day Switzerland. Apart from the nobility, abbeys and monasteries were often essential landowners. The monastery of St. Gallen, for example, acquired vast land holdings up to the High Middle Ages. The *Acta Murensia* (1160) listed the property for the Benedictine monastery of Muri from the Alsace to Central Switzerland. The monasteries had a reputation for being mild and generous, unlike many aristocratic landlords. Bonded peasants used to say: "Under the crosier (of the Abbot) life is good!"

Quite often, a multitude of different landlords existed side by side. For instance, in the High Middle Ages, a significant number of bigger and smaller holdings were scattered over the territory of today's canton Zug. Religious landlords, often just owning single estates, were the Fraumunster in Zurich, the monastery of Einsiedeln, the monastery of Muri, the monastery of St. Blasien in the Black Forest, the monastery of Engelberg. Furthermore, the monastery of Beromünster, the monastery of Kappel, the monastery of Frauental and the Commandery of the Order of St. John in Bubikon. Among the secular landlords were the Kyburgs and Lenzburgs, later the Habsburgs, the Barons of Ruessegg, the Nobles of Hünenberg, the Barons of Wolhusen, the Nobles of Cham, the Knights of Ebnat and the Nobles of Hertenstein.

Free peasants

Besides the bondsmen, there were always free peasants. Especially in the alpine zones of central Switzerland, the manorial system could not prevail. In the territory of today's Switzerland, the number of bonded people was much smaller than in other parts of Europe. Moreover, around the 14th century, a cessation movement started, in which entire valleys of the Alpine and Pre-Alpine region redeemed themselves from the manorial system. Thus the image of the "free Swiss" emerged abroad. However, this showed only a part of the reality since, until the 19th century, some ground rents resulting from the redemption from the manorial system were still on the political agenda.

2.6 Tribal rights

Transcription of legal norms

Apart from the legislation of the Frankish kings, various tribal rights were handed down since the second half of the 5th century. The transcription of previously lived and orally passed on the law was an expression of the Latin culture of writing, with which the formerly illiterate Germanic tribes came in touch during the Frankish period. These tribal rights were records of the legal norms existing in a tribal area. They were also called *leges barbarorum*. However, they hardly ever contained purely Germanic law. The authors, called *prudentes*, who were usually clerics with legal education and distinguished lay clerics, did not strictly adhere to the customary law for the transcription. On the contrary, they often mixed it with imperial ordinance rights and with Canon and Roman law. In addition to Germanic legal thoughts, the late Roman law existed further. The authors changed the legal norms according to the requirements of their time. The tribal rights formed by this a multifaceted picture of the legal concepts of the Early Middle Ages. Not only different cultures but also different legal traditions mixed.

Personality Principle

Tribal rights usually did not apply to a specific territory, but to a particular group of people. According to modern interpretation, the personality principle was applicable. The Burgundian and Frankish rulers recorded not only the right of the various Germanic tribes but also the right of the descendants of the Roman population in their dominion. In these *leges*, the proportion of late Roman law was unusually large. Only after an increasing mixing of the people, the community in one territory adopted the same legal norms. Hence occurred a transition to the principle of territoriality: People's rights became territorial right.

The determination of rights served to strengthen the rule of tribal leaders and to reinforce peace in tribal territory. If these tribal laws were applied, is another question. Sometimes it was just the desired code. The recorded tribal rights were by no means exhaustive and often contained only a part of the entire legal tradition of a tribe. From a modern point of view, these texts included norms of state, private and procedural law as well as first elements of criminal law.

Lex Romana Visigothorum

Scholars of legal history have discovered many different tribal rights. A detailed comparison of surviving manuscripts explored their origins, contents, and consequences. As a vital source of law in the transition from the Late Antiquity to the Middle Ages served the *Lex Romana Visigothorum*. Commissioned by the king of the Visigoths, Alaric II (484–507), it is a record of the law of the Romands, who lived in the South of France and Spain which belonged to the Visigoth Empire in the 5th and 6th century. According to the personality principle, it does not consist of Germanic but the late Roman law. The Lex Romana Visigothorum, written in 506, served for a long time as a source of legal records for other Romands of the defunct Western Roman Empire. As a result, it strongly influenced the subsequent Frankish law. The text has been handed down in about 70 manuscripts and allowed researchers to gain valuable knowledge of the late Roman law.

Legal records

For the territory of today's Switzerland, the following four legal records are of particular importance:

- The *Lex Burgundionum* is attributed to the Burgundian king Gundobad (480–516) and his successor Sigismund († 523). Like the Lex Romana Visigothorum, it is an indispensable source of law in the transition period from the Late Antiquity to Early Middle Ages. It also conveys valuable knowledge about the history of the Burgundians, since they, unlike other Germanic tribes, did not have their own historiography. It applied to the Burgundian population and contained, such as norms for the marital and inheritance law, for the liability and criminal law as well as for the slavery law. For the descendants of the Helvetii and the Romans with whom the Burgundians lived together, the *Lex Romana Burgundionum* was issued, which consisted of a compilation of late Roman law.
- The *Lex Romana Curiensis* dates back to the first half of the 8th century. Unlike the already mentioned leges, it has no official character but is a private work. It originated in Churrhaetien, which is today's Grisons. This province of the Frankish Empire experienced a strong after-effect of the Roman law. The author of the text was probably a notary working for the Church. His work is a contemporary adaptation of the Lex Romana Visigothorum, thus essentially containing late Roman law. The text served in legal education and instruction and later often used in the legal practice of Grisons. It is also of great importance for the cultural history of Grisons.
- The *Edictum Rothari* dates back to the year 643. As the other leges mentioned above, the edict is written in inferior ("vulgarised") Latin, since Latin was the universal language of the time. The Langobardi army commander Rothar had the tribal elders questioned by legally trained persons, who then recorded the hitherto only orally handed down law. At an army meeting near Pavia, the armed men of his tribe accepted it as their law. Subsequently, this rule was applied in Northern Italy, but also in Southern Switzerland. Roman law influenced this code, but much less than in the above-mentioned leges; the original Germanic law appears more distinct. Regarding content, the edict regulates fines for violating legal interests. To limit feuds, a comprehensive catalogue of casuistic cases defined how to atone for different kinds of injury. Additional chapters established rules for the family, the house community, and the clan.
- The *Lex Alamannorum* originated in the period of the 712–725 AD, the Pactus Alamannorum slightly earlier. Both claimed validity in the Alemannic region, such as in south-west Germany and German-speaking Switzerland. Like the

> Edictum Rothari, they contained a list of fines. With these, the tribal leaders tried to prevent conflicts erupting into violence between the clans, for the tribes often took the law into their own hands via the blood revenge, which usually led to long-lasting feuds. Therefore, the leaders tried to channel the resolution of conflicts. A means for this was the determination of precise compensation sums for all kinds of violation of legal interests. Retaliatory violence should be prevented by the provision of compensation for breach of legitimate interests. The Alemannic tribal rights contained long lists of compensation sums for each injured limb or any destroyed object. The amounts for these fines were unrealistically high; they probably should deter potential perpetrators from harming and so avoid subsequent actions of revenge by the aggrieved clan.

The earlier Pactus Alamannorum mainly consists of this catalogue of fines. In the Lex Alamannorum, it is the last of three parts. The first part deals with "Church matters", i.e. the formation and preservation of the Church's property and protection of the persons belonging to it. The second part deals with "Duke matters", like the privileged treatment and protection of Alemannic dukes.

The catalogue of fines in these two people's rights gives intriguing insights into the social structure of the Alemannic society. The penalties were tiered, depending on whether there was a violation of a free, half-free, or un-free person. Within the social stratum of the free, another distinction was made between major-free, like nobles, middle-free, and minor-free persons. The un-free persons, at the lower end of the social ladder, had no rights. They could be killed without any penalty for their owner. However, the legal status of the different degrees of freedom allows no specific conclusions about the actual economic situation of people.

More than 50 manuscripts of the Lex Alamannorum have survived from the period between the 8th to the 12th century. It is proof of broad dissemination and explains why individual rules and principles of this legal text in late-medieval urban and rural law in Switzerland reappear. The private and criminal law of late-medieval German-speaking Switzerland shows many Alemannic features, whereas coeval sources of law in the Western part of Switzerland can be traced back to the Lex Burgundionum.

2.7 Clan, household, marriage

The aforementioned tribal rights allow some remarks on family-related structures in the Early Middle Ages and their legal regulation. Since these are legal records of very different people, there may be considerable deviations from the following general statements. Attention will be drawn to the early medieval situation. In the High- and Late Middle Ages, the Church exerted considerable influence on the legal regulations on family-related structures, as well as on the feudal system, the founding of cities, and the formation of sovereign countries.

Clan

In the case of kinship, three related structures are identified in tribal law: the clan, the household and the marriage.

The clan was made up of those members of a tribe that were related by blood to each other. The kinship came not only by descent from the father (patrilineal) but also by those of the mother (matrilineal). Persons belonged to the clans of both parents. The clan offered legal protection to the individual in pre-state times: it protected the individual from external violence and avenged injustice done to him/her. The duty of the relatives to support acts of revenge could lead to violent clan feuds because the circle of potential perpetrators and victims of further acts of retaliation were continually expanding. The catalogues of fines in the tribal rights document how they tried to prevent this. The obligation to cooperate with the relatives also applied when the act of revenge was to be averted by atonement (Bussleistung).

The relatives were obliged to contribute their part to a fine. Conflicts among relatives were regulated by the clan, for instance by the arbitration of the elders. In some cases, a member could also be rejected (*Entsippung*), which rendered it unprotected and deprived of all rights. On the other hand, a member might also renounce his clan, for example, in order not to become the target of an act of revenge of different clans, or not to have to contribute to atonement. The clan was not, as assumed by prior research, a (constitutionally) legal institution, but a de facto existing peace union. This function lost its importance in the wake of the 13th century public peace movement, where superior rulers began to regard the preservation of peace as their task.

Household

The smaller social unit, the household, consisted of an adult mature man and the people living together under his patrimonial authority (*Munt* - *Mund*). These were his wife, the immature children and other relatives living in the household (e.g., the widowed mother or the unmarried sisters) and the servants with their families. The patrimonial authority of the father gave him power and authority over his household members and their property. Thus, the father had the right to marry his children, under certain circumstances even against their will. He represented his children and his wife in court, managed and utilised their assets. On the other hand, he was also liable with his fortune for wrongdoings committed by them. The father of the house had the right of chastisement against his household members, and until the 8th century, he could even sell them into bondage. Nonetheless, he also had a duty of provision and endowment. The children remained until their *relinquishment* (Abschichtung) under his authority; that is until they left the household according to their personality and proprietary rights. In the case of the sons, this occurred when they came of age, established their household and for this purpose received a share of their father's property; for the daughters, this was the case when they were married. The term Mund means hand or protection; this legal figure is the Germanic counterpart to the Roman legal figure of patria potestas. The present institution of guardianship (Vormundschaft) has not only the same etymological root in German, but is also modelled on the father's authority over the children.

In the Frankish era, the inheritance law was also tied to the household. At the death of the father in the house, chattels, money, and if need be even the estate was passed over to the members of the household which were under his authority. Properties went primarily to sons. As the Lex Burgundionum shows, daughters only inherited if no sons were present. The man of the house could not freely dispose of his property since the children had individual entitlements to their part of the inheritance. The inheritance right of the offspring was absolute. Freedom of disposition only developed in the High Middle Ages under religious influence. Equal rights for the heirs did not exist yet. The disadvantaged position of the daughters was partially compensated for by the endowment for the marriage that had been given to them by the father. First attempts toward a kind of gender equality are found in city rights of Western Switzerland in the 11th and 12th century.

Marriage

At the *wedlock*, the woman changed from the Mund of the father to the Mund of the husband. This was preceded by a kind of engagement, a public ceremony in which the bridegroom pledged to pay a certain amount (the Mund treasure or the Wittum) for the acquisition of the Mund authority (Muntgewalt) over the bride and to provide for her in the future. At the same time, the bride's father, as the owner of the Mund, pledged to transfer the Mund over the daughter to the bridegroom. The engagement was thus a first step in the scope of a contract between the bride's father and the bridegroom. The bride was not part of a contracting party but instead was legally arranged. The amount of the Mund treasure was, as the tribal rights show, considerable; it was established by common law and haggling was not customary. The Mund treasure had the function of providing for the woman materially in case of death of the husband. The wedding, which followed the engagement, was a purely secular act. The bride and with her, the

Mund authority, was solemnly handed over to the bridegroom accompanied by a series of symbolic actions. The bride's father handed over his daughter and at the same time symbols of protective power, such as a sword, a spear or a hat. On his part, the bridegroom demonstrated his new position as a husband by seizing the bride's hands, kicking her foot, or placing her on his lap. The ceremonial hand-over was followed by the solemn repatriation (Heimführung) of the bride in the house of the husband (Brautlauf). There, in the presence of relatives as witnesses, the "treading" of the marriage bed took place, for only through sexual intercourse did the bride become the legitimate spouse of the husband. The last part was to hand over of a portion of his fortune to the wife, the so-called morning gift. With this grant, the woman was officially recognised as a housewife and spouse, and received some monetary security in case she became a widow.

Apart from the Mund marriage there also existed the form of the *Friedelehe*, in which the wife was not transferred to the authority of the husband but remained in that of her father (or other former Muntwartes). The engagement and wedlock were skipped, and the ceremony limited itself to the Brautlauf, sexual intercourse and the morning gift. With these actions, the bride became a publicly acknowledged wife and mistress of the house. The Friedelehe was thus distinguished from simple concubinage. It was usually chosen when the wife belonged to a higher social status than her husband did, or when he was not able to pay the Mund treasure. The woman retained the social status of her original family and by this also her inheritance rights.

In the Frankish period, ecclesial blessings and consecration of the marriage emerged. They were initially religious acts, which did not justify a wedding, but strengthened it. It was not until the High Middle Ages that the doctrine developed in late Roman law and taken up again by the Church, according to which it was the consensus of the bride and groom that constituted the marriage, prevailed.

Part 2: The Confederation

3 Formation and Consolidation of the Confederation

3.1 Holy Roman Empire

From a constitutional point of view, in the early modern era, the territory of today's Switzerland still belonged to the Holy Roman Empire. Through the reinforcement of an alliance system between individual cantons (Orte; The term *canton* was imported from France in the middle of the 15th century and is now the standard translation for *Ort*) in the Late Middle Ages, the Confederation emerged, which emancipated and distanced itself increasingly from the Empire. To understand the emergence of the Confederation and its process of emancipation, we need to show how the Empire was structured and how it developed.

Conception

After the disintegration of the Frankish Empire in the High Middle Ages, the significance of the German monarchy as a political power rose significantly. The German kingdom had emerged from the union of Franconian, Saxon and Bavarian dukedoms, later the Swabian dukedom and the old kingdom of Hochburgund also fell to the German king. Like Charlemagne, King Otto I was crowned as Emperor by the pope in the year 962. Charlemagne had endeavoured to create an Empire, which represented a third great power against the East Roman Empire and the Islamic Empire of the Abbasids. Accordingly, at least the idea of the perished Roman Empire of antiquity was to continue. The Frankish and, later, the German Empire intended to be a continuation and renewal of the Roman Empire. Due to the high importance of the Church, the King sought not only secular but also religious legitimation. He received this through the papal coronation to the Emperor. The Empire became the *sacrum imperium* (Holy Empire). According to this concept, the church regarded the Emperor as the patron and bailiff of the church; he was at the same time a political ruler and a sacred person, symbolising the unity of the Occident and *Christendom*. The coronation by the Pope in Rome served as a symbol of the continuity of the Roman Empire as well as the secure attachment to the Church.

Formal and actual rule

The Emperor's formal rule extended over the kingdoms of Germany, Burgundy, and Italy, but also dukedoms, earldoms, ecclesiastical dominated territories, and cities. In consequence, it consisted of multiple people and languages like the Roman Empire in ancient times. The Empire, however, was not a territorial state with high central power, but rather a sort of loose union of state (ständisch) rulers. The Emperor's relations with the rulers were often tense and conflictual. The same applies to his relationship with the Church, which was in the High Middle Ages, a political "world power" like the Empire. Thus, the Emperor's power and political importance was subject to fluctuations. In the Late Middle Ages, this power decreased. On the one hand, great rulers within the Empire asserted their authority against the Emperor, and on the other hand, some peripheral geographic regions, like the Confederation or the Netherlands, de facto seceded from the Empire. In the part of Switzerland, the real power at the beginning of the 15th century was in the hands of aristocratic dynasties like the Habsburgs and Savoys. The noble families such as the Earls of Toggenburg and Greyerz, urban and rural entities of the Empire, namely the cantons of the Old Confederation also gained power. At the end of the 15th century, the Empire retained only a political significance for the diminished territory of Germany and hence was called the Holy Roman Empire of the German Nation.

Election of the Emperor

The king was chosen from among the most important religious and secular rulers of his ranks - a circle of around 100 to 200 imperial princes - and after that crowned by the pope as the Emperor. He was *primus inter pares* (one amongst equals) among the royal princes. With the Golden Bull of 1356, the number of electoral princes was reduced to seven, and the Emperor's crowning in Rome was abolished. From then on, a small clique of princes elected the Emperor and the imperial constitution enabled a sort of oligarchy. Despite the electoral body, the Emperor was typically designated, since the Imperial crown was bound to one ruling dynasty. After the Saxons, Salians, and Staufers, the Habsburgs became Emperors from 1438 onward and, except for a brief interruption, remained in this seat until the end of the Empire.

The Emperor's Rights

The Emperor was regarded as the source of all governing rights in the Empire, and as such he held some imperial competencies and rights. In the Late Middle Ages, these were already in part only formal. The Emperor was first of all the highest commander of the army and thus responsible for the protection of the imperial frontiers. Likewise, he had to ensure peace within the Empire. The Imperial Peace Constitution (Reichslandfrieden – constitutio pacis) was enacted as a framework law for the first time in Mainz in 1103 to achieve this peace. Since the Emperor did not possess an extensive right of coercive police power, he appointed subordinate authorities for their execution. The Emperor also had the power of disposition for the Imperial Estates (Reichsgut), which was the property of the ruling dynasty, scattered throughout the Empire. However, due to donations and pledges, not many of the Imperial Estates remained around 1500.

Coronation of King Sigismund in Aachen (1414). The crowning of Sigismund with the imperial crown by the King of Bohemia, the head of the secular electoral princes, and by the Archbishop of Mainz, the head of the religious electoral princes. The other five electoral princes are also present, on the left the religious ones, the archbishops of Trier and Cologne and on the right the secular ones, the electoral prince of the Palatinate, of Brandenburg, and Saxony. Picture: Tschachtlans Bilderchronik from 1470, original faithful facsimile edition, fig. 132, p. 427, chap. 352, Kantons- und Universitätsbibliothek Freiburg (Cantonal and university library Freiburg).

The Emperor was also entitled to some sovereign rights (iura regalia), enabling him to earn an income. These sovereign rights were, for example, the coin-, customs-, hunting-, mountain-, salt-, market- and Jewish rights (*regalia*). In the 13th century, these sovereign rights were primarily transferred to subordinate rulers through pledges. After all, the Emperor was the highest feudal and judicial authority and therefore the supreme source of secular law. He could set the law, or - as was more often the case - delegate the power of judicial authority to a subordinate ruler. Since the Emperor was regarded as the successor of the Roman Caesars (caesares), the classical Roman law enjoyed a unique position in the Empire. It was considered as the Imperial Law and could thus claim validity in the entire Empire.

The function of legitimising sovereignty

The real power of the Emperor rapidly decreased after the High Middle Ages and passed to constitutionally subordinate rulers. Nevertheless, the Empire survived as a constitutional institution for many centuries. This system can only be understood regarding how power was legitimated in the Empire and the Church. A political sovereign needed a religious legitimation in the Middle Ages. For the medieval individual secular power was anchored in divine power: authority had to come from on high, that is, be given by God. A power legitimised by the people was an alien concept to medieval people. The Emperor got the religious legitimation by a papal coronation and by granting rights and regalia to subordinated rulers, their power was further justified. Up to the early modern age, any authoritarian power could only be legitimised through imperial privileges received. With the theory of sovereignty developed by the French lawyer Jean Bodin (1529–1596) a new model of government emerged, that was independent of the church. The decisive factor became the actual power held by a sovereign. However, Bodin's doctrine of the indivisible power of the monarch only got minor acceptance in the Empire with its complex distribution of competences between the Emperor and the state rulers.

Reform legislation

From the beginning of the 15th until the middle of the 16th century, the Emperors attempted to reform the Empire. The growing political significance of regional powers required a reorganisation of the Empire's relationship with its members. At the height of this reform epoch in 1495, there was at the Imperial Diet (Reichstag) in Worms an *eternal peace constitution* (Ewiger Landfriede) enacted, with which the feud should be contained in the Empire. For its enforcement, six, later ten, *Imperial Circles* (Reichskreise) were set up as regionally divided entities, in which the imperial army and the imperial taxation were to be based. The highest court, the Imperial Chamber Court was reorganised with the *Legislation on the Imperial Chamber Court* (Reichskammergerichtsordnung). It became institutionally separated from the Imperial House, and the Emperor and other sovereigns of the Empire jointly occupied the seats. An *Imperial Government* (Reichsregiment) was also envisaged, which would replace the previous Imperial assembly of monarchs during the Imperial Diet. Finally, a special tax (Common Penny - *Gemeiner Pfennig*) should be raised to finance the war against the Turks. At the start of the 16th century, various *Ordinances of the Imperial Police (Reichspolizeiverordnungen)* were issued, the contents of which were in part taken over by the legislation of territorial rulers. In 1532, Emperor Charles V released the *Carolina (Constitutio Criminalis Carolina)*, which had a lasting influence on the criminal and criminal procedural law in the Empire.

The emergence of territorial states

In the course of the Late Middle Ages and early modern times, many of the rulers subordinate to the Emperor solidified their rights in the territory entrusted to them to form a self-contained territorial rule. With the increase of their power, their ties to the Emperor and the Empire diminished. The modern regional states emerged from this process of consolidation and detachment. As a result, the German kingdoms, principalities and city republics, but also the city-states of the Old Confederation developed. The relationship of the Empire to these territorial states was like that of an old tree to its undergrowth. The young regional entities used the protection of the Empire until they were strong enough to survive on their own.

Dissolution

In the late phase, the Empire was just a symbol; the Emperor no longer had any real power. With the *Principal Decree of the Imperial Deputation* (*Reichsdeputati onshauptschluss*) in 1803, various territories of religious and secular rulers were dissolved and incorporated into other territorial sovereignties. In 1806, some German states founded the Confederation of the Rhine *(Rheinbund)* prompted by Napoleon and withdrew from the Empire. In 1806, Emperor Francis II resigned from the imperial crown and released all principalities from their constitutional rights and duties; the Empire was dissolved.

3.2 The Land Peace Pact of 1291 and its interpretation

Local peace alliances

The territory of today's Switzerland was located in a geographic border area of the Empire. The preservation of peace was left to the local authorities such as the officials appointed by the king or Emperor and the local families. For this purpose, they concluded mutual pacts since the second half of the 13th century, which were treaties reaffirmed by oaths. The treaty parties vowed to punish cruel acts of violence in their territories such as murder, robbery, arson and unauthorised seizure to help each other in the fight against trans-regional violence and to resolve conflicts using arbitration. To assure the public prosecution of injustice instead of vigilante justice, they started to establish a court system.

Omnipresent vigilantism

The Land Peace Pacts should help to contain the feuds among both the nobles and the clans. These pacts needed to be seen against the background of a society with an extremely low threshold to use violence. In the Middle Ages, violence was omnipresent. Men were always armed with knives or swords and consciously showed their physical strength. Young virile men shaped public life. If they felt their rights were hurt, they took the law into their own hands, since not to stand up for oneself was against the honour and deemed cowardly. Vigilantism was therefore not only tolerated but also legitimate as a means of enforcing one's legal claims. The feud, with which the use of violence repaid injustice, was – complying with certain formalities - also a permitted way of self-administered justice for the nobility. However, not only the conflicting parties used vigilantism. In the case of manslaughter, for which disputes often degenerated, there existed a duty to revenge by the relatives. Such conflicts would increasingly threaten further circles of the clans and could lead to a massive disruption of public peace.

Divine Peace

Since the 12th century, Land Peace Pacts already existed in Northern Italy and the South of France. There some cities evoked peace, modelled on a Church concept. As early as in the 11th century, the Church had established laity councils with the aim of maintaining order (*Divine Peace, pax dei*). In large public gatherings held open air, the participants were obliged to observe peace and to provide non-armed groups (peasants, women, children, and clerics) with special protection. These spiritual peace movements, which could also be found in the territory of modern Switzerland, were part of a religious campaign in the High Middle Ages with features like processions, reliquary convictions and the belief in miracles.

Other Land Peace Pacts

Secular Land Peace Pacts were not only concluded between cities at the border area of the Empire but also between princes, knights, and peasant communities. Such pacts often collapsed after a short time or then continued with modified structures. Within the area of today's Switzerland, several allied regions existed in the 13th century. Based on a contract between Berne and Freiburg in the year 1234 the *Burgundian Confederation*, a fabric of different overlapping peace pacts emerged between Berne, Freiburg, Solothurn, Bienne, Morat and other cities. In the Northeast, the *Rhine Confederation* from 1254 included Basel and Zurich along with others, and the *Lake Constance City Confederation* from 1327, consisted of i.a. Zurich, Schaffhausen, and St. Gallen. In the alpine regions, valley communities concluded rural Land Peace Pacts.

Clan feuds in Central Switzerland

The traditionally dated foundation of the Confederation in 1291 was such an alliance - possibly succeeding an earlier pact - which was concluded by the valley communities of Uri, Schwyz, and Unterwalden in Central Switzerland. Like other alliances, this one should contain violence and vigilantism throughout these valleys. In the 13th century, protracted clan feuds went on and caused a constant disruption of peace. A dispute between the families Izzeli and Gruoba 1257/58 in Uri could only be settled by direct involvement of Rudolf I of Habsburg. By threatening high fines or embarrassing punishments for actions of revenge, family clans should be forced to abandon feud and allow tribunals to punish the perpetrators. Since the valleys were the gates to essential mountain passes and trade routes, peacekeeping was also crucial for economic reasons. Many people lived from trade and transportation over the mountain passes. Around the turn of the 13th century, the opening of the Gotthard Pass rapidly gained importance as a quick and easy-to-reach alpine crossroad.

Political Significance

The political significance of the Confederation, which went beyond peacekeeping, becomes visible when one dates the conclusion of the alliance after the election of Count Henry of Luxembourg as head of the Empire in 1308 and not 1291. Henry planned a military expedition to Italy and to facilitate the recruitment of mercenaries from Central Switzerland in 1309, appointed Earl Werner of Homburg as a reeve of Uri, Schwyz, and Unterwalden. One aim of the Confederation was also the enhancement of the position of the reeve. Since it also served to strengthen their position, it is not coincidental that leading native families had prompted the conclusion of the alliance. The Confederate Charter of 1291 explicitly mentions that the existing feudal rights should remain intact; this meant, in particular, the feudal rights of outside monasteries and nobles, but also the landed property of indigenous families. The Confederate Charter also mentions, that only unscrupulous countrymen should be elected as judges. Such terms served the efforts of the local rulers to take over their jurisdiction. The same objective was also pursued by cities to emancipate themselves from a city lord.

Formation of the founding myth

Contrary to the historical view propagated for a long time, this alliance does not correspond with the historic founding document of the Confederation. This interpretation is also not supported by the provisions of the Confederate Charter. The allies did not vow to resist the tyrannical power of the Habsburg bailiff, and there are neither references to Wilhelm Tell in the Charter's text nor the destruction of castles of the Habsburg officials ("Castle Breach - Burgenbruch") or the Rüetli Oath (Rütlischwur). Where and when did this traditional historical view start then? The grouping of the various, partly historical, but also purely fictional narratives about the Land Peace text was compiled by Hans Schriber, a keeper of records from Obwalden. To create a "founding myth" he recorded in 1474 the various stories in the *White Book of Sarnen*. Under the historiographical tradition of his time, Schriber tried to prove that the rule of the Habsburgs was tyrannical, for only a tyranny justified an insurrection against a legitimate ruler in the late medieval times. The usurpation of governing rights by the Confederates could only be explained with this kind of description. The keeper of records of Obwalden tried to strengthen the Confederation system of his time, which was threatened by internal conflicts, by creating a shared heroic historical view.

Other chronicles from early modern times such as the *Chronicon Helveticum* of the historian and politician Aegidius Tschudi (1505–1572) from Glarus consolidated this historical view. The drama Wilhelm Tell (1804) written by Friedrich Schiller contributed actively to the popularisation in the 19th century. In the young Swiss Confederation of 1848, this view of history helped people to identify themselves with the newly created nation. As a national holiday, August 1st was celebrated for the first time in 1891, now in a logical relationship to the Rüetli Oath. The idea originated in the city of Berne, which wanted to combine its city founding ceremony of 700 years with the celebration of the "Federal Foundation". This founding myth was again revived during the *Spiritual Defense Campaign* against the national socialist threat before and during the Second World War.

Compendium Saxonis

Since the middle of the 19th century, historical research pointed to the fact that this founding myth of freedom is only partially based on evidence. The conclusion of the confederation and the Rüetli Oath did not take place at the same time. The legend of William Tell did not originate in Central Switzerland but was known in the Middle Ages under a different name in Northern Europe. In the 12th century, the Danish clergyman and historian Saxo Grammaticus had recorded this story. A copy of his *Compendium Saxonis* probably arrived in Central Switzerland through the Council of Basel (1431–1449), which was known for its flourishing trade of handwriting. Research has also shown that the house of Habsburg never played such a negative role as assigned to them, but that the central Swiss themselves brought about the conflicts with the Habsburgs in the struggle for political autonomy.

3.3 Rudolf of Habsburg

The Earls of Habsburg

Originally from Alsace, the dynasty of the Earls of Habsburg had been holding feudal rights in the area of today's German-speaking Switzerland since the 10th century. Through purchase, the foundation of cities, forced annexation and a selective marriage policy they increased the number of their rights to free and manorial estates, earldoms and bailiwicks as well as to jurisdictions and sovereign rights (regalia). Thus, they secured a politically dominant rule, but not an entire united territorial sovereignty. At the beginning of the 13th century, the Habsburgs existed as landgraves of the Zurichgau and Aargau, as Reeves in Uri as well as feudal bailiffs of various monasteries such as Wettingen, Muri, and Murbach, who owned estates in Central Switzerland.

Rudolf of Habsburgs policy of expansion

Rudolf of Habsburg (1218–1291) was a particularly determined ruler, and in 1264 after the extinction of the Kyburgs - another local dynasty of rulers – he grabbed their rights. Rudolf sought political domination in the region from the Alsace to the Alps to gain access to the Gotthard Pass under his rule. For whoever gained control there, was able to levy lucrative tariffs through the customs rights (Zollregal). Rudolf's expansion efforts since 1264 led to violent clashes with the Savoys, the dynasty dominating the West of Switzerland, and the Bishop of Basel, who also tried to expand his dominion. However, the events took an unexpected turn. During the siege of the city of Basel in 1273, Rudolf received the news, that the electoral princes in Mainz had elected him as the German king. Set for new tasks, he stopped his political aspirations in today's Switzerland and devoted himself to the functions of the Empire. In the battle against Ottokar of Bohemia, Rudolf acquired a vast territory as house estates in today's Austria in the eastern part of the Empire. He only continued in 1281 the policy of expansion in Central Switzerland. In 1291, shortly before his death, Rudolf acquired the governing rights over the city of Lucerne from the heavily indebted Abbot of Murbach.

Focused on other tasks, Rudolf left the valley communities in Central Switzerland comparatively great leeway. As a German king, he confirmed "immediate" attachment of Uri to the Empire in 1274, which had already been granted to them for the first time in 1231. In 1282, he guaranteed Schwyz that only one judge in the valley or the king himself could decide on their legal disputes. The mayors (Ammann) who were employed by him led the administration independently. These officials were not only recruited from the House of Habsburg, but also from the class of the long-established regional noble families, as well as from wealthy peasant families, who owned large estates in the valleys.

Thus, the parties to the Land Peace Pact enjoyed a comparatively large room for manoeuvre. They concluded the pact with the aim to secure peace in the valleys. The autonomy demanded in the Confederate Charter on the determination of judges was not new, but had been one of the previous privileges. Moreover, the provision that existing governing rights of the landlords would not be affected served not only the foreign landlords but also the local families ruling over large estates in the area.

3.4 The formation of the Confederation of eight cantons

The Confederation of 1315

A few years later, in 1315, the Confederation of the three allied cantons was confirmed, but this time with significant changes. The feudal rights of outside landlords who tried to attack the valley communities should be suspended until a peace settlement was in place. Moreover, it was forbidden for the allied cantons to recognise or conclude treaties with foreign landlords without consulting the others. These stipulations should prevent foreign landlords from exerting increased influence on municipalities or individuals in the valleys and with it an expansion of the rights to sovereignty. These provisions were directed against Habsburg and were the result of several previous conflicts. The successor of Rudolf of Habsburg, King Albrecht, had started to compile an inventory list of rights and revenues of the Habsburgs in 1303 (*Habsburg Urbar*), with the aim of creating a defined territorial sphere of influence. This list also recorded rights for the monastery of Einsiedeln, which the inhabitants of Schwyz through previous military campaigns had already usurped from the Habsburgs. Peasants of Schwyz had for many years been contending with the tenants of the common pastures (Allmend) and other pastures from the monastery which were under Habsburgs bail. On the day of Epiphany in 1314, they invaded the monastery and abducted the monks. This event triggered a punitive action, which ended in a defeat of the Habsburgs. The Habsburg troops led by Duke Leopold, the brother of the king, were thwarted by armed fellow countrymen of Schwyz and put to flight in 1315 (Battle of Morgarten). This victory strongly increased the political self-confidence and local autonomy of the leading families in the valleys. With the renewal of the alliance, they intended to create the basis for a standard policy against foreign powers. The internal peace alliance soon became a defence alliance against Habsburg.

Battle of Morgarten. A single soldier from Schwyz holds up the vanguard of the Habsburg army. From the mountain slope, the others reach the main part of the ducal army, when the latter leaves the cover of the forest. The Duke, recognisable by his helmet decorated with gold, was accompanied by his fool who had warned him about this war. In the foreground are knights, who were driven into the water by the soldiers of Schwyz. Picture: Tschachtlans Bilderchronik from 1470, original faithful facsimile edition, fig. 28, p. 93, chap. 91, Kantons- und Universitätsbibliothek Freiburg (Cantonal and university library Freiburg).

Further Alliances

On the heel of the alliance of 1315 followed further pacts with other cantons until 1353. Besides and later instead of the provisions for the containment of feuds, there were even agreements for the provision of mutual aid in the case of impending wars. The efforts of Habsburg to extend and consolidate their rule should be repelled with united strength. In 1332, Lucerne concluded an alliance with the three founding cantons. In 1351, Zurich joined these four cantons called four Waldstaetten. Both unions came about because of increasing tensions with the Habsburgs. The cities were seeking political backing and military aid from the three founding cantons in the event of a major war. Further alliances followed between Glarus and Zurich and the three cantons (1352), between the town and countryside of Zug with Zurich and the four Waldstaetten (1352) and between Berne and the three cantons (1353). All these pacts had a similar content:

- a peace zone comprising the Swiss Plateau and the Prealps was established;
- in the event of war or a siege by foreign troops, a joint consultation should take place;
- Finally, an arbitration court was established for the case of disputes between the allied cantons.

Fight against mediatisation

In these most recent alliances, the term Confederation (Eidgenossenschaft – Confederation by Oath) was mentioned the first time. It meant the association of comrades with equal rights by an oath sworn to God. The Confederation consisting of eight cantons in the middle of the 14th century, however, was not a united, self -contained political entity. Apart from these alliances, which laid the foundation, others existed in the same territory. However, the Confederation between equals was remarkable since the countryside, and the cities had very different legal and social structures. It aimed at preventing a further increase of Habsburg's rule, and so avoiding the threat of *mediatisation (Loss of imperial immediacy)*, which would have meant a full subordination to the Habsburg's. Mediatisation was rapidly expanding elsewhere in the Empire. The decline of the political power of the Emperor was accompanied by an increase in power of the great ruling dynasties. These dynasties attempted to establish their territorial sovereignty by incorporating the rights of lower nobles and cities under their rule. In the Late Middle Ages, the noble families and cities struggled to remain *immediate* (reichsfrei) that is, the Emperor's direct vassals, to retain their rights and political freedoms granted by the Emperor. Most of them did not succeed as well as the free cities of Lucerne, Zurich, and Berne. They used the confederation system with the valleys of central Switzerland in an efficient way to resist a mediatisation. Later the consolidation and enlargement of the confederation system served the same purpose.

3.5 The extension of the Confederation to 13 cantons

Associated cantons

From the mid 14th century onward, the eight cantons entered into further alliances. On the one hand, they closed existing gaps in the alliance system among themselves, as in the case of the pact between Berne and Lucerne (1406) or that between Zurich and Glarus (1408). On the other hand, they established ties to other cities and counties, with just a few or even only one of the eight cantons as an allied partner. Allied parties of cantons, called *Associate cantons* were Bienne, the Grey Covenant, the Covenant of the House of God and the Covenant of Ten in today's Grison. Furthermore the Earl and the city of Neuchâtel, the bishop of Sion, and the Zenden (municipalities) in the Valais, the Prince-Abbot and the town of St. Gallen as well as Schaffhausen, Rottweil, Mulhouse, and Geneva.

Old Confederations from 1291 to 1513

Year	**Parties involved**												
1291	**UR**	**SZ**	**NW**										
1315	**UR**	**SZ**	**UW**										
1332	**UR**	**SZ**	**UW**	**LU**									
1351	**UR**	**SZ**	**UW**	**LU**	**ZH**								
1352/ 1473	**UR**	**SZ**	**UW**	-	**ZH**	**with GL**							
1352/ 1365	**UR**	**SZ**	**UW**	**LU**	**ZH**	-	**ZG**						
1353	**UR**	**SZ**	**UW**	-	-	-	-	**BE**					
1406				**LU**				**BE**					
1408	-	-	-	-	**ZH**	**GL**	-	-					
1421	-	-	-	**LU**	-	-	-	**BE**					
1423	-	-	-	-	**ZH**	-	-	**BE**					
1481	**UR**	**SZ**	**UW**	**LU**	**ZH**	**GL**	**ZG**	**BE**	**with FR**	**SO**			
1501	**UR**	**SZ**	**UW**	**LU**	**ZH**	**GL**	**ZG**	**BE**	**FR**	**SO**	**with BS**		
1501	**UR**	**SZ**	**UW**	**LU**	**ZH**	**GL**	**ZG**	**BE**	**FR**	**SO**	**BS**	**with SH**	
1513	**UR**	**SZ**	**UW**	**LU**	**ZH**	**GL**	**ZG**	**BE**	**FR**	**SO**	**bs**	**SH**	**withAP**

UR: Uri SZ: Schwyz NW: Nidwalden UW: Unterwalden LU: Lucerne
ZH: Zurich ZG: Zug GL: Glarus
BE: Berne FR: Freiburg SO: Solothurn BS: Basel SH: Schaffhausen
AP: Appenzell

Since an alliance usually meant a disadvantage for an Associate canton, the underlying legal texts were not called confederation but *protective and land rights (Burg- und Landrechte)*. Thus, a protectionist relationship of the fully entitled cantons over an Associate canton was established.

The reason for an alliance was often the fight against mediatisation by the Associate cantons. In the south and west of the Confederation, the Savoys, who had already succeeded in taking over the Vaud and the lower Valais valleys in the 12th century, tried to expand their rule. To ward off these rulers, the Bishop of Sion and the seven municipalities (Zenden) of the upper Valais allied themselves with the Confederates (1416/17, 1475). The city of Geneva also defended itself against this same, perpetually highly successful territorial power (1536/1584). In the Northeast, when Habsburg got the rights of the Earldom of Tyrol as an award, the Bishop and the city of Chur, as well as other municipalities joined in

1367 to form the Covenant of the House of God, which in 1498 allied with the Confederation.

Expansion of the Confederation

Some of the Associate cantons were admitted to the Confederation at the turn to the 16th century, namely, Freiburg and Solothurn in 1481, Basel and Schaffhausen in 1501 and Appenzell in 1513. Even as allied (dazugehörende) cantons the five new ones of the now 13 cantons in the Confederation still faced various disadvantages. Only with the consent of a majority of the eight old cantons were they allowed to enter into pacts with other cantons or states. They also had no share in possession of subject territories (Common Dominions - *Gemeinen Herrschaften*) acquired in the 15th century, i.e. those regions which had been integrated into the territorial sovereignty of the Confederation using violent conquest or purchase of pledges. These territories were after the conquest of Aargau in 1415, the bailiwick Baden and the Freiamt, the Thurgau (1460), Sargans (1483) and the Rhine Valley (1490). The new Allied cantons became only involved after the conquest of the bailiwicks of Lugano, Mendrisio, Locarno and Valle Maggia in 1512.

As a consequence, the Confederation established a basic structure at the start of the 16th century, which mostly remained the same until the end of the 18th century:

- the 13-strong Confederation with its eight old and five new cantons,
- the Associate cantons,
- the Common Dominions.

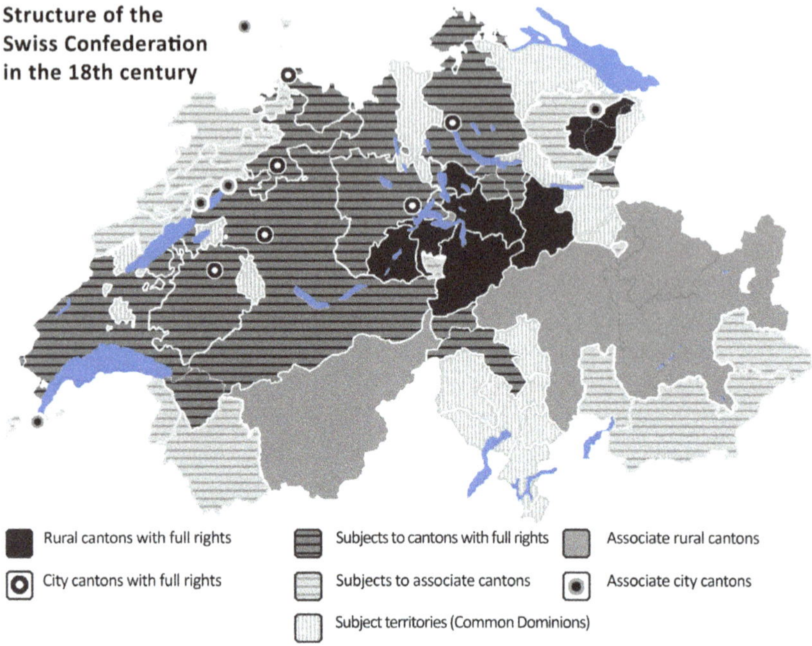

3.6 The consolidation of constitutional structures

Territorial sovereignty of the Confederation

The above-delineated form of the Confederation and its functioning did not develop straightforwardly, or in a targeted way and it was not the result of deliberate planning and consolidation, but rather that of coping with internal and external conflicts. In particular, the cities of Zurich, Lucerne, and Berne played a leading role due to their disputes with Habsburg and Savoy. The territorial sovereignty of the Confederation and the awareness of shared interests were formed more by chance, as sort of a side effect of conflict resolution. Over time, the Confederation had also been perceived externally as a political unity in a geographically more or less defined territory. The intricate legislative history in the Late Middle Ages, which led to this result, cannot be analysed here in detail. At least some critical stages on the way to the consolidation of the – rather modest - constitutional structures of the Confederation shall be portrayed.

3.6.1 The Pfaffenbrief (The Priest's Letter)

In 1370, Bruno Brun, provost of the Zurich Cathedral (Grossmünster) and son of Rudolf Brun, the powerful mayor of Zurich, who was bound to the Habsburgs, illegally arrested Peter von Gundoldingen, the mayor of Lucerne. When he should be brought to justice, he refused to step before a secular judge because he was a cleric. The church usually claimed jurisdiction over clerics and religious matters at this time.

To resolve the conflict, the cantons of Zurich, Lucerne, Uri, Schwyz, Unterwalden, and Zug agreed to a contract:

- External clergymen ("priests") shall not be allowed to appeal to outer courts on complaints against residents of the Confederate cantons, except for religious matters,
- Laypeople must be prosecuted in secular affairs at the court of their place of residence,
- Vassals and service providers of the Habsburgs must comply with local law,
- The contracting cantons in this treaty are obliged to protect the trade routes from Zurich to the Gotthard.

Restrictions of external jurisdiction

This contract (Pfaffenbrief) of 1370 subsequently pushed back the jurisdiction of external, i.e. ecclesiastical, but also the Habsburg courts, and the application of church law was primarily forbidden. In this way, foreign law should be kept away from the Confederation, and instead, the local law of the countryside and the cities should be enforced. The use of court and criminal justice mentioned in the Pfaffenbrief was the first step towards overall territorial sovereignty. For the first time, the law did not originate from an individual canton, but from a collective and therefore, in addition to the Confederation, the first universal right emerged. Instead of the validity of the personality principle, the validity of the territoriality principle was also used for the first time. In addition to the bilateral peace provisions stipulated in the Confederate Charter, a general peace was postulated. This postulate corresponded with the fact that in the Pfaffenbrief for the first time the *Eydgnosschaft* (Confederation) was mentioned not only as a union of people but as a geographical territory.

3.6.2 The Battle of Sempach and the Sempach Letter

The emergence of the Confederation in the Late Middle Ages was accompanied by a long series of minor and major military conflicts. In changing coalitions, the Confederates engaged in different battles from which they often, but not always, emerged victoriously. The rise of the Confederation is, therefore based, among other things, on pure and naked violence. The strength of the Confederates was their motivation: they fought for the freedom and independence of their cantons. With elemental force, the confederate's squadrons equipped with halberds pushed on the battlefield into armour-clad cavalry formations of the opponents usually armed with lances. Unlike in the patriotically romanticised historiography, today's research considers the so-called "noble Confederate comrades-in-arms" in a slightly sober light as a grouping of pugnacious, ravening and sometimes even criminal young men, who went from one battle to the next. However, it can be assumed that the respective opponents also did not go to fight with honest intentions. The society of the Late Middle Ages was extremely violent.

Battle of Sempach

The battle of Sempach (1386) stands out from a series of actions because the Confederate troops defeated the Habsburg's military superiority. Both sides had given cause for this battle. Duke Leopold III of Habsburg had attempted to increase his influence in the territory of the Confederate cantons by granting fiefs and pledges. The Confederate cities, on the other hand, had disregarded Habsburg sovereignty by concluding alliances with cities hitherto under Habsburg's rule and by a comprehensive policy of granting city rights to free people (Stadtbürgerrecht). The latter also included people in their city rights, who did not live in the city and were hitherto bound to the Habsburgs; thus they won additional *expatriates* (Ausbürger).

Chroniclers mention that on an unusually hot day in July 1386, the battle on a hill above Lake Sempach started after many previous skirmishes. Troops composed of young peasants and town-dwellers from Lucerne, Uri, Schwyz, and Unterwalden, fought on the one side and the Duke of Habsburg, accompanied by a large number of earls, barons, and knights with their mercenaries from South Germany on the other. The decisive factor for the Confederates victory was less the heroic deed of a man called Winkelried - a figure historically unproven - but the fact that the Habsburg knights were impaired in their iron and leather guard by the summer heat. Even the personal intervention of the duke, who fell in battle, could not turn the outcome.

The lost battle, an event noted with profound shock in the whole Europe, had brought about a decline of power for the Habsburgs, which led to the end of their territorial sovereignty in the region of the Confederation. For the Confederates, the battle was the prelude to a more expansive regional policy, and they invaded the defenceless dominions of the Habsburgs. In Sempach, the town-dwellers and peasants had also won over the noble chivalry. The Battle of Sempach is a mosaic stone in the overall picture of the aristocratic crisis of the Late Middle Ages. A large part of the nobility became extinct by death on the battlefield, by plague and childlessness. The nobility could no longer perform its function as rulers. These circumstances have shaped the character of the Confederation for the subsequent period. It became a country in which social and political importance was attached to citizens and peasants and not to the nobility.

After the battle, the eight cantons of the Confederation concluded an agreement. The Sempach Letter of 1393 set up general rules for the prosecution of injustice, and behaviour in a war. Furthermore, the feud was forbidden among Confederates and security was guaranteed for merchants and the trade. In a battle, the looting of the enemy was to take place only after a victory, and just after the loot was divided up by the captains. Deserters and war criminals should be prosecuted, and churches, monasteries and women were to be spared. The regulations draw a vivid picture of the war's reality at the time. With the Sempach Letter started a long struggle of the Confederation against unlawful acts of conflict within the country. Following the Pfaffenbrief, the Sempach Letter was a second step towards the realisation of an overall monopoly on the use of force throughout the Confederation. At the same time, the battle of Sempach, like that of Morgarten, represented a second myth, which, in times of crisis, could be used to invoke unity and confidence in the Confederation.

3.6.3 Confederate Assembly (Tagsatzung)

First Common Dominions

In 1415, the Confederates had a risk-free opportunity to close a gap in the centre of their territory. The German Emperor Sigismund of Luxembourg-Bohemia the chief rival of Duke Friedrich IV of Austria had him excommunicated through the Imperial Ban (Reichsacht) because he had supported Pope John XXIII, who had been deposed by the Council of Constance (1414–1418). Consequently, Duke Friedrich lost his territorial rights in the Aargau. The rural towns of Aargau - now without landlord - were occupied by Confederate troops in a swift military campaign, with only a few major combat operations. They acquired the Imperial Lien (Reichspfandschaft) from the Emperor over the Earldom of Baden and the Freiamt region, and for the first time, the Confederation became as a collective unity the sovereign over a territory.

The need for discussion and decision-making on matters relating to the administration of these first Common Dominions (Gemeine Herrschaften) led to the formation of a joint assembly at regular intervals, the Confederate Assembly (Tagsatzung). This institution was the only central body until the fall of the Old Confederation, and even the Federal Constitution of 1848 had to be enacted by the Tagsatzung.

Competencies

Except for the administration of the Common Dominions, the Tagsatzung had little legislative and even less executive power. These competencies laid mostly in the alliances between the cantons. The Tagsatzung only mediated in conflicts between the cantons and made decisions on foreign policy issues. The negotiations held covered relations with the Emperor and other European powers and the preparation of military expeditions as well as on problems of the mercenary system (Reislaufen). As the assembly protocols - the adoptions (Abschiede) - show, to a lesser degree also church-, customs-, mint-, and trade-issues were decided. The competencies of the Tagsatzung were in modern terms limited to the security-, foreign- and economic policy, for everything else, the cantons themselves remained responsible.

A two-page description of the Confederate Hearing in Baden 1537 from the manuscript "Circkell der Eidtgnosschaft" of 1597 by Andreas Ryff.
Image: Historisches Museum Mülhausen (Historical museum Mulhouse) (coll. SIM), © photo Ville de Mulhouse.

Function and composition

The functioning and composition of the Tagsatzung was not put down in writing but was exercised under customary law. At the Tagsatzung, which took place several times a year, the cantons participated with one or two representatives, mostly a mayor, a chief magistrate (Landammann), or another member of their political elite. Bienne and the Prince-Abbot of St. Gallen also held a permanent seat, whereas the Associate cantons were not or only invited for a limited time. Based on a strictly adhered, official order, the participants sat in a large square. At the presidential table sat the representative of the Head canton (Vorort) of Zurich, which as a rule had convened the Tagsatzung and next to him, on high chairs, were the representatives of the eight old cantons seated, then the rest of the representatives. Behind every envoy usually stood his bailiff, dressed in the standard colours of the canton.

The representatives voted based on written instructions taken along with them. Except in the case of the administration of the Common Dominions, where a majority vote was sufficient, any other decision had to be made unanimously, which slowed down the decision process. The resolutions of the Tagsatzung had to be brought back by the envoys and needed to be submitted to the rulers of their canton for ratification. They were not binding for the cantons and were therefore sometimes not implemented. Until the Reformation, the locations of assembly were alternately Lucerne, Zurich, and other cities, after that Baden became the permanent location of the Tagsatzung and from 1715 onward Frauenfeld.

Significance

In the course of its long existence, the Tagsatzung went through many testing times. The cohesion of the cantons was always threatened by the challenge of single cantons to increase their power and to expand their territory, or by other particular pursuits running contrary to the collective's interests. Considerable tensions and several armed conflicts since the Reformation arose because of the confessional split within the cantons. From the 16th century onward, there were also individual denominational assemblies of the Confederates convened besides the general Tagsatzung. Furthermore, many problems arose from the sharp contrast between the countryside and the cities with their different governmental systems, social structures and different levels of economic prosperity. In light of all these difficulties, recent historical research emphasized the fact that it played a significant role in the integration of the Confederation and mentioned less the considerable slowness and inefficiency of the Tagsatzung. The political leaders of the Confederate cantons met for opinion- and decision-making and here the partisan spirit of a united confederation developed, that led to the Swiss Confederation founded in 1848.

3.6.4 The Treaty of Stans

Unanimity

The principle of unanimity of the resolutions at the Tagsatzung made the implementation of significant projects considerably more difficult. At the same time, it promoted cohesion among the very different confederate cantons because it prevented the minorisation of individual cantons. The principle of unanimity became an unwritten but compelling rule with the Treaty of Stans (Stanser Verkommnis) in 1481; a treaty between the eight old cantons with which they settled an existential crisis between the rural and urban cantons.

The crisis had been triggered by the rising political significance of Berne after its successful wars against Burgundy (1474–1477). In addition, Freiburg and Solothurn wanted to be admitted to the Confederation, which threatened a shift of the political centre away from the first five founding cantons towards Western Switzerland. At the start of the year 1477, armed young central Swiss men formed a troop of insurgents (Freischar) called the Hog-Banner Campaign (Saubannerzug) and moved westward. Although the march ended in Geneva with a financial compensation of each insurgent, the cities of Berne, Freiburg, and Solothurn after that concluded a treaty of protection (Municipal Rights - Burgrecht) with the cities of Zurich and Lucerne to arm themselves against similar incidents. The rural cantons of the Confederation fought against this alliance of the cities because it seemed like a departure of the cities from the coalition. This conflict over local rights between the cities and the rural cantons threatened to escalate into an open war. It was only through the mediation of the hermit-saint Nikolaus von Flüe (1417–1487) that they succeeded in adopting a treaty in Stans in 1481, which reconciled the conflict. On the one hand, Freiburg and Solothurn were admitted to the Confederation. On the other hand, the cantons committed themselves to renounce armed assaults on fellow confederates, to prosecute criminal offenders and to renounce warfare against foreign powers without the explicit consent of the majority of the other cantons. From then on, the foreign policy of individual cantons was limited for the benefit of the Confederation as a collective.

Basic confederate law

Like the Pfaffenbrief and the Sempach Letter, the Treaty of Stans accordingly created elementary confederate law; which also emerged from the decisions in the Tagsatzung. These also strengthened the cohesion of the Confederation as a political unity. However, it remained a fact that apart from the spheres of security and foreign policy, the Confederation as a collective had no constitutionally legal powers. These were either in the hands of the urban and rural cantons or the local officials under their rule. Until the end of the Old Confederation, people lived primarily according to the law of their city or countryside. A tendency toward centralisation was only partly adopted in the sphere of jurisdiction of the cantons, but not in the Confederation as an entity. The Confederation preserved its late-medieval, state-alliance character until the 18th century.

3.7 Confessionalization of the Confederation

The religious schism in the wake of the Reformation posed a critical test for the alliance system of the Confederation. In particular, the issue of which confession the subjects of the Common Dominions should adhere to led to numerous conflicts and several civil wars between the two confessional camps. The relatively early establishment of the faith-based territoriality principle prevented the break-up of the alliance system, but the differences were not ironed out.

The Reformation strengthened the rule on church matters (*Kirchenregiment*) exercised by secular authorities since the Late Middle Ages in the interior of the cantons. Consequently, this also consolidated their territorial sovereignty as a whole. Therefore, the Reformation was an essential phase in the emergence of the early modern state.

3.7.1 Pre-Reformation Developments

Grievances in the Church

The church of the Late Middle Ages played not only a religious, but also an influential economic and political role. Bishops and abbots, such as the Prince-Bishop of Basel, the Prince-Abbot of St. Gallen, or the Abbot of Einsiedeln, exercised territorial sovereignty alongside their religious functions, and churches, cathedral chapters and monasteries were significant landlords. The clerics lived off the income from feudal estates and the tithe of the parishioners. A large number of different fees for official acts and the system of indulgences also served as sources of income. Formerly with an indulgence, a temporal, but not eternal *punishment of sin* could be averted or alleviated if God had already forgiven this sin in the sacrament of penance. In the Late Middle Ages, the indulgence was increasingly understood as a – theologically abridged - instrument for the forgiveness of sins. The various ecclesiastical revenues were often not used according to the administrative foundation laws (stiftungsgemäss), i.e., the income from indulgences was used for the construction of religious prestige buildings such as urban cathedrals. Many priests, who enjoyed lavish sinecures, said only mass and employed *lay priests* (Leutpriester) to perform all other activities in the parish. The cleric concubinage was widespread and broadly tolerated by the bishops. The bishops of Constance and Chur collected taxes from their clergymen for their concubines and their joint children.

Urban reform efforts

Already before the Reformation period, some secular rulers took action against these and other ecclesiastical grievances. As Christian authorities, the municipal councils and the provincial authorities felt justified and obliged to rule on certain church matters. In many places, they exercised the patronage over the parish church and decided on the appointment of the priest and the use of ecclesiastical sinecures and foundations. In other areas, the authorities supervised as church advocates

(Kastvogt) the administration of monasteries and religious organisations. The city councils delegated their members as guardians to control the use of church estates. In 1484, the city of Berne incorporated a dozen monasteries and ecclesiastical foundations into their Vinzenz Foundation (Vinzenzstift). This new self-consciousness, which already existed before the Reformation, explains why many cities of the Confederation swiftly supported the efforts of the Reformers.

Parish Principle

Even before the Reformation, the bourgeoisie or middle class grew in the cities as a new social class. The Renaissance and the ideas of humanism stimulated them to participate in intellectual life. Education in the Middle Ages was a monopoly of the Church, but now the bourgeoisie wanted to join in. The thirst for learning also included philosophy and theology among others. Thus, even the laity in the church increasingly understood them as empowered. This element, which had already been emerging in the Late Middle Ages, was reflected in the reformatory *parish principle (Gemeindeprinzip)*. According to this, the responsibility for the Church should no longer lie exclusively in the hands of the priests, but with the whole parish.

3.7.2 The introduction of the Reformation in Zurich

Zwingli and the Zurich Council

At the suggestion of leading political figures in 1518, the lay priest (Leutpriester) Huldrych Zwingli (1484–1531) was called to the Grossmünster in Zurich. Zwingli, strongly influenced by the reform principles of the great Erasmus of Rotterdam (1469–1536), who was active in Basel, also acknowledged the Bible as the supreme, religious authority. Zwingli combined his endeavours for a church renewal skilfully with economic and political demands. His efforts to reduce taxes for the church, but also the fight against pension schemes and the mercenary system, ensured his support by the urban artisan's guilds, whose labour force was diminished by warfare. With their weight in the Zurich Grand Council, the guilds pushed through that Zwingli was able to defend his stance in a theological disputation before the Council in 1523. As a result of this debate, the Council allowed Zwingli to proclaim the gospel as he had done before, based solely on the text of the Bible and independent of the doctrine of the Church. In addition, the Council enacted the Bible principle for other preachers in the city and the subject territories ruled by the town. This revolutionary act was wholly opposed to the ecclesiastical doctrine and canonical law. The secular authority replaced the church leadership not merely in an organisational matter, but in a fundamental clerical issue. Where so far the Bishop of Constance had been responsible, the Grand Council was now taking action. The Council thus unleashed an avalanche with which a large number of religious customs, norms, and institutions were challenged such as the sacred images and the masses, the processions and pilgrimages, the celibacy of clerics, and the matrimonial law, which so far had been regulated by the church. In quick succession, the Grand Council issued relevant new regulations. Many of the solutions proposed served as a model for other confederate cantons, which introduced the Reformation in the following years.

Of critical political and economic importance was the issue of the use of the Church property and their financial assets (*Kirchengut*), as well as the fate of the religious foundations and monasteries in the territories ruled by the city. The peasants living in the ecclesiastical domains of the region sensed the favour of the hour. In the Reformation sermon, they heard about the freedom of Christian people. This liberty was, in their view, incompatible with the obligations to the nobility and the clergy to which they were still subject. Therefore, they attempted to shake off the burden of the feudal system- the tithes and the feudal rights (regalia) of hunting, fishing and forestry. Suddenly, the late medieval feudal order was called into question. As had happened before in South Germany, an uprising of peasants and urban dwellers (*Peasant's War*) started in Zurich in 1525.

Rebellious peasants forced their way into the monastery of Rüti and the Johanniter commandery Bubikon. The events influenced other regions of Eastern Switzerland, and there were insurgencies and complaints in many dominions. A commission appointed by the Grand Council and composed of a group of reformed theologians, including Zwingli, drew up an expert opinion on the question of primary charges (Grundlasten). It refused to abolish the tithes in principle because existing contracts had to be recognised. However, bound individuals received partial relief; a portion of the levy was lifted, as was the prohibition of the non-cooperative marriage (ungenossamen Ehe). The other feudal rights remained. The church estates were secularised and not only used for church affairs but also for education and the provision of the poor and in part for the rehabilitation of the city's finances.

3.7.3 The Formation of Confessional Camps

The Catholic cantons

The Grand Council of Zurich stood at first alone with its regulations on the Reformation. In 1522, the Tagsatzung recommended not to protect the new doctrine, but to remain with the old faith. Lucerne, Uri, Schwyz, Unterwalden, and Zug threatened in 1524 to no longer meet with Zurich, should the city not return to the old faith. From the start of the Reformation, these five cantons formed a closed group within the Confederation, since they were not only closely related regarding their mindset but also through regional, constitutional and political ties. Zwingli's criticism of the mercenary system and pensions schemes met with strong disapproval from them. The war service for foreign powers was an economic necessity for many young central Swiss men for the lack of other income opportunities. Dignitaries and war entrepreneurs (Kriegsunternehmer), on their part, lived well from the money pouring in from successful mercenary recruitments for foreign powers.

These five cantons formed the hard core of the Catholic Confederation. Later Freiburg and Solothurn joined them. There, as in Lucerne, the artisan guilds were politically not very influential, and the Reformation had little appeal.

The Reformed cantons

At the Tagsatzung of 1525, the five cantons introduced a faith mandate. In this, they confessed themselves to the old faith, and at the same time offered a series of measures to rectify the church's conditions. However, this mandate failed due to the principle of unanimity. Not alone Zurich, but also Berne, Basel, and Schaffhausen declined to agree to this term. A clarification of the confessional situation of these cantons came along in particular through the Bernese disputation of 1528. Berne decided in the same year for the Reformation; Basel and Schaffhausen followed in 1529. Together with Zurich, they formed the core of the reformed cantons in the Confederation. In Glarus and Appenzell, the two other of the thirteen cantons of the Confederation, no confession could become predominant. These circumstances led to the division of Appenzell into the Catholic Innerrhoden and the Reformed Ausserrhoden. Glarus did not divide, but in 1683 it created confessionally separated organisational structures.

The decision of the cities to adopt the Reformation was often based on political and economic considerations. For with the adoption, one's domination could be extended to the now suspended ecclesiastical rule of bishops and monasteries. Zurich, Berne, and Schaffhausen were able to considerably increase their territorial sovereignty by appropriating local rights, which had previously been exercised by ecclesiastical authorities. At the expense of the Bishop of Basel, the city of Basel extended its dominion in the Birstal and the allied city of Biel extended its territory in the South Jura; the Three Covenants of Grison (Drei Bünde) and the town of Chur took over the remaining estates of the Bishopric of Chur.

The Reformation took a strong foothold in economically dominating cities and included two-thirds of the population in the Confederation. The allied cities of St. Gallen, Bienne, Neuchâtel, and Geneva joined as well as the Vaud, conquered by Berne in 1536.

Through the Reformation, the Confederation split into two confessional camps, which were increasingly drifting apart due to the treaties of protection with foreign powers. The Reformed cantons allied with Constance and Mulhouse in 1527/1529, the Catholic cantons with Habsburg in 1529. With this kind of defensive alliances, both camps tried to prevent being encircled geographically by the opposing party and so be cut off from confessional confederates in neighbouring countries. The foreign powers, on the other hand, secured access to the potential of mercenaries in the respective cantons.

3.7.4 The Land Peace Orders

First Land Peace

The issue as to which confession the inhabitants of the Common Dominions should belong to caused many conflicts. Because the bailiffs appointed by the Tagsatzung were changing in turns, these territories were under Catholic and then again under reformed rule. So emerged the question if the bailiff from the Catholic Unterwalden was allowed to suppress the Reformation in the Freiamt. This problem led to controversial discussions at the Tagsatzung of 1528 since there were neither legal norms nor a practice to clarify them. After tedious negotiations in 1529, at Kappel, where armed mercenaries of both confessional camps faced each other, bloodshed was prevented by the conclusion of a land peace treaty that led to a first settlement of the faith-based question. In the Common Dominions, the individual parishes themselves should decide by a majority on their faith. The Protestant cantons were given the freedom to carry out the Reformation in their dominion; the five Catholic cantons in return were guaranteed the right to their faith. This first Land Peace, a constitutional supplement to the late medieval Confederate Charters, embedded the territorial principle of the religious belief (*cuius regio, eius religio*). The confessional co-existence of the cantons, respectively the Common Dominions, was therefore constitutionally recognised.

Second Land Peace

The confessional conflicts did not end despite this Land Peace, in particular, because the reformed places cut off the food supply to Central Switzerland, and

Zwingli continued to pursue the policy of protective treaties with foreign powers. In 1531 at the Battle of Kappel in which Zwingli was slain, the Catholic troops beat Zurich. The ensuing second Land Peace went a step further than the first. The winners enforced that Catholic minorities in the Common Dominions could demand the reinstatement of their faith. This pact enabled the two confessions to co-exist in the same community, and thus the strategically essential allies of Uznach and Rapperswil, as well as Gaster (the region around Rapperswil) and the Freiamt turned Catholic again. However, the same right of reinstatement to the previous faith was not granted to the reformed minorities in Catholic Dominions.

Third Land Peace

Individual freedom of faith did not exist then. This situation led to tensions in 1655 when the authorities of Schwyz took action against a clandestine reformist church in Arth (The Arth Affair - Artherhandel). A part of the Anabaptists fled to Zurich; several were executed or handed over to the Inquisition in Rome. This event was the cause of the Battle of Villmergen in 1656, after which the Third Land Peace came into force. It determined that religious disputes between the cantons should be settled peacefully.

Fourth Land Peace

The full constitutional equality of the confessions (parity) was created for the Common Dominions only with the fourth Land Peace of 1712. Like in Thurgau, this pact led to the establishment of two separate parishes, to equitable use of the church property and a strictly balanced appointment of local political offices as well as individual rules for education and matrimonial matters. Similar parity arrangements also existed in Glarus and Grison. These agreements were an attempt to avoid friction and conflicts between the confessions and to a certain extent de-confessionalise politics.

Apart from these exceptions, confessional exclusivity was enforced in the cantons until the end of the Old Confederation. Individuals who did not want to participate in the official religion could move but had to leave their possessions behind. A right to emigrate (ius emigrandi) was only granted - for the sake of clemency - by some reformed cantons. Only later, in the young Swiss Confederation, was freedom of religion recognised.

The four Land Peaces followed the tradition of late-medieval Confederate Charters. Like these, they constituted sort of a confederate constitutional right and intended to preserve peace in the Confederation, though now under a new omen, that of the confessional split.

3.8 The relationship of the Confederation with the Empire

3.8.1 Up to the late 15th century

Achievement of the Imperial Immediacy

The territory of the Confederation belonged, as stated above, to the Holy Roman Empire. There the Emperor was the supreme bearer of the law. However, he extended his rights to subordinate rulers who used these privileges to build up their territorial sovereignty. Uri, Schwyz, and Unterwalden, as well as cities such as Berne, Solothurn, and Zurich, gained such rights as early as the 13th century. They were allowed to hold court on their own and to pronounce the death penalty (*Power over life and death - Blutbann*), but also to pledge fiefdoms and repledge them. In particular, the Emperor Wenceslas (1378–1400) and Sigismund (1411–1437) from the House of Luxemburg, granted complete freedom, which led to the fact that all eight old cantons had the imperial immediacy (Reichsfreiheit). As a matter of constitutional law, these tiny towns and valleys were on equal terms with the vast principalities in the Empire. Like these, they had the legal means to build up territorial sovereignty, at which different cities of the Confederation succeeded.

The free cities and countries got a reaffirmation of their freedom from every Emperor to legitimise their rule. In 1356, Emperor Charles IV (1346–1378) recognised the alliances between Uri, Schwyz, Unterwalden, Lucerne, Berne, and Zurich, with which the coalition of the Confederation as a whole got a kind of legal recognition. As a so-called urban- and rural-alliance, the Confederation existed alongside other similar confederations in the Empire.

Participation in the Imperial Diet

During the late medieval period emerged from the royal court assemblies (Hoftagen) the institution of the Imperial Diet (Reichstag), which became the assembly of the imperial vassals. The circle of those who were entitled and obliged to participate was not always the same, and the Imperial Diet was not regularly convened. In the 15th century, the circle of participants became consolidated and the principle was established that, besides the princes, the imperial free cities were to be invited too. An annual rotation was introduced, and the Imperial Diet was now responsible for all the critical matters of the Empire. From the Confederation, however, only Berne and, above all, Zurich sent delegates to the Imperial Diet, and for some time Zurich engaged in the policy of the Empire, which was very intensive in comparison with other imperial cities. Due to the scarce financial and personal resources but also a lack of interest, the other cantons waived participation.

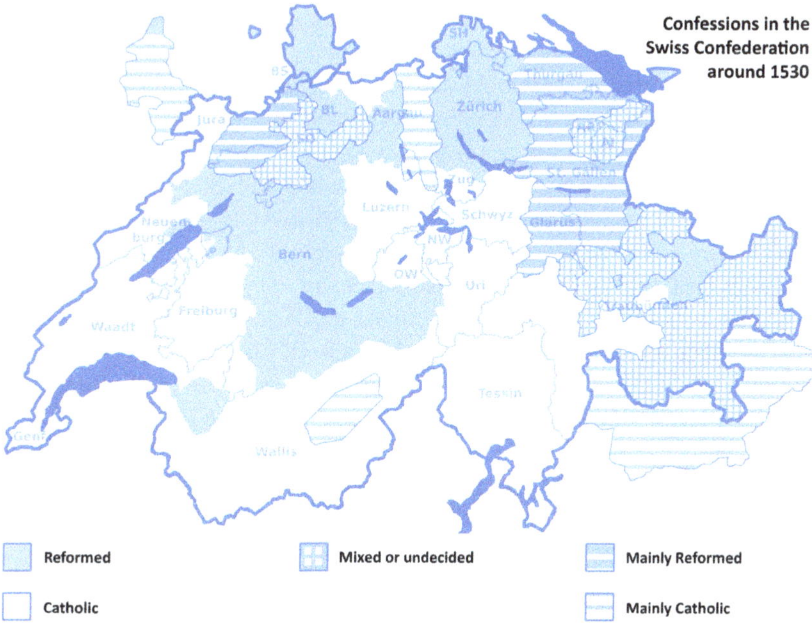

3.8.2 From 1495 to 1648

De facto independence

According to the standard thesis, established by Johann Caspar Bluntschli in the 19th century then expanded by Wilhelm Öchsli and later adopted by many historians, the resolutions passed in the course of the Imperial Reform 1495 in Worms changed the relationship of the Empire to the Confederation. The decisions in Worms led to a de facto independence of the latter. Therefore, this autonomy simply received a legal confirmation with the Peace of Westphalia in 1648.

However, recent research shows that the resolutions of Worms were an event among several, which in their entirety led to a de facto standoff between the two political entities. The ambassadors from Berne, Freiburg, and Solothurn took part in the Imperial Diet in Worms, but due to the lack of formal mandate, they left ahead of schedule and did not initiate a formal complaint against the resolutions. Emperor Maximilian I (1459–1519) wanted to obtain an opinion on the decisions and, in particular, a contribution to the Common Penny (Gemeinen Pfennig). The Confederates refused a donation by arguing that the

Emperor had always freed them from taxes. They also did not comment on the other resolutions.

Even the Peace of Basel in 1499 did not focus on the relationship between the Confederation and the Empire in a fundamental way. This peace treaty came into force after a series of armed conflicts with the Knights of the Swabian League (1488) and southern German imperial cities (*Swabian War*). In the treaty Maximilian said, however, to abolish all feuds and trials against the Confederates and their allies; but this pledge referred only to regional conflicts in Eastern Switzerland, i.e. to the geographic frontier between the Swabian and the Confederates alliance system (*Varnbüler and Schwendinerhandel*). A general exemption from the jurisdiction of the Imperial Chamber Court (Iudicium imperii) was neither intended by the Confederates nor granted by the Emperor.

Political legitimation

The fact that the Confederation still considered itself as part of the Empire shows the fact that all the cantons, except Berne, Glarus, and Appenzell, got confirmations of their freedom by Emperor Charles V (1506–1556) in the following years. They were dependent on this kind of legitimation of their rule because they could rely on neither divine grace (ecclesiastical rulers) nor a ruling dynasty (secular rulers). Without an imperial legitimacy, the jurisdiction at high courts (Blood Court – Blutgericht) and other elements of the magisterial rule, such as the market-, mint-, and customs law, could not be exercised. Even in the mid 16th century, the Confederates applied for a collective acknowledgement of their freedoms; particular allies, especially the religious landlords, such as the Prince-Abbot of St. Gallen, held on to this confirmation by the Empire even longer. A reference to the Empire was also established by imperial symbols. In city halls, on public documents and the money, the imperial coat of arms - with the double-headed eagle and the imperial crown - could be found in many places until the 18th century.

Double-headed imperial eagle surrounded by the coats of arms of the Confederate cantons. Symbol of the affiliation of the Confederation to the Empire.
Picture: Petermann Etterlin, Kronica von der loblichen Eydtgnoschaft Jr harkõmen vnd sust seltzam strittenn vnd geschichten, Basel, 1507.
Bayerische Staatsbibliothek München (Bavarian State Library Munich), Rar. 1517, fol. A1.

The uninvited cantons of the Confederation did not take part in the new institutions created by the resolutions of Worms in 1495 such as the Imperial Circles (Reichskreise), and the assembly of the imperial cities. They received no invitation because most of the cantons had not participated in the previous Imperial Diet and were therefore not listed in the Imperial Register (Reichsmatrikel), a list of the Imperial Estates of the Holy Roman Empire. Exceptions were only Solothurn and Basel, which became members of the Confederation in 1481 and 1501. The Imperial Register of 1521, which remained decisive until the end of the Empire, recorded only Basel, Schaffhausen and St. Gallen, as well as various free bishops and abbots in the Confederates area.

Imperial Chamber Court

The jurisdiction of the Imperial Chamber Court, newly organised in 1495, extended to the entire territory of the Confederation. Contrary to their assumption, the Confederates were not exempted, for their current imperial privileges referred only to the court of the first instance. However, as early as the 15th century, imperial jurisdiction was hardly applied in most parts of the Confederation since the system of Land Peace Pacts had resulted in great legal security and efficient court organisation compared with other regions of the Empire. Only Basel, Schaffhausen, St. Gallen and the free bishops and abbots were involved in rulings of the Imperial Chamber Court.

In the 15th century, the Empire and the Confederation successively started drifting apart. This trend was further amplified in 1495 by the establishment of institutions in which the Confederates did not wish to participate, as they could not see any benefit given their internal degree of organisation and legal security. They did not support the fundamental consolidation process at the Imperial level since they had already reached this for their territory. The confessional split accentuated the alienation process, mainly by the attempts of the Catholic Emperor Charles V to influence the reformation efforts of cities such as Geneva and Lausanne. This attempt increased the distance of the reformed cantons of the Confederation to the Empire even further.

Declaration of Exemption

Towards the end of the Thirty Years' War, the cities of Basel and Schaffhausen increasingly faced problems from the Imperial Chamber Court. Their merchants maintained intensive trade relations with the regions of the Empire. In the last years of the war, this often led to unpleasant confrontations with the Imperial Chamber Court; with court summons and the seizure of merchandise becoming more frequent. The mayor, Johann Rudolf Wettstein (1594–1666) travelled in 1648 to the peace negotiations of the European powers in Munster and Osnabruck, to obtain an exemption from the Imperial Chamber Court. He was insuffieciently and only after initial hesitation supported by most other cantons of the Confederation. However, his complaints were treated as necessary in the peace negotiations. Especially since Basel was near the politically contentious Alsace, both the Emperor and the French ambassadors wanted to preserve good relations with the city. After protracted negotiations, the Emperor declared that the city of Basel and the other cantons had full liberty and exemption from the Empire. Furthermore, they were in no respect subject to the courts and judgments of the Empire (Article 6 of the Treaty of Osnabruck between the Emperor and Sweden and § 61 of the Treaty of Munster between the Emperor and France).

3.8.3 After 1648

This declaration, caused by local Basler autonomy interests, was interpreted differently in the following period. Was it, as the jurists argued in the Empire, just an exemption from the (imperial) courts? Or was it to be understood that the entire Confederation had now been released from the association of states within the Holy Roman Empire (Reichsverband). In some cantons of the Confederation, the latter, broad interpretation prevailed. Basel, for example, from 1651 onward no longer publicly read out aloud the imperial privileges to the citizens and Zurich did not mention the Empire in the *Jury's Letter* (Geschworenen Brief) of the city constitution in 1654 anymore. From 1653 onwards, the Tagsatzung omitted in the official salutation of its members the reference to membership of the Empire. Even the use of imperial symbols as references to the Empire disappeared. In some places, the Imperial eagle survived on official buildings and coins for reasons of tradition.

Theory of Sovereignty

The fact that in the middle of the 17th century the cantons of the Confederation could discard of the legitimisation of their rule by a formal affiliation with the Empire also depended on the development of the doctrine of the state. With the theory of sovereignty developed by the French lawyer Jean Bodin (1529–1596) in his work *Six livres de la République* (1576), another new form of legitimation of state domination appeared. According to Bodin, a state is a law-abiding, sovereign governmental power over a variety of households. Sovereignty means the absolute and temporally unlimited power of the state; sovereign is anybody, who, according to his own free will can set right and abolish it and who, apart from God, must recognise no one else above himself. According to Bodin, the right to legislate is the main feature of sovereignty; from there derives the power to wage war and to conclude alliances, to appoint a government and civil servants, but also to act as the supreme authority over appeals, and to exercise pardons. Bodin's work enjoyed great success as early as the 16th century and was widely acclaimed.

This new doctrine on the legitimacy of domination emerged from the Western part of the territory of the Confederation. In 1609, Geneva, for the first time in an official collection of laws, declared itself as the *City and Republic of Geneva - Ville et République de Genève*; In 1636 the city, in litigation, ruled precisely based on this title that it did not recognise any foreign court. In 1628, the Zenden in the Valais was described as the *free republic* (*libre république*) with *sovereign status (souverainischer status)*. The German-speaking cantons of the Old Confederation learned about these concepts in dealing with their French-speaking neighbours. Solothurn regarded itself as a sovereign state in 1681 and as a consequence removed the reference to the Empire in their citizen's oath. In 1682, the mayor and the city council of Berne demanded authoritative sovereignty over the citizenry and official seals were minted, which denominated the city as Respublica Bernensis. Before this, Berne had already tried to enforce the concept of sovereignty in conflicts with Freiburg concerning the administration of their Common Dominions as well as against newly acquired protectorates. As a sovereign of both French and German subjects, Berne played a hinge function role in the transfer of the French terminology into German. In 1693, Zurich, in a dispute with France, concerning mercenary troops for Holland also appealed to its sovereignty. Around 1700, the modern concepts of autonomy and independence were adopted throughout the Confederation.

With the adoption of the sovereignty concept, the city-states put themselves on the same level as sovereign princes in and outside the Empire who exercised a monarchical rule. They also used the idea of the republic, both for individual cantons as for the Confederation as a whole, in the interaction (based on international law) with the latter, but also in official collections of laws.

Continuing relations

Although most of the Confederation's cantons considered themselves as separated from the Empire in the 17th century, and especially after 1648, some ties continued in individual cases until the end of the Empire. Thus, for example, the Fricktal was subject to the Habsburgs, Tarasp to the Prince of Dietrichstein, or the towns of Arbon, Bischofszell, and Horn, to the prince-bishop of Constance. Vice versa, ecclesiastical landlords still had privileged rights in some areas of the Empire. For instance, the Prince-Bishop of Basel was ruler over Schliengen and Istein in the Breisgau, or the Prince-Abbot of St. Gallen, ruled over Neu-Ravensburg, Ebrigen, and Norsingen, three towns on the northern side of the Rhine. The Prince-Bishops of Sion and Lausanne, the Princes of Muri, Pfäfers, and Einsiedeln, and the Prince-Bishop of Schanis still kept the Prince's title, although they no longer had any sovereign rights in the Empire. Only the Principal Decree of the Imperial Deputation (Reichsdeputationshauptschluss) of 1803 determined in § 29, that all feudal, judicial and honorary rights of the Imperial cities in the territory of the Confederation were abolished.

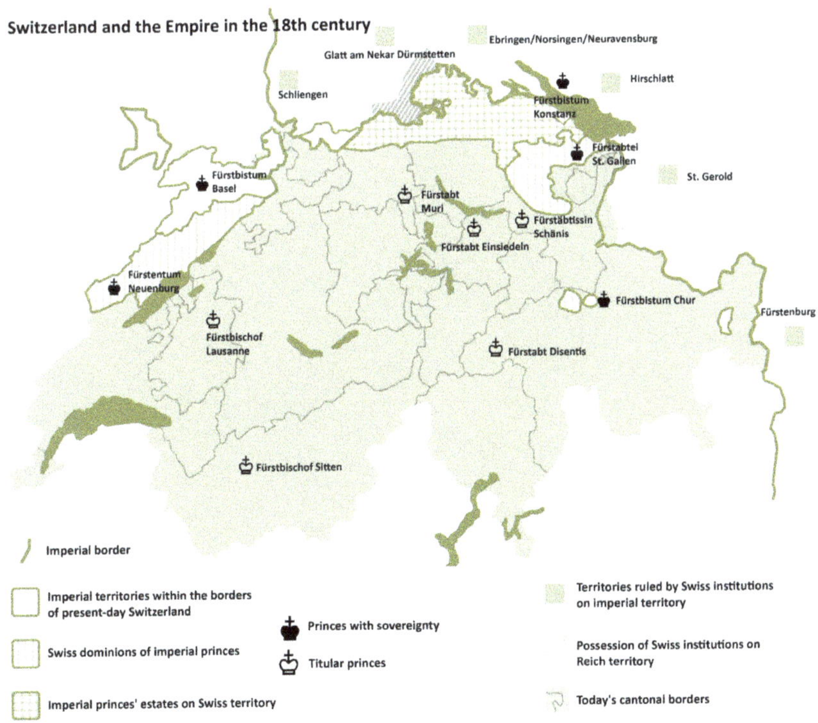

4 The internal structure of the cantons

Chapter 3 illustrated how the Confederation has developed as a whole, on which legal basis it was founded and of what kind of political bodies it consisted. In this chapter, the internal structure of the cantons will be presented, with only a few essential features of the constitutional system highlighted, especially those of the fully privileged cantons. The historical complexity of the Old Confederation, which consisted of around 50 entities, namely the fully privileged cantons, the Associate cantons and the subject territories, warrants this narrow selection. Each of these political entities had its own, often very complicated, but interesting, constitutional history.

The fully privileged cantons of the Old Confederation existed traditionally divided into provincial cantons and city cantons. These two groups not only developed different constitutional structures (Landsgemeinde/Ratsverfassung) but also differed economically and socially, as well as in their way of thinking and their mindset. Among the provincial cantons were Uri, Schwyz, Ob- and Nidwalden, Glarus and Appenzell. Lucerne, Zurich, Berne, Basel, Freiburg, Solothurn and Schaffhausen belonged to the second group, the city cantons, where the city was the starting point of the development of a constitution. Zug took a middle position but was counted among the provincial cantons, because of its provincial community assembly, although its charter also held elements of a city constitution. Among the Associate cantons, St. Gallen, Bienne, Mulhouse, and Geneva belonged to the city cantons and the Zenden communities in the Valais as well as the three Rhaetian Covenants in Grisons to the provincial cantons.

Other Associate cantons like the Principality of Neuchâtel, the Prince-Bishopric of Basel and Prince Constance of St. Gallen did not fit into this two-tiered system since they had monarchical constitutional structures.

4.1 Provincial cantons

4.1.1 The emergence of the provincial community assemblies

Imperial Freedom as a prerequisite

In the early 13th century, the provincial cantons of Central Switzerland already attained the Imperial freedom. It was a prerequisite for the formation of their political structures. If previously the bailiff, appointed by the Habsburgs, held court with a fair say of the people living in the area, this competence now passed to the compatriots of the canton based on the Imperial freedom. Besides the jurisdiction, they were also responsible for the legislation, either by recognising existing customary law through transcription or by issuing new norms. In place of the bailiff, the local assembly elected from their ranks a chair of the meeting and the court, the *Ammann*.

Historical sources refer to these meetings in general as *fideles* or *universitates*. In Uri, it was referred to as the "Gemeinde der Leute des Tals" (community of the people of the valley) from 1231 and in Schwyz as the "Landtag" (County Assembly) from 1294. At the end of the Middle Ages, the term "Landsgemeinde" (Provincial Community Assembly) was adopted.

Prevalence

Provincial community assemblies also took place since 1309 in Unterwalden (after the separation in mid 14th century: Nid- and Obwalden), since 1387 in Glarus and since 1404 regularly in Appenzell. The confessional separation of Appenzell in 1597 led to two separate assemblies. In Glarus, from 1623, apart from the general provincial community assembly, there were also distinct Protestant and Catholic community assemblies.

The model of collective decision-making spread widely from the provincial cantons to their protectorates and subject territories, such as the Ticino (Leventina and the bailiwicks of Bellinzona, Blenio, Riviera, and Valle Maggia). It also spread to Uster, to the March and Einsiedeln, to Gaster as well as to the countryside of Oberhasle, Obersimmental, and Saanen. Like the Valais and the Grisons, the provincial cantons were located in alpine and pre-alpine regions without town centres (except for Zug), where collective decision-making processes made sense. In the mid 18th century there were still nine sovereign cantons and 17 dependent regions with a provincial community assembly. In the latter group, the provincial community assembly only had limited competencies.

4.1.2 Political bodies and competencies

Competencies

The provincial community assembly was the supreme political body in the fully privileged cantons. It decided on critical political issues of the territory and the relations with the Confederation, in the latter case mainly about matters concerning the conclusion or confirmation of alliances or the participation in wars.

The assembly was also responsible for appointments of officials, the administration, legislation, and jurisdiction:

- They chose and confirmed the chief magistrates of the canton (*Chiefs*) such as the Landamman, the standard-bearer, the bursar and the alderman. Moreover, other magistrates, such as the county scribe, the judges, and the envoys, as well as the bailiffs for their own and the collective subject territories.
- They appointed the Council (Rat), such as in Schwyz the "Council of Sixty", a committee composed of representatives of the individual village communities, which took care of the administrative business together with the Chiefs in between the ordinary community assemblies and often enacted the law without a meeting.
- In *Community Documents* (Offnungen) and local *Land Rights* (Landrechten), they collected and upheld existing law. They also established new norms for the preservation of peace, the persecution of injustice, the use of collectively owned pastures (*Allmenden*), forests and alps and among others also for matrimonial, hereditary and peasant's land rights.
- They decided on essential questions of *foreign policy*, that is, about war and peace with other powers, about alliances and military aid to alliance partners.
- In the earlier days, they also issued court judgments. Since it usually met only once a year, independent judicial bodies were established, first for minor legal cases, and later also for the *high jurisdiction including the death penalty* (*Blutgerichtsbarkeit*). The assembly chose the judges and remained the highest appellate court.

Procedure

In ordinary terms, the provincial community assembly gathered annually on a fixed date in spring, if needed more often. It was summoned and led by the Landamman. The meeting place was always the same and usually known as the location of the former bailiff's court. All *able-bodied men with good standing* (ehr-und wehrfähig) from the age 14 or 16 years on were entitled to participate and to apply. Solemn and symbolic rituals accompanied the opening and procedure of the provincial community assembly.

Preservation

During the Late Middle Ages, the size of the provincial community assemblies, their organisation, and competencies, as well as those of the Chiefs and councillors changed. At the end of the 15th century, they had established those structures, which remained in place until the demise of the Old Confederation.

After the Helvetic Republic (1798–1803), which was a centralised state for a short time, the provincial community assemblies resumed in some places until 1848, and in others until the late 20th century. In the still existing ones (Appenzell Innerrhoden, Glarus), an element of the internal confederate constitution of the Late Middle Ages is still breathing on.

4.1.3 Root of modern democracy?

The significance of the collective

According to a conventional assumption, the historical roots of the democratic system of present Switzerland lie in the provincial community assembly democracy. In fact, these alpine peasant organisations, having freed themselves from the feudal structures, did undergo a mediatisation similar to other parts of Europe, but their corporate freedom remained. Here is the distinction between the federations of the freed people (Freienverbände), such as those existing in Swabia, Franconia, the Allgäu, and Alsace.

However, modern concepts of democracy do not apply to the ancient self-government of the provincial community assemblies. These concepts are rooted in the natural law (Naturrecht) of the Early Modern Period, which granted political participation to every individual by its capacity as a human being and were later adopted from foreign models in the 19th century. The countrymen of central Switzerland were not allowed to participate in the provincial community assembly as a result of their individual personalities, but because of their affiliation to a local collective, a village community or an agricultural cooperative. Consequently, the formation of the political will first occurred in this local organisation, and the voters decided under "line whip" (Fraktionszwang) at the provincial community assembly. The collective represented was more relevant than the individual, which meant that there existed a concept of democracy as a collective rather than an individual and it excluded part of the population. Women, *petty citizens* (Bei- und Hintersässen) and strangers were excluded from the process of the political will formation. So, for example, were the inhabitants of the March region as subjects to Schwyz excluded from the provincial community assembly. They had to struggle to win their political equality during the constitutional fights in the 19th century. Thus, as with the council governments of the towns, the provincial community assembly was instead more of a collective sovereign than a representative body.

The political domination of the provincial community assembly was not an antithesis to the aristocracies and monarchies, the then dominant ruling arrangements in Europe until the French Revolution in 1798. On the contrary, this kind of rule was legitimised through the royal and imperial freedoms and privileges attained in the 13th and 14th centuries. Also, the legitimate right of opposition against tyrannical rulers was another feature adhering to the typical feudal legal concept. The relationship to the Holy Empire was also preserved by the provincial cantons until the early modern period.

Dominance of the Chief families

The egalitarian concept of modern democracy is also in stark contrasts with the fact that individual families in the provincial cantons had a real – but not legal – dominance in political life. Such families were initially predominantly coming from the high and official nobility. After their decline in the 14th century, families with substantial farming estates, who had acquired wealth and influence through land ownership and mercenary service, took their place. At the end of the 15th century, real chief-families (Häupterfamilien) emerged, and key offices were passed on for generations within these families. These included the Reding and Weber in Schwyz, the Beroldinger in Uri, the Tschudi in Glarus, the Zelger and Wyrsch in Nidwalden and the Wirz in Obwalden. The rivalries between the chief-families shaped the political events at the provincial community assemblies and led to promises in the voting and election behaviour. The chief-families were forced to buy loyalty for critical decisions and the election to lucrative offices by way of financial donations. In the early modern period, oligarchic tendencies were rising in these provincial cantons, following the overall trend towards aristocracy in Europe. The circle of the families with access to central offices narrowed. In the 18th century, 18 families in Uri were eligible for the highest positions, but 77 % of the magistrates were members of the seven most influential families. The tendencies for exclusion, however, were not as high as in the cities. The chief-families always were accountable to the provincial community assembly. Besides, the common man retained his power at the meeting and sometimes refused his loyalty. The chief-families could not always prevent members of other families from gaining access to the political offices. Unlike in the city of Lucerne, there existed no strict nomenclature of families with *the capability to rule* (*regimentsfähig*).

Another difference between a modern democracy and the provincial community assembly was the absence of the division of power. The meeting held legislative, executive and judicial power: the Landamman, the chiefs and the councils governed by delegation. The same was true of the courts; their judgments were often appealed at the provincial community assembly.

Provincial community assembly in Appenzell. At the bottom of the photograph, one can see the grandstand called the 'chair' on which the government stands. Those entitled to vote are in the 'ring'. As soon as the Landamman opens the discussion, they will be allowed to address the assembly by entering the 'chair' and present their concerns from there. The voting slip and the "side gun" (sword) for men serve as the entitlement for voting. Photo: Landsgemeinde in Hundwil vom 24. April 1949, Werner Friedli, ETH-BIB-Hundwil, Landsgemeinde-LBS H1-011774.

4.2 City cantons

4.2.1 The emergence of cities

Roman cities

In the Old Confederation, there were not only rural areas but also numerous towns. Some of them, such as Basel, Chur, Geneva, Lausanne, Martigny, and Sion, dated back to Roman towns or episcopal sees of the late Antiquity. As a result of the destruction by Teutonic invasions in the Early Middle Ages, they had considerably lost in importance, and many places had stopped the settlement activities entirely. In the 10th and 11th century new urban settlements appeared at marketplaces. Due to general population growth in this period, agricultural productivity also increased, and excess products beyond a farmer's private needs sold in markets. Such market towns emerged at significant traffic intersections, such as forks in roads, river crossings, lake ports, or adjacent to manors, castles, and monasteries.

Foundations in the Late Middle Ages

An intense wave of city foundations took place in the 13th and 14th century. Around 1200, there were only 35 towns in the area of today's Switzerland, one hundred years later there were almost 200. Many were just small boroughs, and most had no more than 500 inhabitants, some of them even went under because of lack of inhabitants. The economic upturn and the expansion policy of secular and religious territorial sovereigns led to the foundation of numerous townships. With a strategic location of towns, they wanted to consolidate their territories and to secure their borders. They also wanted to economically benefit from the city's collection of fees from sovereign rights (regalia) such as market-, mint-, customs- and court-fees. From the diverse group of aristocratic founders of towns emerged a few dynasties as prominent. The Savoy founded more than 20 municipalities. The Habsburgs, the Kyburgs and the Counts of Neuchâtel and the Zähringer founded more than ten each. The Froburgs, the Seigneurs of Grandson and Cossonay, as well as the Bishops of Lausanne, established more than five each. The founding of these towns occurred mainly in the area of the Swiss Plateau since the alpine and pre-alpine regions did not allow the erection of such political and legal "extraneous bodies" in their territory.

City fortifications

What did "founding a town" really mean? The answer in each case is different. Sometimes an existing town was provided with specific legal norms, which was the beginning of an autonomous city right but often there were also foundings "on the green field". Often, the exact founding process is historically unknown, and sources all of a sudden mention a new city. Visible and indispensable mark of the city was its fortification with walls and towers. Their permanent fortification distinguished them from the village but also a rural hamlet.

Many cities changed their sovereigns in rapid succession. As was the case for the city of Freiburg, which Berchtold of Zähringen had founded in 1157 at a small market settlement to keep the nobility of Western Switzerland in check and set as a boundary against the Savoy. After his death in 1218, the city fell to the Kyburgs and as early as 1277, after a series of armed conflicts, to the Habsburgs.

Part of the fortified wall of Morat. The wall was built in several stages and with different materials. The lower part (pebbles) was made before the founding of the city in the 12th century at the request of King Konrad IV. The middle section (drop stones) was built approximately 100 years later and the highest part (sandstone) shortly before the siege by the Burgundians in 1476. Photo: Author.

4.2.2 Increase in political and personal autonomy

Emancipation from the town ruler

The first town-dwellers differed little in their legal position from the inhabitants of the countryside and were also often bonded to a landowner. Their source of income was different: instead of farmers, market traders, merchants, and artisans lived in the cities. The secular or religious rulers first set the norms applicable to a town. As vassals of the Emperor, they had the right to fortification but also the market-, mint- and customs-rights, the right to raise troops, and they acted as the judges in the city. An essential duty of the town ruler was the preservation of peace and order. If he did not succeed in doing so adequately, the inhabitants of the city took care of it. They would invoke a *City Peace*, a catalogue of norms, which penalised acts harmful to peace. Accordingly, manslaughter, bodily injury, brawl and unlawful carrying of arms could be prosecuted. In their intention and content, the City Peace resembled the Land Peace Pacts.

Origin of the city of Bern. Above: Duke Berchtold V of Zahringen (left) gives the order to the Lord of Bubenberg (right) to build the city of Berne, 1191.

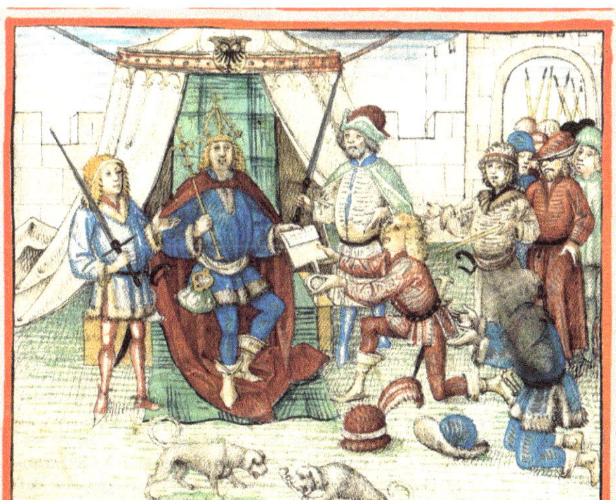

Emperor Frederick II hands over the Handveste to the Imperial free city of Berne, 1218. Pictures: Diebold Schilling, Amtliche Berner Chronik, originated 1478–1483, Burgerbibliothek Bern, Mss.h.h.h. P. 11/Mss.h.h.I.1. p.17; Photo: Codices Electronici AG, www.e-codices.ch

In these legal texts, the citizenry becomes visible as a corporate political body. In other areas of the town life as well, legal norms gradually arose from the citizenry, once they had obtained the relevant regulatory authority from the town lord by way of granted privileges. The more rights acquired by the town's citizenry, the less the influence of the town lord. The autonomy of the citizenry increased and with it the competencies of the municipal organs. This process of replacement from the ties of town lords can be observed not only in the Old Confederation of the 13th and 14th century but also in other regions of Europe. It developed differently from city to city and often not in a continuous way. At the end of this process, the citizenry was able to set their legislation and to exercise the jurisdiction for the area of the city and to conclude treaties and alliances with other sovereigns. The provision of the Imperial freedom from the Empire legally secured this autonomy. That was the case in all eight Old cantons of the Confederation by 1415.

Development of personal freedom

The increase in political autonomy had repercussions on the city inhabitants as legal personalities. A large part of them had migrated from the countryside because they had no means of subsistence there due to the population growth and more efficient agricultural techniques; whereas in the city, they found a livelihood in various craft and trades. However, the move to the town did not abolish their bonds to the provincial landlord. If the previous landlord was at the same time the town lord, nothing changed for the migrated inhabitants. Otherwise, they had to break their *ties as a bonded person* (Hörigenverband), and even then the former landlord could still reclaim them from the town lord *within a year and a day* (innert Jahr und Tag). Thus besides a few free people, mainly the officials of the town lord (the ministerial), many unfree people lived in the early cities. With the political emancipation of a town from the town lord, their legal position improved.

The more rights the town ruler surrendered to the city, the weaker became his control over the unfree people, and their legal position became similar to that of the free people. Therefore, in many towns the development towards personal freedom has progressed faster than in the countryside. In the Late Middle Ages, the cities formed islands of freedom and private rights in an otherwise feudal legal environment. The saying: "town air makes you free" held true then. Although this concise formula, coined by researchers of legal history in the 19th century, was only applicable in the free Imperial cities. Just very few towns in the Confederation were free Imperial cities since most of them were under the rule of one of the principal city cantons. The municipality of Berne, succeeding former feudal town lords, incorporated a whole series of towns under their sovereignty in the rural regions of Berne, Aargau and the Vaud, whereby their town rights, and also those of their inhabitants had to comply with the freedoms granted by the principal city.

4.2.3 The Councils of the City

City Council

In the early cities, the City Peace was only invoked by the ministerials of the town lords and by merchants, because their interest in peace and order corresponded with that of the town lord. They also constituted the council of the city, a small body of ten to twenty persons, whose members were appointed by the town lord, and later extended by self-suffrage (co-optation). The general population was therefore not involved in the appointment of this council. Some City Peace also contained constitutional provisions to safeguard the government and administrative functions of the councillors. The more significant part of the city inhabitants, especially the craftsmen, were thereby excluded from the political will formation.

In the 13th century, craftsmen began to form co-operative associations, the guilds. The purpose of these guilds was diverse. One of the essential objectives was to ensure the livelihood of the members by protecting them from external competition, as well as measures to ensure the quality of the products and the level of training of their journeymen. The guilds also took over functions serving the general public, such as the economic care of the widows and orphans of deceased members, and they participated in the town guard, city defence and fire control.

Guild Struggles

With their rising influence in urban life, the guilds also pursued political participation. They wanted to curb the power of the current council and put the legislative rule in the city on a broader base. During the first half of the 14th century in many towns of today's German-speaking Switzerland and Southern Germany, their demands caused unrest. As a result of these mostly peaceful but occasionally violent guild battles, the guilds were included in various city councils. In many cities a new town law was ratified, which allowed representation of the guilds in the city council, such as in Zurich (1336), Basel (1337), St. Gallen (1354), and Schaffhausen (1411). That was also the case in smaller towns like Rheinfelden (1331), Winterthur (1344) and Chur (1456). As these examples show, this movement only affected German-speaking Switzerland. In the French-speaking Switzerland and Ticino, the guilds emerged later and played no political role.

A well-known example was the *Guild Revolt of Zurich* (Zürcher Zunftrevolution) in 1336. With the grant of the Imperial freedom in 1218, the Council and the citizenry were the constitutional bodies of the city in Zurich. The citizenry was invited by the Council to attend community meetings to discuss important political issues. But only knights, city nobles, and merchants had access (Einsitz) to the Council. The city nobles lost their influence at the beginning of the 14th century because wholesale merchants, who had come to a fortune with silk and overseas trade, marginalised them. Knight Rudolf Brun wanted to use the dissatisfaction of the craftsmen to break the power of the increasingly dominant merchants. Under his leadership, the Zurich artisans stormed the town hall in 1336 and deposed of the council being in session there. In the *Juror's Letter (Geschworenen Brief)* of 1336, they agreed the following: The Council needs to consist of two groups. In the one, the Constaffel-Guild, the nobles, and merchants who had previously ruled should delegate 13 council members. In the other, the guild masters of the 13 newly created artisan guilds were to take a seat. In addition to these 26 Council members, a second *resting* Council of the same size is to be appointed. The two Councils would change every six months so that every member of the Council could pursue his occupation at least during half a year. Brun created for himself the office of mayor, who presided over the Council.

Minor and Grand Council

In addition to this *Minor Council*, the "Council of the Two Hundred" was founded in the mid of the 14th century, to which both the members of the Minor Council, as well as a proportional representation of the Constaffel and the other guilds, belonged. As a committee of the citizenry, this Council advised the Minor Council on critical issues. It was involved in legislation and was the highest appellate body against judgments of the Minor Council. With the establishment of this *Grand Council*, the City Councils lost their importance; it was later only convened twice a year for the citizens' declaration of commitment to the city law.

The development in Zurich is exemplary for other municipalities. In the 13th and 14th century, the cities emancipated themselves from their town lords and became independent sovereigns. At the same time, the political power spread to other strata of society. Besides the Minor Council, there emerged the Grand Council, the purpose of which was to involve the citizenry in the decision-making process.

The development in the cities was reflected in the emergence and development of the provincial community assembly democracies. Here as there, the political power, after the separation from the existing aristocratic sovereigns, went over to a small body of Chiefs, and a corrective was needed in the form of a more extensive political body. As a result, the provincial community assembly and the Grand Council in the city had the highest judicial and legislative power.

The Grand Council usually had 60 to 200 members, depending on the area. Together with the citizenry, it formed the sovereign of the city, based on the reception of the doctrine of sovereignty. However, in the early modern period, the citizenry in many places was no longer convened, and if they continued to exist, their competences were often limited. The Grand Council elected the Chairs of the Minor Council such as the mayor (called Bürgermeister or Schultheiss), the heads of the town districts (Venner), the bursar and other officials, but also the bailiffs and the judges. It also approved critical domestic and foreign policy matters prepared by the Minor Council and concluded protective- (Burghery) and other alliances. It enacted the municipal law, and for court judgments of the Minor Council or the Town Court, it was the highest appellate body.

Since the Grand Council merely met weekly or even only monthly, the Minor Council carried out the day-to-day business and was thus the executive body of the Grand Council. Depending on the town, it had between 20 to 60 members and convened several times a week. Through this increased presence, the Minor Council developed everywhere to the de facto government and the real centre of power. It filled all the principal offices in the city, conducted the day-to-day business, negotiated with foreign envoys and exercised jurisdiction, where no separate court existed. The Minor Council, like the council of the 12th and 13th centuries, developed into the actual authority and the Grand Council in the longer term acted only as a representation of the citizenry.

In some places, a *Secret Council* was formed as a small political body consisting of those members of the Minor Council who were responsible for essential governmental affairs such as finance, economics, and the military. This institution had far-reaching powers.

As in Zurich, guilds were represented in the Grand Council of Basel, St. Gallen, Schaffhausen and Bienne. In other cities such as Berne, Lucerne, Freiburg, Solothurn, and Geneva, they did not achieve an institutionalised representation in the Grand Council. There the councils were supplemented by self-suffrage elections, without taking into account particular political bodies. In the 16th century, this fostered the development of family dominance. Historiography defines this second group as *Patrician cantons* and the first group as *Cities of Guilds*. The difference laid more in social than in legal terms. Although the guilds in the Patrician cantons had no institutionalised access to the councils, there was little difference in the organisation, the elections and the competencies of the councils.

Patrician cantons and Cities of Guilds

The constitutional system of the city cantons was based on the representation of artisans-associations and members of different rank (Standesverbände - nobles, clerics, etc.), and the co-optation. Only those who belonged to these associations or were part of a corresponding social network could have a say in politics. The differences of city cantons to a modern democracy were even more evident than those of the provincial community assembly democracies. With a strong tendency to block newcomers, they de facto developed into oligarchies.

4.2.4 The city administration

With the replacement of the town lords in the 13th and 14th century, not only the councils emerged, but also autonomous administrative organs of the city developed. The keeper of records, bursar, tollkeeper, master builders and master of the granary, together with their clerks, took care of the supervision of markets, crafts and trades, the collection and administration of taxes and duties, public and private buildings, and the safeguarding of food supplies.

Keeper of Records

The centre of the administration remained the municipal chancelleries with the keeper of records presiding over it. It drew up the *Councils minutes*, carried out the correspondence of the Council and produced documents. The first keepers of records were often clergy, who, in addition to their activities in an ecclesiastical chancellery, also led the chancelleries of the city. Since they were literate, unlike most of the laity of this time, besides often having legal or notarial training, they had a lead in education, which predestined them for this office. In the Late Middle Ages, a separation of the ecclesiastical and city keeper of records emerged. The keeper of records, now often a member of the urban upper class with a legal education, was likewise a famous person in the political life of the city. He served as the "memory" of the town, as a provider of information and counsellor as well as an envoy to diplomatic negotiations with other sovereigns.

Transcription of administrative activities

In the 15th century, the set-up of subject territories in the surrounding areas of the city not only led to the establishment of decentralised administrative structures

(Bailiffs), but also to the expansion and professionalization of the municipal administration at the principal canton. The increasing complexity of the administrative structures made the transcription of governmental activities necessary. In addition to the Council minutes, which recorded the Council decisions, they now also kept *Records of Missives – Messages* (Missivenbücher) containing copies of the outgoing Council correspondence. Furthermore, *Records of Copies* (Kopialbücher) providing copies of the crucial documents of the government such as privileges granted by the Empire, city statutes or alliances with other cantons. Within these various transcripts, the Records of Copies displayed the current constitution and the city right. These collections of documents, such as the Red Book of Zurich (1428), the Book of Freedoms of Berne (1430/31), the Silver Book of Lucerne (1433), or the White Book of Obwalden (1470) also showed the self-image and self-awareness of the canton. Critical legal-historical sources are also the various *Court Records* (Gerichtsbücher) containing the protocols of interrogation and the judgments of the municipal courts.

Cameralistics

In the second half of the 17th-century, simultaneous administration or cameralistics was adopted in the more essential city-states of the Confederation. As in the German principalities, *commissions* or *chambers* were created for the different spheres of government activities. Delegated by the council these new institutions administered and supervised the financial-, legal-, church-, school-, welfare- and military-affairs.

4.2.5 Dominance of families in modern times

The democratic nature of council elections was kept in almost all City cantons to the same extent as in provincial cantons until the end of the Ancien Régime. However, this official "republican" concept of a constitution had been undermined by the formation of dominant families since the 16th century. The participation in the political rule was limited either by written or by unwritten law to members of defined upper-class families and so political offices became virtually hereditary. This process of aristocratization also befell other parts of Europe. In various countries, powerful territorial princes of the Late Middle Ages developed the royal houses of the Early Modern Period. How they organised their political life, but also their lifestyle became a focal point for the European nobility. With the demise of the old aristocracy in the 14th century, wealthy bourgeois families in Switzerland were now aspiring to the model of the foreign nobility.

In the Confederation of the Late Middle Ages, only a few families succeeded to stay in the upper class for more than a century. After the demise of the old ministerial families, the families of peasants and merchants who had become wealthy and well respected, emerged. Often after only a few generations in the highest offices, hunger and plagues, battles and wars led to the extinction of the families in the male line. Sometimes economic failures caused a social decline, or they were forced out of their offices by political upheavals and unrest. Only a few families like buoys in the rough sea succeeded in remaining in the upper class for a longer time. Within 30 years, a generational span, all members of a council in a city were usually exchanged. Consequently, anyone who had only just acquired the civil rights of a city or a county had a real chance of getting a seat in the Grand Council and later gain a place in principal council offices for his sons, if not for himself.

Restriction of citizen rights

Various events had diminished the permeability of the social strata since the 16th century. Lost battles, such as the one against the French King at Marignano in 1515, ended the expansion policy of the Confederates and they waged fewer wars against foreign powers. With the Land Peace, internal confessional conflicts were not eliminated but contained. The population grew, which led to fear of the habitat, the workplace, and food security. Artisans were afraid of competition, the citizens with the capability to rule were suspicious of the rising rush on financially lucrative government offices, and the Council was worried about the increase of *poor inhabitants (Armengenössigen)*, and the burden on the community because destitute persons were entitled to welfare support in their place of citizenship. Where previously civil rights had been generously granted, mainly to compensate for the population decimation caused by plague and war, non-locals were now only hesitantly accepted into civil rights. Purchasing citizens rights had become more expensive in specific places or sometimes even impossible. The group of those who were able to participate in the political rule shrank in size both in the provincial cantons as well as in the City cantons. Even cantons that had not completely closed off their citizens' rights initiated legal hurdles to prevent or delay the participation of the newly registered incomers in the local political government.

The city of Berne, for example, decreed in 1635 that only the sons of newly registered incomers could be elected into the Grand Council and only their grandchildren into the Minor Council. With the *New Ordinance* (Nüwen Ordnung) of 1643, the city created a secondary category of *citizens* (Burgern), the so-called *inhabitants* (Habitanten) or permanent residents (Ewigen Einwohner).

They were prohibited from being elected into the councils and should stay with their traditional handicraft or trade. The acquisition of the citizens' right (Burgerrecht) was now no longer automatically linked to the *capability to rule* (Regimentsfähigkeit), meaning the right to be elected to the Grand or Minor Council. Only those families who had acquired the citizens' rights before 1643 were regarded as capable of ruling. Similar resolutions as in the capital were also launched in the provincial towns. Without the *capability to rule*, public offices such as a bailiwick, a judicial authority or the administration of secularised monasteries connected with revenues could not be retained.

Access to public offices

In other cantons, access to the Councils was influenced differently. For the electoral process, there were official and usually very complicated rules. However, especially in the case of the Minor Council, there was not an election by the citizenry carried out, but instead, an internal supplementary poll by the councillors themselves was allowed. Through various forms of bribery, whether by donations or promises, the candidates could influence the election through their social prestige and wealth. This kind of *practice* (Praktizieren) could not be prevented despite various prohibitions. Anyone who had won a Council seat for himself ensured that he would keep it throughout his whole life, and then allow it to pass over to his son or another male relative. The Council seats became de facto hereditary.

The Reformation led to an intensification of this kind of autocratic administration in the Confederate cantons. An occupation in the Minor Council, which convened several times a week, but also the performance of other duties was time-consuming and not possible without an appropriate material basis of the occupant of the office. As elsewhere in Europe, only those could devote themselves to political posts, which were either entirely or in part relieved of the obligation to earn their daily living. Affiliation to the Council and political participation in the early modern age was therefore only open to members of wealthy families. These families had acquired their wealth mainly through property ownership and the possession of sovereign rights, the transport business across the Alps, trade and financial transactions, but also due to the mercenary- and pension-system. With the acquisition of subject territories, the bailiwicks were also opened up to them as another lucrative source of income.

Family crests of councillors. There were also family sovereignties in Freiburg. The family crests of the council members were included in the flag book. The picture shows those of the years 1647/48. Picture: Staatsarchiv Freiburg i. Ue. (State archive of Freiburg), Legislation and Miscellaneous 53, Flagbook, Parchemin - 42 ff. - 31 x 48 - Freiburg CH - 1647–1648, 7r.

Contuinal exclusion

For artisans and small-scale traders, it was increasingly difficult to take a seat in the Councils, even though, based on their civil rights they were capable of rule and so eligible. The magistrates in the Foreign Service (Soldoffiziere) and wholesale merchants ousted them as well as the state officers (Staatsspezialisten), who were employed by and for the administration. The circle of the families participating in the government successively shrank. In 1525, 198 families represented the Bernese Grand Council counting approximately 300 members. In 1691, there remained still 104, in 1730 just 88 and 1798 only 73 families. The citizenry divided increasingly into an ever-smaller circle of governing families and the growing number of others excluded from the government despite their capacity of rule. Similarly, in other cantons, the number of ruling families decreased. In Zurich 1530 some 143 families had access to the councils, in 1637 just 106 and 1730 only 87. In Freiburg, the number of families in the Minor Council decreased from 64 (in the years 1490–1520) to 36 (1700–1730). In Lucerne between 1501 and 1510, there were still 104 families represented in the two councils. Between 1591 and 1600 only 68 and in 1680 there were less than 50. In the 17th century, only a solid core of 17 families existed who could retain their seats in the Minor Council and thus monopolised around three-quarters of the 36 council seats. In 1798, just 13 of them still belonged to the Minor Council. The families represented in the Minor Council were also increasingly dominating the Grand Council of Lucerne. In 1620, half of the 64 members of the Grand Council were blood-related to members of the Minor Council and in the 18th century almost 80 % of them. In the last decades of the Ancien Régime, the circle of the families with access to the Council in Lucerne was utterly closed. The Fundamental Law (Fundamentalgesetz) of 1773 limited the number of ruling families with access to the Councils to the existing remainder of families.

In Lucerne, as well as in Berne, Solothurn, Freiburg, and Geneva, factual aristocracies established themselves. Based on the model of the patrician nobility in the Roman Republic, who had occupied the Senate and the magistracies, they called themselves in the 16th-century *patricians* and their rule the *patriciate.* Likewise, in the provincial cantons and the covenants of municipalities in Valais and Grisons, a few families specialising in state services held the political offices, despite the existence of a provincial community assembly. In the Guild Cities, the obstruction process was less widespread, but here too, some families gained overweight in the Councils by winning access to the various guilds, which were entitled to vote. Zurich and Basel, in particular, knew a regiment of wholesale merchants, textile entrepreneurs, officers, and *pensioners* (Rentner), who lived off the revenue of their agricultural estates. Only in the city of St. Gallen, the wholesale merchants remained in the minority as political opponents to the craftsmen.

Status Symbols

In order to document and increase their importance, the dominating council family lines adopted status symbols known from foreign nobility. These included monumental residences in the city, a territorial jurisdiction or a private Manor (*Campagne*) in the country as well as a marriage appropriate to the family status of their children. The acquisition of coat-of-arms and nobility titles, which were granted by foreign monarchs as gratitude for military and diplomatic services, was equally important. In many respects, they emulated the French nobility. In the patriciate cantons, all families capable of rule, including those who were not represented in the Council, were considered noble. Their members could request confirmation of their nobility by the Grand Council as the sovereign, for example, when they went abroad as officers of the Foreign Service. The acquisition of culture and education was also a part of a strategy to "stay on top", which different privileged families pursued with different means and not necessarily with the same success. With the adoption of the written form of administration at the cantons, the ability to read and write became the prerequisite for the participation in political power. The new law schools established in some Confederate cities in the early modern period taught the theoretical know-how primarily to the sons of the council family lines for their future as government officials.

Urban unrest

As in the provincial cantons, the amassing of council seats and lucrative state offices by a few families led to tensions with other segments of the population. Representatives of local families with the capability to rule but not represented in the Councils protested and stirred up unrest. To mention here are the *Knab Dispute* (Knabhandel) (1609/1610) and the *Burgher Dispute* (Burgerhandel) (1651–1653) in Lucerne. The *Henzi Plot* (Henziverschwörung) (1749) in Berne, the *Chenaux Dispute* (Chenauxhandel) (1780–1784) in Freiburg, but also the riots in the Guild Cities Schaffhausen (1689), Basel (1691) and Zurich (1713). Similarly, in Geneva of the 18th century turmoil and constitutional struggles erupted repeatedly between the various population groups. These disturbances led in some places to improvements of the system, such as in Basel and St. Gallen, where the Grand Council appointed by the guilds again became the supreme political body. Or in Glarus, Freiburg, Berne, Basel and Schaffhausen where the election by lot was introduced to combat the corrupt practice of buying a seat (Praktizieren).

Population groups without political rights

The dominance of families led to the exclusion of most of the population from political life: The members of families capable of ruling but not involved in the government as well as the *inhabitants* (Habitanten) permanently settled in the city but not entitled as capable of ruling, and finally the *"petty citizens"* (Hintersässen). The latter had to renew their residence permit every year against the payment of the petty citizen's money (Hintersässengeld), had no political rights, only partial or no access to the guilds and other associations, and were largely excluded from the lower municipal offices and services. They did not participate in the cooperative property of the city (i.e. pastures and forests) and could only purchase limited land in the town. It was no different in the provincial towns and villages of subject territories where the upper social strata of wealthy merchants and farmers, publicans and millers divided the administrative offices subordinated to the city government, such as the sub-bailiffs, ushers and bursars. There was also a lower class of small-scale farmers (Tauner), day-labourers and secondary citizens, who could not participate in any of the privileges and possessions. They often hired themselves out for mercenary service and since the 18th century also as workers in the emerging textile industry.

The dominance of families in the 16th to the 18th century is not a peculiarity of the Confederation. They also existed, for example, in the German Imperial cities or in cities, which had belonged to the Republic of the Netherlands since 1597. A circle of families also dominated these cities in the 17th and 18th century, despite a democratic or republican political foundation.

With the Helvetic Revolution of 1798, the constitutions of the different cantons were abolished, and a unified state emerged. The dominance of the guilds and the patriciate was abolished. In the Mediation period after 1803 they were partially restored, and it was only in the Regeneration period after 1830, that some of the cantonal constitutions enshrined the sovereignty of the people and freedom rights.

Muenchenwiler Castle (BE). The castle was built from the stones of a former Cluniac monastery. Bernese patrician families owned it from 1535 until 1932. Photo: Author.

4.3 Cantons with a monarchical constitution

In addition to the provincial community assembly cantons and the City cantons, there were also cantons with a monarchical constitutional model among the Associated cantons. Among the most important was the Principality of Neuchâtel-Valangin, the Prince Constance of St. Gallen and the Princely Bishopric of Basel.

Neuchâtel

The Earldom of Neuchâtel and the confederate domain Valangin came to the Princely House of Longueville-Orléans at the beginning of the 17th century and in 1707 under the rule of Prussia. Neuchâtel became the absolute property of the House of Hohenzollern but retained its rights and freedoms within the framework of this monarchy. Apart from the royal "gouvernement", the *Three Ranks* (*Trois Etats*) exercised local government in the form of a municipal assembly. This consisted of three groups such as the four civil officers (*officiers civils*) or the four oldest state councillors, then the four bailiffs (*châtelains*) and the four ministerial (*ministeraux*) as representatives of the city. In this way, the Three Ranks gradually gained the power of legislation and judicial authority.

Ecclesiastical territorial domains

Of the numerous ecclesiastical territorial domains which had formed from the 10th century onwards, at the end of the Ancien Régime, only the micro territory of the Engelberg Abbey, the Princely Bishopric of Basel and Prince Constance of St. Gallen remained. The others had fallen victim to the expansion of cities and rural communities as well as the emigration of citizens from the towns of bishops and monasteries in the Late Middle Ages and the Reformation. The bishops of Sion and Lausanne and the abbots of Pfäfers, Einsiedeln, Muri, and Schänis, still bore the title of an Imperial prince, but they owned no secular domains anymore.

The ecclesiastical territorial domains featured the dual function of the Prince-Bishops or Prince-Abbots as secular landlords and spiritual leaders of the Catholic Church. Their secular territory was subject to the Emperor, which granted them the title of Imperial Prince with a seat and vote in the Imperial Diet. Due to historical developments, the secular territory was often not identical with the religious area of the bishopric or monastery.

The Prince-Abbot was elected by the convent of his monastery, while the Prince-Bishop mostly by the cathedral chapter of the diocese, a body of clerics who worked at the bishop's church (cathedral). The election of the bishop took place through the cathedral chapter based on a rule from his ranks; so that the elected bishop received his religious power; the pope then had to confirm him.

In their secular territories, the Prince-Abbot and the Prince-Bishop had the position of a monarch. They enacted or confirmed their territorial rights and exercised, mostly by delegation to other functionaries, the high and low jurisdiction.

Princely Bishopric of Basel

With the inclusion of the City of Basel in 1501 in the Confederation, the Prince-Bishop of Basel lost the secular jurisdiction over the city and in 1529, with the Reformation, also the spiritual authority. The Reformation also led to the move of the Prince-Bishop's residence to Porrentruy. In the early modern period, the secular territory of the Prince-Bishopric included only the Jura, the northern parts of Baselland, and some exclaves on the Upper Rhine. Divided into 17 bailiwicks or domains, in which bailiffs and mayors, as representatives of the Prince-Bishop, exercised power. Before the 16th century, the central administrative functions of the Prince-Bishopric were predominantly performed by the cathedral chapter and then increasingly by secular counsellors. Councils were established, which, on behalf of the bishop, exercised the executive and judicial functions. The *Court Council* (*Hofrat*), as the supreme judicial body in the Prince-Bishopric, served as an appellate body against judgments of the courts in bailiwicks. Its decisions in civilian affairs were passed on to the Imperial Chamber Court in Wetzlar. The assembly of the ranked landlords (*Landstände*), which consisted of representatives of the clergy and the subjects, took an active role in the distribution of extraordinary tax revenues.

The Prince-Bishops' institutions in the Princely Bishopric Basel in the 18th century.
Artwork: Historisches Lexikon der Schweiz HLS, Basel (Fürstbistum).

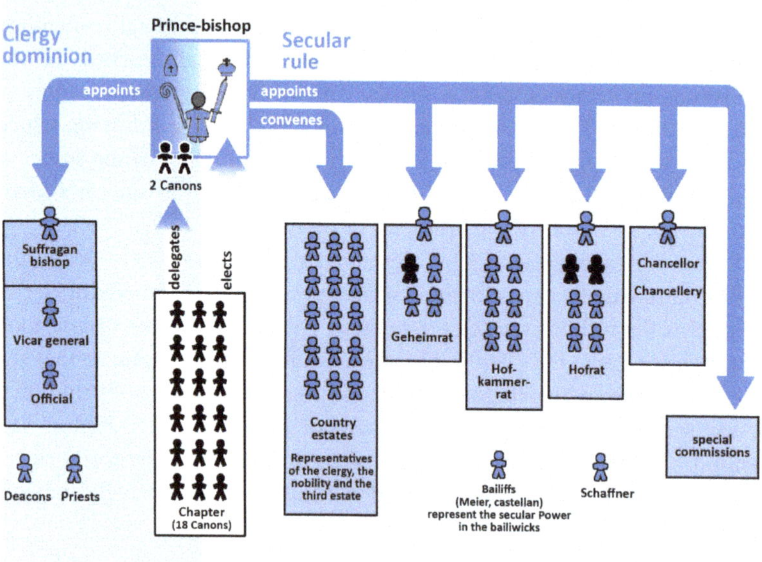

The Prince-Abbot of St. Gallen had already lost his rights to the city in the 15th century. In the short period of 60 years, the Prince-Abbots Ulrich Rösch (reigned from 1463 to 1491), Gotthard Giel von Glattburg (1491–1504) and Franz Gaisberg (1504–1529) succeeded in expanding the sovereignty, and the regional administration from Wil to Lake Constance as well as in Toggenburg. The Prince-Abbots *aide* (*Adlatus – Hofmeister)* as the highest secular representative exercised the high jurisdiction (Blutbann) likewise the bailiffs in Wil, Rorschach, and Oberberg, while the rest of the bailiffs and mayors only exercised the low jurisdiction.

Prince Constance of St. Gallen

The monarchical constitutional structure did not necessarily lead to autocratic rulership. As in the provincial and city cantons, there were offices and committees in the administration of the monastery state, which enabled individual persons to participate in its economic resources and its political rule. In this way, representatives of the local leadership were bonded with the abbey.

4.4 The constitution of Sovereignty

Privileges as a prerequisite

As illustrated in chapter 3, the cantons of the Confederation acquired rights and freedoms through Imperial privileges. They formed the legal basis for their political autonomy, which they often had to defend forcefully against the other competing powers in their territory, especially the Habsburgs and Savoy, later also Milan and France. Due to an accelerated consolidation process in the 15th century, they allied themselves to form the political structure of the Old Confederation, which had not yet clearly defined territorial boundaries, had only limited competencies and was entitled to just a modest collective domain, the Common Dominions.

However, the privileges granted by the Empire and by town lords served the cantons as a basis for the autonomous organisation of their realm. In *Land Peaces, Land Rights, Hand-Bindings (Handfesten), Jurors Letters* and similar legal texts, the first constitutional structures were established, and rules for peace-keeping and the coexistence of people in cities and the countryside were adopted.

Different types of sovereignty

In the 14th century, the cantons of the Confederation began to extend their dominions besides the Common Dominions. By acquiring and consolidating sovereign rights, a majority of them set up real internal sovereignties by the end of the 15th century. These survived as larger or smaller regional states until the end of the Ancien Régime. During the formation of the new federal country, after the constitutional changes of the first half of the 19th century, these territories formed the basis for the territorial organisation of a part of the cantons. The most impressive example of the establishment of sovereignty was undoubtedly Berne, whose area in the Ancien Régime included 11,000 km^2 with a population of 400,000 comprising a large number of other cities besides the capital. Therefore, Berne was the most significant *city-state* north of the Alps – if this expression seems adequate given its spatial expansion. Likewise, the sovereignties of other cities such as Zurich, Lucerne, Basel, Freiburg, and Solothurn were not insignificant.

On the other hand, the provincial cantons were unable to establish any or then only modest territorial dominions due to the lack of financial resources. In 1517, Glarus, for example, acquired the Earldom of Werdenberg and the House of Wartau from the Baron of Hewen for 21,500 florins. Schwyz owned quite a vast territory with the rural land of the March and Uri with the Leventina. Like the city cantons, the provincial cantons also took part in the Common Dominions, which were a source of political self-confidence and income. Several Associated cantons also established sovereignties such as the Prince-Abbot of St. Gallen, who acquired the Old Countryside (Alte Landschaften) and the Toggenburg. Or the Zenden communities of the Upper Valais, who ruled over the Lower Valais, as well as the three Rhaetian Covenants governing Maienfeld, Bormio, Chiavenna and the Valtellina valley.

Between the cantons of the Confederation existed considerable economic and social differences and likewise between the different subject territories. In addition to rural, agricultural areas, there were some provincial towns where crafts and trade dominated. The legal relations to the principal canton could also be different according to how it had acquired them, and the administration on-site was also not uniform. Thus, the internal sovereignty of the cantons found its tangible form in many different ways.

The early-modern sovereignty as a form of autocratic rule replaced the feudal system, based on personal ties and became a prerequisite for the emergence of the modern territorial state. Sovereignty was an essential part of the historical development of modern statehood.

The right of Citizenship Contract of 1330 of the city of Berne with Earl Aymo of Savoy. The members of the Grand Council swear an oath to the Right of Citizenship Letter, with which the city gave the Earl the Right of Citizenship (ius burgense) but released him from the constitutional tax obligation. Because an oath was made before God, the swearers raise three fingers of their hands, which symbolise the Trinity in the Christian religion. On the pedestal with the Chair of the Minor Council, the Keeper of records reads the letter, the Mayor and the Earl take the oath. On the wall two Bernese coat of arms, above it the Imperial shield with the Imperial crown. Picture (Photography): Diebold Schillings Spiezer Chronik, facsimile edition of the manuscript Mss. Hist. Helv.I 16, Kantons- und Universitätsbibliothek Freiburg (Cantonal and university library Freiburg).

4.4.1 Causes for the acquisition of Sovereignties

Excessive debt of the nobility

The statutory basis for the acquisition of influence beyond the legal sphere of the city walls was the acquisition of sovereignties in rural environments, for which there were different possibilities. The fact that these were accessible for the cantons of the Confederation was a direct outcome of the crisis of the feudal aristocracy in the 14th century and furthermore the result of the declining productivity in the countryside. The founding of cities had led to migration and plagues and wars added to the decimation of the country's population. Many estates were no longer cultivated, and so no more revenues were channelled to the landlords. Their demand for money rose with the development of trade and the monetary economy, which had led to a price increase of commercial goods. However, the natural and financial contributions of the tenants could not be increased at will, as they were often set out in community statutes (*Offnungen*).

The decline in the material livelihood affected the members of the lower nobility more than the princes and monasteries. To make a living, they had to incur debts. To save themselves from the high indebtedness they sought to pledge and later definitely sell their estates and jurisdictions and even bailiwicks. Those noble families who had survived the wars and plagues of the 14th century suffered a material decline resulting in a loss of political influence. Those noble families, who did not move out of the territory of the Confederation, either sought the protection of more powerful sovereigns using the Right of Citizenship or tried to integrate themselves into the new ruling classes of cities and provincial states.

Acquisition by dynasts and cities

Other sovereigns also exploited the crisis in the feudal aristocracy. Wealthy and resourceful dynasts, such as the Dukes of Savoy, Habsburg, and Milan started to acquire bailiwicks, estates, and jurisdictions and also urban and rural municipalities did the same. Several cities gained ground within a few decades in the surrounding rural region. Lucerne gained influence over Weggis (1380) as its first bailiwick and later after the Battle of Sempach (1394) over the feudal territories of Sempach, Rotenburg, Hochdorf, and Root, as well as the Entlebuch and Merenschwand. In 1406, the city acquired the scattered feudal rights of the Habsburgs, and later the Earldom of Willisau. It extended its municipal high jurisdiction to the estates of Baldegg and also to the bailiwicks of Ebikon, Malters, and Littau. In Sursee, Lucerne had the right to appoint the mayor; here as elsewhere, the city was the legal successor to the Habsburgs. Lucerne also incorporated various secular and religious landlords in its Right of Citizenship.

4.4.2 Forms of acquisition

There were different ways of acquiring rights and gaining political influence:

Acquisition by pledge and purchase

A first option was the *acquisition* of a *pledge*, but better the *proprietorship* of estates, sovereign rights, and regalia. Among the last two are the high and lower jurisdiction, tax- and customs-rights, the right to raise troops (*Mannschaftsrecht*) but also hunting-, fishing-, mining- and forestry-rights. These kinds of rights were not only acquired by the city and provincial cantons, but also by wealthy citizens and countrymen. Around 1400, a large part of the dominions was privately owned and therefore not under the direct influence of the cantons. Only the jurisdiction and taxation were centrally organised. Anyone exercising these elementary public functions could exert considerable authority on the local people.

Right of Citizenship and Territorial Rights

A second possibility was the conclusion of contracts for the *Right of Citizenship and Territorial Rights* with neighbouring, usually politically or economically weaker sovereigns such as nobles, monasteries, cities or provincial municipalities. The conclusion of such a treaty was a kind of barter trade and established a protection and shield relationship similar to that of the citizenship: one party promised protection and shield, the other went under the latter's rule. The city of Berne used this option on a large scale, so that half of the 68 larger territorial domains, acquired during the late medieval period, were based on a right of citizenship. Zurich, Lucerne, Solothurn, and Schwyz also used this option to break down the legally binding obligations of their contract partners with their sovereigns.

Patronage

Another possibility was the acquisition of a *patronage*. These were acquired from monasteries and religious foundations covering ecclesiastical bailiwicks existing since the 11th century. The patrons were obliged, as before the clerical bailiffs (Kastvögte), to provide military and judicial protection of the monasteries, and to exercise the secular jurisdiction in these territories. The patronage also allowed direct influence on the vast estates of the monasteries and the participation in their revenue. In these sovereignties, the patrons claimed the rights to raise troops, the high jurisdiction and the power of taxation.

External citizens

One of the cities preferred possibilities was the conferring of *External Citizens Rights (Ausbürgerrecht)*. An External Citizen Right could be granted to the peasants living in the surrounding region of cities. External Citizens had the same rights and responsibilities as the citizens living in the town; and like the inhabitants of the city, they had to purchase citizenship, pay taxes and contribute to the military defence of the city. In war and unrest, they were able to seek shelter in the town. By granting city rights to numerous inhabitants of their surroundings, cities such as Berne, Zurich and Lucerne increased their legal and political influence in the rural regions. This policy, of course, conflicted with the interests of the former landlords of these external citizens such as the noble and ecclesiastical sovereigns, whose authority was undermined. The aggressive politics of granting External Citizen Rights of the city of Lucerne, at the expense of the Habsburgs, was one of the causes for the Battle of Sempach.

Conquest

Another possibility was military conquest. This alone did not in any way alter the feudal status, but a conquest led to the compulsory sale of sovereign rights to the victor.

4.4.3 The streamlining of domination

The enumeration of the various possibilities of acquisition underlines that the areas dominated by a single canton were not a "state territory" in the modern sense, but rather a mixture of the most diverse rights, which allowed access to different associations of persons and entities. These sovereign rights were acquired by the provincial and the financially much more powerful city cantons for different reasons. They often wanted to weaken political rivals, to realise strategic interests or to safeguard the Land Peace better and usually, it would also include the development of new revenue sources and markets or the elimination of supply bottlenecks.

The cantons subsequently made efforts to streamline and consolidate their rule. For this purpose, they used various methods:

Consolidation of jurisdiction

The claim and consolidation of the different forms of jurisdiction: the jurisdiction, besides the right to raise troops and the power to levy taxes as elementary forms of "statehood" was the backbone of sovereign authority. To whom the gallows belonged, belonged the rule. The legal subjects regarded anyone, who dispensed justice or decided on damage claims, imposed and enforced punishments, as an authority, which ensured peace and order. Therefore, the places attempted to gain control of the lower and the higher jurisdiction, and then, with the *Privilege of Evocation (privilegium de non evocando)*, to eliminate the courts of appeal of the former rulers. Through their own appellate body, they were able to influence the court practice and thus also the right in the dominated territories. The cantons even tried to eliminate private judicial authorities. In the Bernese *Dispute of the Twing Lords* (Twingherrenstreit) of 1470, for example, the Council of Berne abolished in specific regions the right of private individuals for *Force and Jurisdiction* (Twing and Bann), which included, among other things, the ability to exercise the lower jurisdiction. The existing *Twing Lords* (Twingherren), members of the wealthy and prestigious bourgeois families, lost their public functions in their dominions and became just landowners.

Harmonisation of the law

Influence on the law in subject territories: The right to enact an ordinance law did not go readily hand in hand with the acquisition of a jurisdiction. The subject territories retained the power to issue regulations for their region themselves. At the beginning of a reign, the new bearers of sovereignty confirmed the existence of local law. Every area, however small, had its own civil and penal code, which led to a tremendous *fragmentation of law* in the territory of the Confederation and thus rendering a legal unity in the subject territories of specific cantons impossible. In the 16th century and increasingly in the 17th and 18th century, some cantons made extraordinary efforts to influence the right of their urban and rural subject territories. They had to submit their new laws to the Council of the principal canton for approval, or the law of the latter was considered as supplemental law if the law code of the subject territory contained a gap or uncertainty. The practice of the appellate instances also led to a legal harmonisation, since the law of the principal canton applied as the basis for decisions. Until the end of the Ancien Régime, a complete legal entity was not realised, but a gradual harmonisation of the judicial order in subject territories with the law of the Principal canton was possible.

Mandates

Enactment of *mandates*, which also applied to adjacent subject territories: With the elimination of episcopal power in the reformed areas, the secular authority claimed the right to enact norms for the order of church life, but also for marriage and on the general conduct of life. In the Early Modern Period, from the first church and marriage ordinances evolved in reformed but also in Catholic cantons many norms for religious, marital and moral discipline, for the economy, and the mercenary system. To preserve the public interest and to live together according to Christian ideas, a policy to implement a state of good order (*guten Policey*) started and the authorities in some places issued a flood of norms with which they interfered in the life of the subjects. Until the end of the Ancien Régime, Zurich released several thousand mandates and ordinances.

Taxation

Increased use of tax sovereignty: The cantons extended their right to the collection of indirect levies on trade and transport (import-, export- and customs rights, with high taxes on salt, alcohol and luxury goods) from the city to the dominated territories. This secured them a stable income, which allowed them to set up a local administration in the dominions and to invest in financial reserves (*state treasury*), which guaranteed their full capacity to act in times of need. After the secularisation of the church estates, the reformed cantons also used tithes, which had previously been donated to the church, to cover the costs for the church and the welfare of paupers and schooling. A few cities even collected a wealth tax but, in most cantons, attempts to introduce regular direct taxes since the 16th century failed due to the opposition of citizens and subjects.

Pledge of Allegiance

The loyalty of the subjects to the sovereign through a *pledge of allegiance*: Like the vassals to their feudal lord and the citizens to the city rights, the subjects were now obliged to bind themselves to the sovereign authority by an act of *homage* (Huldigung). With their oath before the bailiff, they vowed obedience and compliance with obligations to the authorities, such as taxes and duties, jurisdiction, corvée and military services.

Outcome of this process

Using the methods mentioned above, the cantons gradually reached a transformation of the power structure in three areas:

- Domination was increasingly exercised over individual citizens or subjects instead of associations of persons and collectives,
- Acts of authorities were no longer confined to the preservation of peace, but extended to more and more aspects of the life of the citizens and the subjects,
- The out-dated freedoms and rights granted by the Emperor lost their importance as a legitimation of rule; the “representative” rule of the cantons was replaced by an “independent” rule.

The attempts to streamline rarely led to a complete monopolisation of the sovereignty, for not all jurisdictions exercised by noble, bourgeois or ecclesiastical beneficiaries could be eliminated. Monasteries and Abbeys maintained their special privileges; the subject territories retained their legislative autonomy, despite the efforts to reconcile and harmonise it. Provincial towns and individual rural regions remained mostly independent in their administrative organisation. Influenced by the concept of absolutism, a centralisation of power was pursued in the Confederation, but as a result of numerous rural upheavals was much less widely realised than in the monarchies of Europe. Thus, the division of power was to a certain extent a genuine phenomenon, but not a legal concept.

4.4.4 The organisation of the administration

Bailiffs

With the acquisition of sovereignties since the 14th century, the cantons were faced with the task of building administrative structures in the subject territories. At first, these structures were hardly institutionalised, inconsistent, and were often based on the decentralised bureaucratic organisation of the previous sovereigns, such as the aristocratic dynasts and private landlords. The new rulers replaced the officials of the Habsburg, Kyburg or Savoy by their office holders. The *bailiwick (Vogtei)*, also called *Kastlanei* or *Amt*, covered as an organisational entity the various sovereign rights in a particular area. Their chief was the *bailiff* (also called Landvogt, Kastlan or Amtmann). He was the most important and often the only direct representative of the sovereign, there to exercise the sovereigns rights and interests. His duties vary according to the size of the bailiwick and the organisation of the sovereignty. Usually, this included the structure of the legal administration (high and low jurisdiction), defence and peacekeeping (police), the management of administrative revenue (interest, duties, taxes) and property rights, as well as the supervision of communities, churches, and parishes. To carry out these tasks, he was assisted by other functionaries, including his deputy, the *Lieutenant-bailiff* (Untervogt), the *bailiwicks secretary* (Vogteischreiber), the *beadle* (Weibel) and the *mayors* (Ammanns). They exercised the sovereign's interests in the villages, as well as the *court assistants* (Gerichtssässen) at the lower court.

Bailiff and Lieutenant-Bailiff

In the provincial cantons, the bailiffs were elected by the provincial community assembly, and in the City cantons either by the Grand Council or the Minor Council. The bailiffs were accountable to their constituency, and they were obliged to do so by an oath of office. Usually, only citizens of the principal city or provincial canton were eligible as bailiffs, whereas the office of the bailiwick secretary and lieutenant bailiff was open to citizens of the local upper class. The position of the bailiff was limited in time and had to be bought by paying a cash sum to the treasury. The bailiff had a right to part of the revenue (fees, taxes, and fines) of a bailiwick. In many places, the bailiwick was a coveted source of income, so much that members of wealthy families capable of rule, in particular, strove for a career in a bailiwick's office.

In a bailiwick close to a city, the bailiffs were also members of the Minor Council and therefore had their residence in the city. They were only in their bailiwicks for court hearings and on accounting days. The day-to-day business was carried out by his lieutenant-bailiffs: they chaired the lower court, levied taxes, executed inheritances, auctions, and bankruptcies, and investigated in criminal cases. In the more distant subject territories, usually taken over at a later stage, the bailiff often resided in the castle of a noble Dynast, a chateau or in a provincial town. The bailiff and his assigned charges were essential links and communication organs between the sovereign and the subjects. By order of the bailiff, ordinances of the authorities were often read from the pulpits during mass on Sundays and complaints and petitions of the subjects were deposited with him.

The administration of a bailiwick was not uniformly organised, and larger provincial towns often had far-reaching administrative autonomy. Some of them like Aarau and Burgdorf ruled over their small territory despite their subjects' status, and many of them exercised the high jurisdiction themselves.

In the 17th century, a reform of the administrative structures in principal cities and subject territories took place. The administration was expanded and increasingly centralised. Besides the bailiffs, executive organs from the city started to take over tasks throughout the entire subject territories.

Front facade of the Bailiffs Seat in Cevio (TI). Photo: Author.

4.4.5 Rural unrest

With the subject territories, the Confederate cantons in many respects gained a valuable hinterland. With the right to raise troops (Mannschaftsrecht) they were able to recruit soldiers for their numerous wars and armed conflicts and with the taxes and duties levied on the rural population to finance them. In times of war and epidemics, they could supplement the decimated town-dwellers with the rural community. To ensure their supply, they prohibited farmers from selling their products elsewhere than in the urban market (*market constraint*); to protect the downtown guilds from competition, they regulated or banned craftsmen and trades in the subject territories. These measures led to protest and resistance, numerous disturbances and, in a few cases, to violent revolts. The list of troubles – mostly regional and often initiated by the local upper-class peasants – is long and covers the period from the end of the 14th century to the end of the Ancien Régime. Also, disturbances in the Common Dominions and subject territories of the Associate cantons were listed. Riots frequently occurred in the

15th century during the Reformation period, later in the middle of the 17th century and at the end of the 18th century.

Peasant's War of 1653

As a supraregional conflict the *Peasant's War (Bauernkrieg)* of 1653, triggered by an agricultural- and currency-crisis after the Thirty Years' War, is best known and swept through the subject territories of Lucerne, Berne, Solothurn, and Basel. The demands of the insurgents were more radical than usual. Previously, rural disturbances were concerned with the preservation of existing rights and freedoms or the withdrawal of administrative orders in the area of production regulations and levies. Now, however, political participation was called for in general as well as calls for their own "provincial community assemblies" and other assemblies and furthermore an active involvement in legislation.

Towards the end of the 18th century, political participation and a change in existing power structures were once again on the agenda. Under the influence of the ideas of Enlightenment and the Early Industrialisation, new demands were added, such as those for freedom of trade, the elimination of the land tax burdens and political equality with the dominating city and provincial cantons. The protests and conflicts at the end of the Ancien Régime were neither a new phenomenon, nor a symptom of a final general crisis of the existing constitutional structure, but a continuation of a centuries-old habit of resistance. With this opposition, the rural subject territories had de facto compensated for the lack of political representation and the participation in political will formation. Even if the disturbances were politically unsuccessful, they prevented, unlike in other European states, the enforcement of an absolutist government policy. Thus, the streamlining of the military organisation and the introduction of direct taxes could not be achieved in most cantons in the Confederation and also, as shown above, a legal entity could only be realised in small parts.

5 Development of Law

5.1 General information

The early medieval *tribal rights* were the legal records of individual population groups within the Frankish Empire. With the intermixing of the population groups and the disintegration of the Empire, they lost their importance. In the Holy Roman Empire, the preservation of peace was the task of the Emperor and the local rulers who were commissioned by him. It took place through the Great Imperial Peace and Land Peace enacted by local sovereigns of the High and Late Middle Ages. This land peace, however, contained only norms for the communitarian punishment of injustice and self-administered justice. Since the more significant part of the legal system was based on customary law (coutume, consuetudine), that is, on a long-standing constant application of the law. The customary law consisted of an elementary set of rules, such as marriage, child- and hereditary rights, land use, etc. The norms were passed down orally since the written word in the secular realm was still not widely used. The passing on of legal knowledge was carried out by the veteran men; the annual meeting of the lawmakers (Rechtsgenossen) questioned them on applicable norms. From memory, they had to reveal what had always been true.

In the Early Middle Ages, the written word was limited to the sphere of the church and served to spread theological knowledge. Biblical, mainly liturgical texts and the writings of the church fathers among others were copied and disseminated in the monasteries. Since the middle of the 12th century, the written word spread to the secular sphere to enact the local law in the west and the south of the territory of today's Switzerland. Often, only the contested questions were regulated in written form; the uncontested right was passed on as customary law in unwritten form. Thus emerged *Community documents* (*Offnungen)* and *Land rights* in rural areas and *Town Laws* in cities. The arrangement of the material did not follow systematic rules. These new legal norms were applicable only for small and tiny territories, based on the sphere of influence of the sovereign. During the ups and downs of the constitutional and historical changes, they usually emerged and disappeared with a ruler.

In today's judgment, the Late Middle Ages and early modern times are regarded as periods of fragmentation of law. It was the consequence of small-sized estates and jurisdictions, as well as the many small cities and towns with their constitutional autonomy. With the establishment of territorial sovereignty by secular and religious landlords and city cantons, efforts to harmonise and modernise the law went hand in hand. Records of Law (Offnungen) became territorial rights, and these again were partly superimposed by the law of the ruling cities. Later the influence of science led to a *Reformation* of city laws. With *Mandates (Mandate)* widely adopted in the 16th and 17th century, the power of strict regulation expanded and was consolidated. In the Confederation of the High and Late Middle Ages, a large number of sovereigns enacted few norms, whereas at the end of the Ancien Régime a few sovereigns passed many rules.

The description below is not a comprehensive "Theory of sources of Law" of the Old Confederation since a scholastically-dogmatic collection of their types of sources of law was an unfamiliar concept at this time. Instead, only some essential kinds of sources of law will be presented, which also existed in other areas of Europe, but developed their specific features in the territory of the Confederation.

5.2 The Records of Law (Offnungen)

One product of the new written form were the Offnungen or Records of Law. This is a generic term for rural sources of law in the 14th and 15th century. The term Offnung *("offnen"* = proclaim) refers to the custom of orally proclaiming the legal norms at court meetings. The law, which had previously been proclaimed only by legally competent men, had been recorded since the 14th century and was still read out periodically at the court meetings. In the German legal history, the Offnungen are known under the name of *Award (Weistum),* a name, which is only used in the region of the Middle Rhine and the Moselle. In legal research "Weistum" became the general term, based on the monumental legal collection of Jakob Grimm from the years 1840 to 1847, also covering the territory of Switzerland. There were other names such as in the Alsace, where this type of law was called *Dinghofrodel*, in Bavaria and Austria *Taiding*, and in Saxony and northern Bohemia *Rude*.

Regulatory Content

In general terms, a Record of Law clarified an existing legal relationship (a) between landlords and bonded peasants, (b) between peasants themselves, (c) between different sovereigns.

(a) Between landowners and bonded peasants: It determined within the context of the feudal system and often in order to resolve an actual conflict, the rights and obligations of a landlord and his subject; such as the annual basic interest rates and corvée services, the special levy of the best head in the case of death of the subject, the cooperative marriage and the dates and competencies of the manorial court of justice.The Records of Law also had a stabilising function for the authority, since the aristocratic and religious sovereigns secured with them their legal position to their subjects.

(b) Between the peasants among each other: The peasants settled their affairs in the context of the village community, for example, the collective use of pastures (Allmende), waterways and forests, as well as the reciprocal permission of path allowance (Wegrecht).

(c) Between different sovereigns

Different sovereigns furthermore kept their relevant court competencies in a Record of Law, such as the responsibility for the high and the lower jurisdiction, to prove their reciprocal claims in case of a conflict. This indicated that Records of Law were created mainly when legal claims were contested and therefore required evidence. With the Records of Law, one could claim that something had been applicable "for ages" because the village elders or court assistants (Gerichtssässen) had been consulted. Due to the limited ability to pass on knowledge unaltered on an oral basis, assumably, most laws recorded in this way were old; meaning more than 40 to 60 years old. The Records of Law were, therefore, not documents of a long and faithful tradition, but rather the creations of their own time.

The Records of Law give an insight into the rural life of the Late Middle Ages. They are, therefore, not only of interest to legal historians but also for the research of economic and social history.

Records of Law lost their adaptability through the written fixed form. New social and economic conditions in many places made them obsolete. They were still read out in court every year, but they successively lost their relevance. Even without being explicitly rescinded, they were superimposed by a layer of more recent new legal norms.

5.3 Land Rights

Concept and regulatory content

Since the Late Middle Ages, the expression "Land Right" (Landrecht) stands for the law applicable in a defined geographical territory such as a county or valley. A Land Right was usually based on initially unwritten customary law (Record of Law), on privileges, which the secular or religious rulers had ceded, on alliances with other entities, as well as on bylaws for internal matters. In an early phase, these bylaws had the purpose of preserving peace primarily. The *Land Peaces* (*Landfrieden*) with their norms for the punishment of elementary injustices represent early Land Rights. However, the provincial authorities also included provisions on the constitution of the canton, as well as civil norms for the matrimonial property regime and inheritance law as well as regulations on ownership, servitutes, ground rents and seizure. Furthermore, norms of civil and criminal proceedings were also included. With Land Rights, the counties and valleys manifested themselves as independent legal spheres.

Local collections of the Land Rights

The Land Rights were enacted by the assembly of the free *Rechtsgenossen*, usually at the court assembly or by the provincial community assembly. Like the Records of Law, they were read out loud annually. Unlike these, however, they remained open until the modern era for further evolution. If necessary, new norms were added or included. Land Rights, which had become confusing by the growth of new regulations, were occasionally replaced by a new set of laws. For example, in 1448 the provincial community assembly of Glarus wanted to get a complete collection of the norms of Land Rights adopted since the first bylaws of the territory had been enacted in 1387. Similar collections of Land Rights have also been found in Appenzell since 1409, in the region of the March since 1427, since 1432 in Zug and since 1456 in Nidwalden. Further additions and new collections followed in the 16th century. Through continuous additions, the Land Rights of the places in Central Switzerland and the Appenzell changed during the early modern times and became the state right (Landesrecht) of these cantons.

During the establishment of their sovereignty, the cities often had the Land Right of their new subjects collected. The city of Berne, for example, compiled the Land Rights of the Obersimmental in 1509, the ones of the region Hasli in 1534 and 1598 those of the region Saanen. At the same time, the respective local Land Rights were newly systematised and supplemented by municipal law. For the renewal of the Land Rights in the region Emmental in 1559, a large number of regulations from the Berneses statutes of the city court from 1539 were included.

A particularly close connection between the judicial communities and the legal regulations is evident in the numerous Land Rights of Grison.

Although the Land Rights were the rural counterpart to the City Rights, they had different regulatory content, because they did not focus on the regulation of the market, handicrafts, and trade.

Coutumes and Statuti

In the area of today's Western Switzerland, not only Land- but also City Rights were called *Rules (coutumes)*. Coutumes emerged as early as the 13th century, such as in Geneva in 1246, Lausanne in 1236, Moudon in 1273 and the Valais in 1255. The scope of these coutumes was not limited to the territory of the respective cities but also extended to the region dominated by them. In the southern part of Switzerland, the Land Rights were called *Statutes* (Statuti).

A considerable part of the Land Rights from the area of present-day Switzerland is readily available in edited form. Since 1898, the Swiss Association of Lawyers has published the *Collection of Swiss Law Sources* (SSRQ), which today comprises around 100 volumes. It contains in addition to Land Rights, also Records of Law and City Rights since the High Middle Ages until 1798.

5.4 The City Rights

Formation

The first step in the development of a particular right in a rural environment was the granting of *privileges* and *freedoms* to an existing or newly established urban settlement by the town lord. With this award, the town lords wanted to make their cities attractive to newcomers from the countryside. In the late 12th century this was the impetus to the development of a new group of legal sources, the City Rights.

In the first phase, city rights originated from the town lord. Later, with the rising legal autonomy from the citizens themselves, the citizens joined forces in a *Consensus* (*Einung*) committing themselves to the observance of the *City's Peace*, which meant the renunciation of violence and the delegation of the conflict resolution to municipal jurisdiction.

The particular economic structure of the cities was another factor, which fostered the emergence of city rights, apart from the granting of freedoms and the adoption of peace regulations. Market, handicrafts, trade, and commerce needed their regulations. Norms for debt-, trade- and enforcement- rights often used the customary law, then were consolidated as a result of their constant application by the market court, which ultimately led to their written form.

Rights Assurance (Handfeste)

These constitutional, debt, penal and procedural norms were developed in the 13th century, often in an *Assurance of Rights (Handfeste - franchise)*, a parchment certificate with the seal of the town lord as a sign of his assurance. The cities obtained this assurance from the town lord, for example the city of Freiburg in 1249. Here the two Earls of Kyburg, Hartmann IV the Elder and his nephew Hartmann V. the Younger confirmed the newly arranged Assurance of Rights by the town citizens, which initially had been given to them by Berchtold IV in 1157. From today's point of view, it contains provisions on the rights and obligations of the town lord, the mayor, the council and other officials in a somewhat unsystematic arrangement. Furthermore, not only regulations on taxes and communal property, the punishment of manslaughter, theft, unlawful entry of markets and trespassing but also on trade, handicraft and customs duties were included. Moreover, debt, property, family and inheritance law could be found. These regulations had developed continuously since the founding of the city and were then included in different sets of norms into the Assurance of Rights.

Statutory power

In the second stage of development, with the increasing independence of the cities from the town lord, city rights originated at the citizen's assembly. These new rights supplemented the rights contained in the Assurance of Rights, or replaced them by norms, to which it had committed itself by means of a Consensus, as in the Juror's Letter (Geschworenen Brief) of Lucerne in 1252, in the Courts Letters (Richtebriefen) of Zurich, 1218/55, Schaffhausen, 1291 and St. Gallen, 1310, or in the Letter of Venner (Vennerbrief) of Freiburg 1404.

In a third development step, the statutory authority passed to the city council. The right now set by the council was summarised by the keeper of records in *Town Charter Books* (Stadtrechtsbücher) and read out before the assembled citizenship to validate it. By taking the citizen's oath, the citizens committed themselves to the observance of the norms. By taking over the statutory authority, the Council also claimed the jurisdiction. Previously, the council exercised the jurisdiction on behalf of the town lord. Now it did so in his name.

The city rights were initially applied exclusively to the area within the city walls. Later its scope was extended to the precincts outside the city (Bannmeile – Ban Mile), an area where the jurisdiction of the municipal court was enforceable. City Rights also applied to external citizens (Ausbürger).

Cities with the same rights

As elsewhere in Europe, groups of cities with the same city rights (Stadtrechtsfamilien) were formed in the territory of the Confederation. This occurred when city councils transferred all or parts of their city rights to other towns. This was done first by the Zähringer, who transferred parts of the city law of Freiburg i. Br. to the cities of Berne, Burgdorf, Freiburg, and Morat, which had also been founded by them. These daughter-cities (Tochterstädte), in turn, transferred parts of their city rights to other settlements, such as Berne did in Laupen, Kirchberg, and Unterseen, or Freiburg in Erlach, Nidau, Büren, Aarberg, and Arconciel. The Zähringer city rights were also adopted by other dynasties such as the Kyburgs, Habsburgs, and Savoy. As a consequence, regulations in the Assurance Rights of Freiburg can be found in the city rights of the Kyburg- and Habsburg-towns Aarau, Brugg, Zofingen, Sursee, Sempach, and Diessenhofen. The city rights of Moudon passed to the Savoy towns of Châtel-Saint-Denis, Grandcour, Coppet, Morges, Nyon, Romont, Yverdon, Echallens, and Gruyère.

The front page of the Freiburg City Right. "In the name of the Holy Trinity and the names of the Father, the Son, and the Holy Spirit, Amen. This right is of the city of Freiburg im Üechtland." The small image shows the Freiburg battalions with their coat-of-arms at the homage of the Duke of Austria, behind him stands one of his councillors. Picture: Staatsarchiv Freiburg i.Ue. (State Archive of Freiburg) Legislation and Miscellaneous 42, Schwabenspiegel, Parchemin - 166 ff. - 50.5 x 36.5 - Freiburg Switzerland - 1410, 133r.

In the 16th century, when the ecclesiastical and social life was reformed, in many places also the municipal statutory laws underwent a revision. They were rearranged, systematised and completed. These changes became necessary due to the intensification of economic life and the emergence of urban sovereignties. The revisions were based on the Roman law taught at the law schools and universities. Graduates from these institutions such as advisers of the council and the keepers of records introduced Roman law terms, systematics, and legal figures into the established law as editors and compiled scholarly law, primarily in the spheres of private law and in particular in the field of the law of obligations. The type and extent of the compilation depended on the instructions of the council and the personality of the keeper of records. Through these collections, city law usually attained a higher technical and legal level. Examples of such newly conceived statutory rules of a city are the Basel City Court Ordinance of 1539 and 1719, the Bernese Court Statutes of 1539 and 1614, the Zurich Court Book of 1553 and the statutory laws of the city of 1715, the Solothurn city law of 1604, the Schaffhausen city law of 1766 and the Lucerne city laws of 1588 and 1706. Specific city rights also spread to their subject territories. The statutory city laws of Berne, edited by Hans von Rütte in 1539, became the model for the city law renewals of Aarberg (1541/48) and Nidau (1548) as well as for the statutory law of the Emmental (1559).

Regarding the reform of city rights in the area of present-day Switzerland, it is even more important to investigate how far these can be compared with the *city-rights reforms* (Stadtrechtsreformen) in Germany. The numerous records of the Land Rights in the Valais from the 16th century show that the reform efforts in the Confederation were not limited to urban areas. The influence of scholarly law varied from place to place. Sometimes it only led to the adoption of terms and systematics, whereas in other cases to a substantive reception of legal figures from the Roman law. In Western Switzerland, the influence of the scholarly *written law (droit écrit)* was relatively steady since the High Middle Ages. It was applied in the Earldom of Savoy in the vicinity of Geneva, but also in the bailiwick of Chablais in the Lower Valais as the subsidiary law to local law, and elsewhere it had a considerable influence on the *customary law* (droit coutumier).

5.5 The Mandates

The city and land rights contained a basic set of norms, including amongst others those of the private and criminal law. In the course of the Late Middle Ages, the need for regulation increased with the establishment of sovereignties and the intensification of the rule by authorities. New norms were no longer set only by supplementing the city and land rights, but also by own edicts, the *Mandates* (Mandate). This type of legal source can be traced back to the 14th century but their "heyday" was the 16th and 17th century. The mandates were for the most part issued by the councils of the sovereign and subordinate cities. The Tagsatzung hardly ever released one of them. The sovereigns increasingly regulated issues of public life with mandates. In the aftermath of the Reformation, many aspects of ecclesial and moral life were normalised. To proclaim them to the subjects in town and country, they were publicly displayed or read from the pulpit, either by the pastor or by officials. With the end of the Ancien Régime, the mandates lost their validity, but the cantonal legislation of the 19th Century adopted many of their regulatory contents.

This type of legal source is by no means a Swiss particularity. Mandates were issued with different names in many European countries. The Holy Roman Empire also issued mandates at the end of the 15th century and especially in the 16th century (in particular the Imperial Police Ordinances of 1530, 1548 and 1577). In legal historical research they are called *police ordinances (Polizeiordnungen). Policey* referred to the state governance of public order. Police ordinances were laws issued for the sake of good public order in the community. In the territory of the Confederation, this term is rare. This type of legal source is usually called *Sentence (Satz)* or *Ordinance (Ordnung), Admonition (Vermahnung)* and notably since the 17th century, mandate.

Regulatory content

Regarding content, the mandates covered different spheres of public and private life. There existed overlapping areas in private and criminal law with city and land rights. They could include rules for labour, trade, and economies, such as the use and management of landed property or the market constraint for agricultural products of farmers, but also compulsory labour for young, able-bodied workers and the prohibition of employment and competition for non-residents within a city. Furthermore, bans on purchasing and reselling the property to prevent speculation, rules on interest and pension acquisitions and ground rents, quality requirements for goods as well as regulations for measurements, weights and prices. Numerous provisions should limit usury, as well as mercenary service and begging. Concerning the last two matters in particular coordinated efforts of the cantons occasionally took place.

In the 16th century, in addition to these economic regulations, rules to enforce religious and ecclesiastical norms such as the regular and punctual church visit, the observance of Sundays and holidays and rules on refraining blasphemy, swearing, oaths and perjury. Furthermore, rules on the validity of marriage vows and church marriage, on the prohibition of inter-confessional marriages and the practice of Anabaptism as well as on the observance of impediments to marriage. The mandates also contained provisions on the administration of the baptismal-, marriage- and death- registers, as well as the correct management of church property and alms funds and the like. All of these rules were enacted to encourage people to live virtuously from an ecclesial perspective. Even in the pre-Reformation period, the idea existed that the sinful life of man leads to earthly punishments of God in the form of plague, crop failures, inflation and wars among others. Therefore, the secular authorities considered it as their duty to lead their subjects using commandments and prohibitions onto the path of virtue.

Particularly in the 17th and 18th centuries, a further part of the mandates included the moral life of the subjects in general. Restrictions on pub visits, alcohol consumption, and gambling, but also the expenses for baptisms, weddings, and funerals, as well as expenditures for daily luxuries were intended to safeguard public morality and prevent poverty. They should ensure that subjects lived their lives according to their social status. Haughtiness was frowned upon.

The mandates document an intensifying perception of responsibility by the state authorities because with all these norms they interfered profoundly in the lifestyle of their subjects. The boundary between private and public life was barely recognisable. Anyone who broke the rules and prohibitions was fined or given a short prison term. Nevertheless, the mandates did not always lead to the intended social discipline of the citizens. In the 19th century, the old mandates were considered to be the expression of the police state, and the authority of the police was restricted to the protection of peace and order according to a liberal understanding.

The mandates also reflect the roots of modern administrative law, here exemplified by the ordinance issued by the city of Thun in 1777 *for the collective safety, decency and good order of public life because of significant abuses.* In this directive, at first on Sundays, any carting, driving and riding as well as the display of food and the opening of junk shops is forbidden. Further, it is ordered that at night servants and maids should not prowl around in the streets. Stagecoaches, trucks or carriages should not stand around in the streets, and no open fire should be carried through the city. It is forbidden for the innkeepers, to let someone stay overnight in their tavern, that no one should discard scrubbing slurry, construction debris or tares on the street. No one should erect a pigsty on the street, and the master butchers should bring their butchery dregs out of the city to prevent unreasonable stench - and much more. This kind of rules found their way into the modern police and administrative law, albeit with modifications and a less moral undercurrent.

The mandates are an essential and vibrant source of information not only for legal history but also for cultural, economic and social history. Some cantons of the Confederation issued mandates in large numbers. Especially after the Reformation, the city councils considered themselves as a kind of all-competent bodies for the spiritual and physical well being of their citizens and subjects. For Zurich and Berne, the number of mandates issued from the 14th until the 18th century is estimated at several thousand, that is an average of about 15 to 20 mandates per year.

6 The administration of justice

The administration of justice and the court system were always linked to the constitutional order. From the legal system and the real power-relations emerged the forms of justice and the authorities of the local courts. Knowledge of the court's charter requires the tradition of corresponding written sources, which is only the case from the 13th century onwards. Even in the Late Middle Ages and the early modern period, many matters in the administration of justice were still based on unwritten customary law. Only in the 19th century, the division of power emerged with the clear distinction of judicial authorities and an increased reflection on the meaning of sanctions. To use terms like irrationality or inefficiency for the qualification of justice in the cantons of the Old Confederation, however, would fall short of the actual situation. The court system tried, then as today, to settle disputes, to speak justice and to atone for injustice - albeit with much more limited mechanisms and possibilities.

Matching with the complex and continuously changing constitutional conditions, the judicial organisation of the High and Late Middle Ages was indeed extremely diverse.

6.1 Origin of the jurisdiction

Supreme Jurisdiction

During Frankish times, the king was the principal court ruler. Since he could not exercise the jurisdiction himself throughout the empire, he transferred this task to the Earls, whom he had appointed to preserve peace in the provinces of the Empire. The local jurisdiction took place before the court of the Earl. He convened the court meeting (*das Ding*) at regular intervals, where all free and mature men had to gather and decide on the cases that were presented to them.

In the Middle Ages, the Emperor of the Holy Roman Empire was the supreme judge. His Imperial House Court was the Supreme Court in which he was a judge. The Emperor had the right to seize any case that had not yet been decided by another court of law to hold proceedings in his court *(jus evocandi)*. The House Court was also responsible when an immediate imperial vassal was involved in a legal dispute. In the Confederation, these were the imperial free cantons as well as the bishops and abbots in the rank of imperial princes. The House Court was mainly an appellate court for appeals against judgments of regional courts. At the beginning of the 15th century, the House Court was replaced by the Imperial

Chamber Court, which was reorganised in 1495. The Confederates were not exempt from their jurisdiction, contrary to their assumption.

County courts

To enforce the right on site, the Emperor delegated his jurisprudence as previous the Frankish king, using the *Loan of the Ban (Bannleihe)* to the landgraves, who became chairman of the *county court*. The search for justice was exercised by a fixed amount of *sitting court assistants (Gerichtssässen)*, which, as the name says, assembled during the trial at the side of the Landgrave. Their judgment had to be confirmed or rejected by the attendant court comrades (Gerichtsgenossen) who formed the *audience (Umstand)*. The Landgrave had only the task of directing the court meeting, announcing the verdict and then having it carried out. Later the participation of the court comrades was abolished in many places. The separation of responsibilities, such as the non-judicial presiding judge, and the judicial court assistants, however, remained in place.

Mediatisation of the Jurisdiction

Initially, the Emperor would in turn newly assign the office of the Landgrave. By the 13th century, it had become hereditary, and the father could pass it on to his son. It could also be pledged or sold to other persons. Thus, noble dynasties such as the Zähringer and Habsburgs, but also religious leaders came into the possession of the local jurisdiction. A second reason why the Emperor increasingly lost local authority was his way of awarding privileges:

- With the *privilegium de non evocando*, the emperor renounced his right to take court cases to his private court (in favour of the receiver of the privilege).
- With the *privilegium de non appellando*, the Imperial House court lost its function as an appellate court.

Since the High Middle Ages, these privileges were acquired not only by the nobility but also by their legal successors the valley communities and cities. With the imperial freedom, the valley communities of central Switzerland and the other cantons of the Confederation were granted first instance jurisdiction. The court leader was the provincial community assembly in the rural communities, in the cities the city council. In the countryside, jurisdiction initially remained with the nobility, and the lower jurisdiction was often in the hands of a local landlord (Twingherren). With the establishment of sovereignty, the cities sought to enforce their jurisdiction in the dominated territory. For this purpose, they acquired many local jurisdictions by purchase, pledge or, if necessary, by force. As the delegate of the city council the provincial bailiff presided then at the court.

Imperial House Court

The short existence of an imperial county court in Zurich, for example, explains the mediatisation and territorialisation of the first instance jurisdiction. In 1362, Emperor Charles IV granted the city of Zurich, along with other rights, a "county court" for its "constant, faithful service" with all the "rights, freedoms, pardon and good habits that the county court of Rottweil has and has had from time immemorial." The background and motive for this award of an imperial county court after the model of the court in Rottweil was the political situation in the southwest of the empire. In the second half of the 14th century, the Habsburgs threatened the position of the emperor as the central authority with their expansionist desires, such as the usurpation of the Swabian ducal title by Rudolf IV. By expanding his imperial jurisdiction, the Emperor tried to counteract the breakaway movements and the mediatisation of the imperial estates. The county court initially developed a busy activity. However, in 1363, the city council was granted the right to elect the court judge from its ranks, and in 1400 it acquired the higher jurisdiction (Blutbann) over the city. Now the council could exercise the jurisdiction itself. The county court was dispensable and stopped its activity in the same year.

Red Tower of Freiburg. Named Red Tower because it served as a prison and execution site. Photo: Marc Imhof.

6.2 High and lower jurisdiction

Concerning jurisdiction, a distinction between high and lower jurisdiction existed. This division was based on the familiar distinction in Frankish times between *causae maiores* and *causae minores*. After the expansion of public criminal law following the Land Peace movement, the high courts dealt with offences that were punishable by death or mutilation. They were called blood jurisdiction (Blutgerichtsbarkeit) because these punishments were bloody. Consequently, a cane and the gallows symbolised it. In front of the lower court, civil disputes and minor offences were prosecuted, which were not punishable by corporal punishments or life sentences, but by prison terms or fines. However, there was no clear division of responsibility; in particular, the offence constituting bodily harm was often controversial. Therefore, theft, robbery, murder, manslaughter, arson, rape, and defamation were handled by the high jurisdiction.

The jurisdiction was part of the territorial sovereignty. The aspiring cantons of the Confederation made, therefore, great efforts to acquire the high and low jurisdiction from the aristocratic sovereigns. Financial interests were another motivation of the cantons because jurisdiction was an Imperial right (regalia) and revenue source. The parties in dispute had to pay a court fee. A part of a definite financial penalty fell to the court and in many places also the estate of an executed man. Conflicts of interest often led to disputes over the right of the jurisdiction itself or the specific distinction between high and lower jurisdiction.

The Twing Rule

The lower jurisdiction in rural territories was often in the hands of a noble or religious landlord. It was part of the *Force and Constraint (Twing und Bann)*, the complete power over the people of a specific area, such as a village. Within this community, the Twing Lord (Twingherr) was not only the landlord of the bonded countrymen but also decided on the use of common pastures (Allmenden) and waterways. He too exercised the trade restriction (Gewerbebann) for example by allowing the operation of mills, forges, and inns. He handled debt-, ownership- and inheritance claims as well as lighter breaches of peace (Friedbruch) and other lesser forms of delinquency. According to the understanding of that time, the Twing power (Twinggewalt) was the "full domination except for death", so everything was included except the high jurisdiction. The Twing Rule (Twingherrschaft) was associated with revenues, as the Twing Lord collected fees for approvals and permissions granted to the Twing members (Twingangehörige) as well as charges related to a court case.

Court scene during the "Twingherrenstreit" 1471. The Twingherrenstreit was a dispute between the bourgeoisie and city nobility over the supremacy in the city of Berne. In April 1470, the Grand Council elected a master butcher as mayor and not one of the four competing noble Twing Lords. On the same day, the Council renewed a dress mandate of 1464 to ban the use of beak shoes and train again. However, this was very popular with the nobles, because they could stand out from the "common people". They did not comply with the ban and therefore had to appear in court. Against the punishment imposed on them, they resisted with various measures that should force the Council to give in. With the help of envoys from the Confederation, the dispute was settled, and a new contract for Twing Lords was closed. The council after that chose a nobleman as mayor and abolished the dress mandate. Image: Diebold Schilling, Amtliche Berner Chronik, Burgerbibliothek Bern, Mss.h.h.I.3, p. 87.

The lower jurisdiction was not necessarily tied to the Twing- and Landlord-rule since the Twing Lord could sell it to other people or cities. Therefore, there were a large number of people in charge of provincial courts.

For the establishment of their sovereignty, the cities acquired many jurisdictions. Moreover, they increasingly undermined the rights of the Twing Lords. Especially in the early modern period, they used numerous mandates to gradually secure areas, where the regulation had previously been granted to the Twing Lords. As a result, the Twing power and in particular the lower jurisdiction of a Twing Lord lost importance and in turn, the lower jurisdiction exercised by the district bailiff, who was appointed by the city council, became more influential.

6.3 Secular Courts

City Courts

With the acquisition of the jurisdiction by a city, the *city council* became the court body. The city council judged the cases of low jurisdiction and, if it had acquired the blood jurisdiction those of the high jurisdiction. Initially, the city council as a whole, chaired by the mayor (Schultheissen), had to decide on a sentence (Spruchkollegium). With the increase in cases, a *city court* (Stadtgericht) was formed to relieve the city council. This court included the mayor or the aman as chairman and a set number of city councillors as assessors. The assessors were either delegated only from the Minor Council, or from both the Minor and the Grand Council. Depending on the frequency of the court hearings, the city court was also called *daily court* (Tägliches Gericht) or *weekly court* (Wochengericht). Decisions could be passed on to a more substantial body, such as the Grand Council. In the middle of the 16th century, an *appellate chamber* consisting of council members was formed in Berne. If the appellate chamber confirmed the death sentence of the city court, the verdict could be passed on to the Council of the Two Hundred for deliberation. Therefore, Berne had a three-step constitution of the court procedure.

County Courts

Criminal acts, which fell within the high jurisdiction, were usually judged by a *county court (Landgericht)* in the late medieval towns but also in rural areas. It was set up in a square or an alley under the open sky. It was composed of the county judge and the assessors, who were sitting inside a *ring* surrounded by the jurisdictional barriers, and a specially raised group of men surrounding the ring. These men, the court compatriots (Gerichtsgenossen), represented the public, an important factor in times when the power monopoly was still weak. With the consolidation of the power monopoly of the City Council, this court was relieved of its jurisdiction such as in Basel in the year 1622. From then on, the city court judged itself in the sphere of high jurisdiction *(Blood- or Maleficent Court/ Blut-* oder *Malefizgericht)* and often held in camera in the Council Lounge. This involved a change in the procedure.

The county court in Zurich 1383. Within the ring is the judge with a baton in his hand as a sign of his office and the court assessors sitting. Surrounding the ring are the court compatriots standing. The court scene is an illustration by Jacob Hoffmann in "Chronicon Helvetiae" written by Christoph Silberysen (1542–1608). Silberysen was abbot of the Cistercian monastery Wettingen from 1563 to 1594. The first part of the book dates back to 1576, the 2nd and 3rd part to 1572. Image: Aarau, Aargauer Kantonsbibliothek (Aargau Cantonal Library), MsWettF 16: 1, p. 381 - Silbereisen, Chronicon Helvetiae, Part I.

Twing Courts

In the countryside, the Twing Court handled the lower jurisdiction. The local sources of law mention a variety of other names for this kind of court, such as fief - and house court. Different names originated from the court chairman such as Vogt-, Keller-, Ammann- and Meier-Court, or depending on the date of hearings as in Hilarion- (21st October), May- or Autumn-Court. In territories under municipal sovereignty, the rulings of these courts could be passed on to the district bailiff. If the city had also acquired the Twing Rule, the district bailiff was in the first instance responsible, and the city council acted as an appellate court. The district bailiff often did not perform as the judge, but instead commissioned the lieutenant bailiff. The court assessors (Gerichtssässen), whose number varied from place to place and which mostly descended from local dignitaries, determined the sentence. In some regions, the local lower jurisdiction remained in place, despite the transfer of jurisdiction to a city, and the responsibility for the lower jurisdiction was split between the lower court and the district bailiff.

Blood Court (High Court)

The blood jurisdiction was initially in the hands of the district court and later passed to the district bailiff or city council. Since the 15th century, the blood court of Zurich also exercised blood jurisdiction in the countryside. Only in the more distant bailiwicks (Kyburg, Eglisau, Grüningen, Greifensee, Andelfingen, Regensberg, and Knonau), this remained with the district bailiff and the city council acted only as the appellate body. In the cities of the subject territories, the low and high jurisdiction remained mainly with the local city council, but the city council of the principal town kept at least the right to pardon.

In the cantons with provincial community assemblies, the jurisdiction was, as elsewhere in the country, handled by the county court that comprised of a certain number of court assessors and was chaired by the Landamman. In many places, the court assessors were members of the district council. Within this constellation, the provincial community assembly also acted as an appellate body, and the court ruled as a territorial sovereign even on the death penalty in the district bailiwicks. The district council of Glarus also served as blood court (Malefizgericht) in the county of Werdenberg, a rural bailiwick acquired in 1517 by Glarus.

Special courts

In addition to the courts illustrated above, there were several unique forms of jurisdiction, some of which were factually limited:

Bailiwick Court (Vogteigericht) of the religious, territorial sovereigns: In the territories of religious sovereigns, either the bishop or the abbot acted as supreme ruler and as such was the bearer of not only the spiritual but also the secular jurisdiction. As the chair of the *episcopal court (curia episcopi)*, he initially exercised the jurisdiction in person, but from the 14th century onward he delegated it to a bailiff he had appointed.

Free Courts or Free Districts (Freigerichte or *Freiämter)* existed in different regions of the Confederation as courts for people not bound by a landlord, so for free people. In some areas of German-speaking Switzerland, like in Willisau and

Affoltern am Albis, they ruled on disputes in the sphere of the lower jurisdiction. In parts of the Goms and Laax, they also held the high jurisdiction.

Guild Courts: Craftsmen and merchants had their own jurisdiction since the 14th century for the punishment of professional delicts, but also a dishonourable lifestyle among the guild members. Guild courts also judged crimes committed within the guildhalls, where the guild master exercised the jurisdiction as lord of the house.

Guest Courts: For non-residents, especially travelling merchants, a quick and uncomplicated civil jurisdiction was needed. Therefore, the city court met on request outside the regular court appointments, as a guest court, in a smaller cast and without observance of the usual charge and admission periods. Before the guest court, guests could complain against local citizens, citizens against guests and guests against other guests. At Uri, Schwyz, and Nidwalden this court was called *Alley Court* (*Gassengericht*), since it met in the open air, in an alley or on the marketplace.

6.4 Ecclesiastical Courts

6.4.1 In the Late Middle Ages

Diocesan Courts

In the dioceses of the Church existed ecclesiastical courts for the enforcement of canonical law since the 13th century: Since 1250 in the diocese of Geneva, 1252 in Basel, 1265 in the diocese of Constance, to which belonged large parts of the Confederation, 1260 in Lausanne, 1271 in Sion and 1273 in Chur. The chairmen of these courts (*Officials - Offiziale*) appointed by the Bishops often had a legal education and devoted themselves exclusively to case law, unlike judges in the secular courts, where neither was the case. Most of the officials had studied Canon law and even Roman law at a university in northern Italy or France. In the ecclesiastical courts, based on Roman-canonical procedural law, the procedure was in written form, this in contrast to the oral proceedings in the secular courts. The religious judge was free in the appreciation of the evidence and had to justify his judgment. In the case of fluid circumstances, he was able, by canon law, to conduct a summary procedure with shorter deadlines and limited method of taking evidence, allowing for a quick and cost-effective process. The litigations were recorded by a court notary, which limited the arbitrariness of the court chairman and therefore increased legal certainty. With the threat of spiritual punishment, the officials had efficient procedural coercion in their hands. Through an *excommunication,* a condemned man was not only excluded from the sacraments and the church community but also from secular legal relations since personal contacts with an expelled person were forbidden. Officials often threatened to excommunicate when they sent the summons to the court, thus placing intense pressure on the summoned to submit to the ecclesiastical jurisdiction.

Competencies

Due to its rationality and efficiency, the ecclesiastical jurisdiction was approached not only for judgments of religious legal issues but also for worldly affairs. With its rising political influence after the *Investiture Controversy* (1075/77) the Church extended its sphere of competence. Since the Early Middle Ages, she had claimed jurisdiction over the clerics, both as plaintiff and as a defendant. This judicial privilege *(privilegium fori)* was extended to the poor, widows, children, orphans and the sick; so to those who could not defend themselves because of their "weakness" *(personae miserabiles).*

Beyond this personal responsibility, the Church also demanded jurisdiction in all spiritual matters (*causae spirituales*) and issues related to them in a broader sense. These included matrimonial law, except marital property, ecclesiastical offices, patronage, benefices, tithes, and wills. Furthermore, complaints could be brought before the church court for the repayment of usurious interest or for noncompliance of contracts affirmed by oath, since usury and perjury were a sin and therefore constituted a church-law offence. The ecclesiastical courts were also used in other cases: When laypeople had declared by *Prorogation* a clerical instead of a secular judge to be competent; if no secular court was readily available or if a secular court refused to accept a case. Consequently, the officialates decided in many cases on worldly affairs and in particular on financial debt.

In the field of criminal law, all *crimina ecclesiastica* were subject to ecclesiastical jurisdiction. These included stealing, oath-breaking, and perjury, as well as heresy, blasphemy, witchcraft, adultery, bigamy, and fornication. The ecclesiastical court ruled according to canonical law and only when this did not contain a relevant rule of law, did it consult local secular law or Roman law.

Suppression

Since the 14th century, the cantons of the Confederation resisted against these sweeping judicial claims of the church. In particular, the increasingly influential cities tried with continuous prohibitions to prevent their citizens from calling on the church jurisdiction in other than spiritual legal issues. It should be limited to matrimonial matters, usury, and heresy only. Above all, the escalating threat of excommunication was a thorn in the side of the cities. In some cantons, such as in Berne and Freiburg, the local clerics were forbidden to sue a layperson in front of a church court. Therefore, their privilegium fori was already restricted. In addition, the Priest's Letter (Pfaffenbrief) of 1370 was adopted to limit external and therefore ecclesiastical jurisdiction. It belongs in a series of decrees that pushed back the authority of ecclesiastical courts in secular affairs in the Late Middle Ages. This suppression also had an impact on the reception of Roman-canonical law, since the decline of the influence of the religious courts led to percolation of the scholarly code.

6.4.2 In modern times

The diocesan courts continued to exist in those parts of the Confederation that had remained faithful to the Catholic Faith in the 16th century. However, their jurisdiction was gradually reduced to matrimonial law, ecclesiastical offices and duties and the jurisdiction over clerics. The persecution of religious crimes, especially blasphemy and witchcraft, had now become the task of secular courts. The Council of Trent (1545–1563), a reform council for the renewal of the faith and the elimination of existing grievances in the Catholic Church, decided amongst others the formalities for the church marriage and committed the clerics to strict compliance with their duties, in particular of the celibacy. The Catholic cantons subsequently insisted on the enforcement of this last regulation by the church courts. Where these did not take action, the city councils did not hesitate to admonish the bishop, nuncio and even the pope. The city councils interfered quite often in matrimonial matters and yet decided on the validity of engagements and marriages. Thus, the demarcation between secular and religious jurisdiction in spheres for which both powers considered themselves to be competent *(res mixtae)* remained difficult and conflict-laden until the 18th century. As late as in 1723, for example, the respective court jurisdiction of Lucerne and the Bishop of Constance were clarified in detail in a *punctuation*, to avoid tensions.

Reformed Marriage and Moral Courts

In those confederate cantons that joined the Reformation in the 16th century, a new form of clerical jurisdiction, the *Marriage and Moral Courts*, emerged. Since Zwingli and Calvin did not consider marriage as a sacrament, they contended that these legal circumstances should not be subject to the jurisdiction of the diocesan officialate. A new authority composed of representatives of the Church and secular authorities replaced it. According to the concept of the Christian parish, church and state should work together to decide legal issues that arose related to the validity and dissolution of marriages. On the suggestion of Zwingli, the city of Zurich established a marriage court in 1525, which was composed of two pastors and two representatives each of the Minor and the Grand Council. A similar authority *(the Standstill - Stillstand)* was created in the parishes in the countryside: the lieutenant bailiff and two *Marriage Supervisors (Ehegaumer*/gaumen = supervise) and two other honourable men remained after the Sunday service in the church and discussed the upcoming cases.

Following the example of Zurich, similar authorities were created in the other Reformed places as in St. Gallen (1526), Berne (1528), Basel (1529), Schaffhausen (1529), Glarus (1530), Chur (1530) and Appenzell Ausserrhoden (1600). In 1541, Calvin commissioned in Geneva the *Consistoire* with the jurisdiction of matrimonial matters, and in Neuchâtel, an identical authority was created in 1550. Berne established its *Consistory Courts (Chorgerichte)* after the conquest of Vaud. The Zurich court of marriage was also a role model for similar authorities in various southern German cities such as Constance, Ulm, Augsburg, Ravensburg, Stuttgart and Strasbourg.

Chorgericht in Berne. Image: Heinrich Richard Schmidt, Dorf und Religion. Reformierte Sittenzucht in Berner Landgemeinden der frühen Neuzeit, Stuttgart/Jena/New York 1995, p. VII.

The court jurisdiction quickly expanded into a general jurisdiction of morality. It sanctioned not only adultery but also violations of the Sunday sanctuary and sacred duty, as well as cursing and swearing, drunkenness, usury, etc. At first instance, it was responsible for the observance of the norms declared binding by the authorities in mandates. The Moral Courts also took care of the settlement of disputes between spouses or neighbours, which often consisted of insults and defamation and led to assassinations. Therefore, they offered themselves as religiously inspired forums for peaceful conflict resolution. For this purpose, in addition to exhortations, they could also pronounce punishments such as the exclusion from the sacrament or penalties such as the earth kiss, in which the punished had to kneel before the parish church on the floor and repent. At the request of the Moral Courts, the Minor Council could also condemn to jail and exile. In the eighteenth century, the duties of justice of the peace were transferred to a separate authority. In 1798, the *Consistory Courts* were abolished entirely but during the Mediation period, were revived in some places for several decades.

Recent social-historical research has investigated the role of these courts on the social discipline of the people of the early modern state. It was able to demonstrate that the often draconically formulated mandates should not be overestimated in their effect. In the 18th century, these courts were not successful in stopping social change and the inclination to secularise. The vision of a thoroughly Christian community, as the Reformers had intended to create, dissolved. Enlightenment and *Pietism* responded to this trend, but in different ways.

6.5 Arbitration

Disputes of corporations

The arbitration procedure developed in the northern Italian city republics, and was first introduced in the 13th century by legally educated clerics in present-day western Switzerland and soon in the Alemannic Switzerland. The primary task of the arbitral court was the amicable settlement of a legal dispute, and only if this could not be achieved, should judges make a decision. Arbitration was used in conflicts between corporations and individuals. Arbitration clauses for the amicable settlement of disputes between the allies were often observed in the city alliances of the 13th and 14th centuries. The various pacts with which the individual cantons joined the Old Confederation provided for arbitral settlement of conflicts.

Since the middle of the 15th century, the Tagsatzung had devoted a considerable part of its activity to mediation in conflicts between the cantons. Around the year 1500, this accounted for a quarter of their affairs. Particularly conflicting was the administration of the Common Dominions and in the early modern period also the religious and church issues. For the conflict settlement, a procedure was applied, which was first established in the alliance between Zurich and the Waldstaetten in 1351. In a dispute, each ally should appoint two arbitrators. These four could if they failed to agree, select a neutral top arbitrator and make a final and binding judgment with him by a majority vote. Should a state reject the arbitral award, it was threatened with intervention by Confederate troops. This procedure was also used, for example, to resolve the armed conflicts of 1442/43, when Zurich and Habsburg together faced the Confederates (*Zurich War).* It was not until 1450, after protracted negotiations of the arbitrators, that a lasting peace could be achieved under the chairmanship of the Bernese mayor Heinrich von Bubenberg.

Disputes of private persons

Arbitration procedures were also crucial to private persons, especially to merchants and traders. Since they often did their business beyond the borders of sovereignties and jurisdictions, the proceedings before an ordinary court were too cumbersome and time-consuming for them. They preferred a quick and informal judgment based on principles of equity. Sometimes regular judges were also called to judge in an ordinary procedure only after arbitration. The elected arbitrators, often holders of a prestigious office such as mayors, councillors, envoys of the Tagsatzung, bailiffs or keeper of the records, tried to settle the matter in *Harmony* (*Minne*); a procedure to solve the affair by mutual accord after the parties' argument and contradiction were heard and after appraising the evidence. If such an agreement was not reached, they were settled under local law or, at the request of the parties, based on the principle of equity (*Minnespruch*).

6.6 Judges, Advocates and Lawyers

Chairman and Court Assessors

The jurisdiction was, as shown, part of the territorial sovereignty and could be exercised individually by its landlord. The concept of separation of powers was unfamiliar to the constitutional systems of the Old Confederation. In the Middle Ages, usually a noble or religious sovereign as the bearer of the political power occupied the court chair, or he appointed a deputy. The judicial process was carried out by the court assessors (*Urteiler, Sprücher, coutumiers, prud'hommes*), which knew the local law. They were part of the local urban population or village community and qualified themselves through their legal experience gained in practice. With the establishment of the sovereignty by the cantons of the Confederation, the co-determination rights of the local authorities in the selection process of the court assessors were often suppressed, and the principal city increasingly determined these.

The municipal courts met under the chairmanship of the sheriff or mayor. The assessors were members of the city council and took over this office for a specified period. In the criminal procedure, the coroner, who conducted the preliminary investigation, was also a council member. To be able to access the judiciary in the cities it was required that a person belonged to a family or a guild eligible to the council, so in fact, it was limited to the urban elite.

After the establishment of urban sovereignty, the bailiffs or the lieutenant bailiffs oversaw the district courts. Court assessors, six to twelve in number, depending on the court, were elected every year or every two years from members of the rural dignitaries, so they were mostly wealthy peasants. A formal court appointment was organised at the request of the principal city, and then in a noble act the judges were sworn in, and the current court order was read out loud.

Lay jurisdiction

Not only the practical experience in legal matters but also political and economic factors opened the way to the office of judge, legal education was not required. Until the end of the Ancien Régime, civil and criminal jurisdiction remained in the hands of lay people, except for some municipal courts. In the Confederation, the administration of justice in the secular jurisdiction differed from that of the ecclesiastical, where since the 13th century the learned jurists prevailed. They also varied from the development in other countries of Europe, which experienced a professionalisation of the judges through the reception of Roman-canonical law. The evolution towards legally trained and regularly salaried professional judges, which can be observed elsewhere in the Empire since the 15th century, did not occur in most of the cantons of the Old Confederation.

Formal Austerity

In many places, the functional *dichotomy* of the court with the court chairman and assessors remained until well into modern times, unlike in the Empire. The chairman represented the authorities, which was reflected in the judge's baton and his attire in official state colours. He led the trial, gave the casting vote to the assessors in a tie, had the court clerk prepare court records and watched over the execution of the sentence. The assessors were responsible for the determination of justice and the advocacy of the parties. During the 13th and 14th centuries, the trial was characterised by a pronounced austerity of form. Even minor violations of the formal structure could lead to a total loss of rights. The parties were at considerable risk of losing their legal rights if they did not use the right court formulas. To prevent this, they could apply to the court chair for one of the assessors to serve as their *orators (Vorsprecher)*. In their place, the latter spoke the formulas with which a legal claim should be made. If he misspoke himself, there was the right of *recovery (Erholung)*, which meant that a new orator could be appointed.

Advocates and Lawyers

The dismantling of the formalities at the end of the Late Middle Ages changed the task of the orator to that of the *advocate (Fürsprecher)*. He now used arguments instead of set formulas to persuade the other assessors of his client's legal claim. After his presentation, he sat down again on the court bench, took part in the negotiations and said the verdict with the other assessors. He was often the first to vote. The court assessors, therefore, had a strange *double hat (Doppelamt)*. They were both advocates and judges, therefore, on the one hand, they had to represent the individual interests of a party, and on the other hand, they had to help the objective law to achieve a breakthrough. The fundamental conflict of interest inherent in this dual function was not perceived as such for a long time. The separation of the two roles by creating an independent legal assistance, detached from the court appeared in some places belated; in Berne in 1697. In Zurich, the institution of the judge-advocate persisted until 1798, although permanent and salaried council orators (Ratsredner) existed since the second half of the 15th century. Some cantons resisted the separation of magistrates and advocates because the authorities did not want to lose control over this office. As long as the advocates were selected from the ranks of the court assessors, they were subject to the control of the authorities, as the latter were responsible for the election of the assessors.

In some places, mandates were issued restricting the court representation to only the advocates. In 1674, the Tagsatzung also prohibited the representation "by costly legal advisers, bailiffs or procurators, as they call themselves." *Lawyers (Advokaten)* trained in law were excluded from the court proceedings. Based on the Roman model, they did not feel obliged to the objective determination of the law, but the legal interests of their clients. They were independent of the judicial authority, and therefore worked as "freelancers". The first lawyers who tried to work in the Confederation came from neighbouring countries and often encountered mistrust and unease in the courts. The lay courts – probably out of concern of being overtaxed by legally trained representatives of the parties – fought against them with the argument that one-sided advocacy for the interests of a party would lead to unnecessary litigation and that the parties would also be financially exploited. Exceptions to this hostility towards advocacy were those cities, which provided legal education at an early stage such as Basel, where the training of lawyers since the founding of the University (1460) had played a significant role. Also in Geneva, where the Academy founded in 1559 offered a legal education, which led to qualified lawyers and where the first *register for lawyers (matricule des advocats)* was established in 1644.

The rejection of trained lawyers can also be associated with the isolationist political tendencies in the 16th and 17th century. It was not until the 18th century that the Confederation again opened up to foreign countries, which offered many young Swiss the possibility to attend a university. Anyone who had studied law in France or Germany sought after their return to incorporate their studies in legislation and jurisdiction. As a first step, in some places not only the advocates but also "Roman" lawyers were admitted, in a second move, the institution of the advocate was abolished. This development occurred earlier in the cities than in the rural areas of the Confederation. Even there the professionalisation of the judiciary was still less advanced at the end of the Ancien Régime than in the neighbouring countries.

6.7 The proceedings in court

The Frankish trial

Until the Late Middle Ages, there was no distinction between civil and criminal proceedings. This was initiated by the Land Peace, which imposed on the collective the task of sanctioning grave misdeeds, which were threatening security and peace. It was only then that public prosecution and subsequently, criminal justice initiated. Until then, the persecution of any wrong was primarily left to the initiative of the victim. The initiation and the expediting of the process laid in his or his clan's hands. In this respect, the procedure was similar to modern civil process. The purpose of the system was primarily the awarding of compensation and not necessarily a prison sentence, corporal punishment or life sentence. This would have required enforcement options, which the rulers in Frankish times did not have at their disposal. The tribal rights partly contained catalogues of compensation for wrongdoings. Disputes on the amount could be decreased, and actions of feud restrained.

The Frankish trial was conducted publicly and orally, and the population took part in the jurisdiction. Only with the progress of the writing in the Late Middle Ages, parts of the procedure were transcribed, which subsequently restricted the public nature of the jurisdiction. In many places in the Old Confederation, however, this change to the written form occurred, if at all, only in the early modern period. Publicity and the spoken word in the civil process were so retained for a long time.

During the Frankish period, it was not the task of the court to clarify the facts; the parties had to provide the evidence. Paramount was the proof of the defendant that he had not committed any wrong. Since the plaintiff had sued him in court, the defendant had to demonstrate that he was not guilty. Initially, there was no free evaluation of evidence by the judge. The proof was satisfactory if it had been submitted by preserving the prescribed forms. The defendant could more or less "prove" his innocence with an oath that he had not committed the alleged crime. The influence of Christianity is evident. Since the perception of perjury as being punished with severe penalties in the afterlife was pervasive at that time, it was thought unlikely that someone could commit it.

Allegory of justice. 5. Rectorate of Johann Jakob Faesch 1630/1. Faesch was principal of the University of Basel six times between 1612 and 1645. For his fifth term, he painted a Justitia in combination with his family crest on the first page of his entries. The family crest Faesch is in blue and gold. It shows two golden stars on a blue background and a black house sign on a gold background and above it a helmet with three golden clasps as a sign of nobility. For 'his' Justitia Faesch did not allow painting the helmet over the stars and the house sign, but on Justitia's head. In her hands, she holds the symbols of the judiciary, on the right a raised sword and on the left a scale. Her eyes are covered, but with a transparent veil. Image: Rektoraktsmatrikel der Universität Basel, Volume 2 (1568–1653); Universitätsbibliothek Basel (University Library Basel), Sign. AN II 4, f. 173v.

6.7.1 The Civil Proceedings

In the Late Middle Ages and the early modern period, most cases in the secular courts were, according to recent understanding, related to civil law. There were proceedings for debt, property and inheritance claims, for trade and commerce as well as for the purchase and rental of municipal and agricultural properties. In the countryside, especially manorial and leased property concerns led to conflicts. In such cases, the lower courts were responsible, such as the City- or Twing-Court. The rules of procedure at the Twing courts were based on unwritten customary law; those of the city courts were at least partly transcribed in court statutes.

The influence of civil proceedings – developed in the Late Middle Ages by the legists and canonists of northern Italy – varied from place to place and were more pronounced in the bigger cities than in the countryside. This Roman-canonical form of proceedings was developed by legal science and characterised by the written form of the procedure and the exclusion of the public. It featured fixed procedural rules and a clear division into individual procedural steps, and it rejected irrational forms of proof such as God's judgment and the duel. The clerical courts were already using these proceedings since the end of the 13th century. Some cantons introduced certain principles into their secular jurisdiction such as Basel and parts of western Switzerland. The Imperial Chamber Court, committed in 1495 to the scholarly procedure by its court order, could not influence the secular jurisdiction, since it did not play an important role in most parts of the Confederation.

Introduction of the proceedings

The proceedings usually ran as follows: The plaintiff sued the defendant orally in court, which gathered at regular intervals; in the city weekly or even daily. Outside the regular court appointments, court sessions could also be purchased *(purchase court/Kaufgericht)*. The plaintiff presented the subject matter of the claim and requested an advocate from the ranks of the court assessors. In early modern times, written lawsuits were also filed in some places. If the defendant was not present, the court summoned him. Persons with a higher status were asked in writing, others orally by the court clerk (Gerichtsweibel), in fact on the doorstep of their home. The time limit of a summons varied depending on the place, cause and frequency of court sessions, and lasted from twenty-four hours to even one week. If the defendant did not appear, the court could order a fine or temporarily commit the defendant's assets to the plaintiff.

If both parties were present, they first had to decide whether they wanted to settle the matter amicably or through a court decision. The court usually encouraged the conclusion of an amicable settlement to the best of its ability. This happened not only to spare the effort of a lengthy procedure but also from the understanding that a friendly solution was usually the better guarantor of legal peace than an official court decision. If the parties decided that the court should *justify the case*, the defendant was also assigned an advocate from the ranks of court assessors. In many places, the involvement of external lawyers was frowned upon or even forbidden.

The plaintiff or his advocate then presented in the trial the claim and its legal grounds as well as the evidence. From the 14th century onward, the hearing was mostly informal, but later, a formulaic structure of the lawsuit emerged again in many places, especially in regular and frequent trials, such as against debtors, involuntary loss of property, or inheritance. However, this did not lead to the formation of a numerus clausus of the rights to litigate. The defendant either lodged a substantive position on the action in the answer or raised objections, such as the statute of limitation, the lack of jurisdiction of the court or the out-of-court settlement already reached. Over time, replicas and duplicates became common with the subsequent taking of evidence.

Evidence

The opposition of the church against irrational forms of proof such as duels and God's judgments (trials by water and fire) led to their demise by the end of the Middle Ages. Afterwards, documents became meaningful as evidence, due to the dissemination of writing and the advancement of the notary. Witnesses were able to provide proof *(Kundschaft – awareness)* as well. In some places, as in the church law, the testimony of only one witness was not sufficient (*testis unus, testis nullus*). Elsewhere, a woman's statement was worth just half that of a man. The oath, by which the court was denied consideration of the evidence, continued to be significant. On the other hand, the court was able to check testimony by witnesses and writings in a critical, material appreciation. Depending on the legal system, this was handled in the form of a free recognition of evidence or according to fixed rules of proof. Since the Late Middle Ages, both parties had to provide testimony and not just the plaintiff.

Reaching a verdict

When the taking of evidence was closed, the court chairman asked the assessors *what was legally valid (was rechtens sei)*. They then, in turn, put forward their views, usually the advocates of the parties first. If the opinions diverged widely, the consultation was interrupted to seek advice from learned lawyers or higher courts. If the court assessors held differing views, the majority vote decided and in case of a tie, the court chairman. The verdict drafted by the registrar was in many instances imperative. Occasionally, it contained a summary justification in addition to the decision. It called on the losing party to do or refrain from doing something, such as to pay the required sum of money or to refrain from a particular behaviour. The court also decided on the cost of the proceedings. The parties had to reward their advocates, and the losing side had to pay the court fee and the expenses of the winning party. The court costs included, for example in the city of Zug, the feast, which the court members enjoyed after work.

In the early modern period, the possibility of appellation developed from the provincial lower court to the district bailiff or the superior City court or from the City court to the City Council.

6.7.2 The Criminal Proceedings

Consolidation of the monopoly on the use of force

In the Late Middle Ages and the early modern period, the safeguarding of the legal concord was always tricky. Self-(administered) justice was a regular and legitimate approach to punish infringements of property rights, especially after the disintegration of the Frankish royal power and the court organisation installed by it. The God's- and Land Peace were the first attempts of a sovereign conflict settlement. The increasingly successful struggle against self-justice and crime was one of the several factors that promoted the emergence of the "statehood" of the cantons in the Old Confederation. It took a long time until the authorities could not only claim a monopoly on the use of force but also be able to enforce this claim. Local enforcement became in actual circumstances downright an emergency and touchstone of authority and territorial sovereignty. Until the end of the Ancien Régime, the monopoly of the use of force in the large and small territories of the Confederation gradually consolidated. The early modern use of mandates had also contributed to this. However, the development of the monopoly on the use of force was not a straightforward process. Revenge as a form of vigilante justice survived until the beginning of modern times.

The criminal proceedings developed with their own characteristics in the lower and the high jurisdiction. Lower jurisdiction included in addition to the settlement of disputes in civil matters, the sanctioning of minor breaches of the peace, which meant lesser offences that were not punishable by death. The high or blood jurisdiction, however, was responsible for capital crimes. Depending on the nature and severity of the infringement of rights, this resulted in a variety of different procedures, especially since these were carried out before different judicial authorities.

Rules of Procedure

The local criminal trials were based on customary law and since the 13th century on the Land Peace. In the early modern period, unique *rules of procedure (Malefizordnungen)* were issued in some places for the blood jurisdiction. A reference to the law of the Emperor and the Empire was often found in these rules. For the blood jurisdiction, which decided on the lives of people, the legitimisation by the Imperial Law was considered indispensable until the early 18th century.

The Carolina (*Constitutio criminalis carolina*) of the Emperor Charles the Great of 1532 was only applied in a few cantons, such as in the Princely Bishopric of Basel and the monastery state of St. Gallen, but also among the Swiss mercenary troops. It was used as a subsidiary source of law, for example, in the city of Basel and Schaffhausen. Traces of its application can also be found in the legal sources of the League of Ten (Zehngerichtebundes) in the Valais, the Principality of Neuchâtel and some cantons in today's central Switzerland.

6.7.2.1 *The procedure for minor breaches of the peace*

Proximity to civil proceedings

In the case of minor delinquencies, the procedure was mostly similar to civil claims. The injured party had to file a lawsuit before the competent court, for instance for assault, bodily harm, defamation or insult. The court's activity was in such minor cases aimed at settling the dispute and preventing further escalation of the conflict. Following the taking of evidence, the court ordered a fine, which included the compensation for the injured party and remuneration for the court. Perpetrators were often expelled for a limited time from the judicial district, and therefore the court could liberate the district of hotspurs for a while.

Fines and exile were also provided for offenders who had violated mandates of the sovereign or the city council, such as the prohibition to wear weapons or to participate in brawls, which had been issued for peacekeeping. In such cases, an envoy of the council (Ratsbote) took over the role of the plaintiff, and the penalty went to the court in full.

6.7.2.2 *The procedure for capital crimes*

In the case of capital crimes, other procedures existed. Over time, a gradual replacement of the district jurisdiction by the criminal jurisdiction

(Malefizgerichtsbarkeit) took place. In connection with this, the accusatory proceeding was replaced by the inquisitorial system.

6.7.2.2.1 The accusatory proceedings before the district court

Initiation of the trial

The *district jurisdiction* (*Landgerichtsbarkeit*), with its roots in Frankish times, was predominantly responsible for homicides, though initially it also handled other serious offences such as robbery, rape and heresy. In case of such a crime, the sheriff or bailiff, in his function as a district judge, summoned the people to a court session. The meeting place was always easily accessible and symbolic, it was either located in front of the town hall, or on the ground of the provincial community assembly and sometimes under a tree (*Court Linden/ Gerichtslinde*). As soon as the district judge with the judicial sword in his hand had settled in the court chair, the proceedings were opened. This always began with the complaint of the injured party, such as the widow, the mother or the sister or any other relative of the person killed. Their chosen advocate initiated the trial in a ritualized "question and answer form" with the district judge, in which the correct convocation of the district court and the summons of the defendant were clarified. If the defendant was not present, which was often the case in homicides, he was summoned three times by the court courier outside his house. If he did not appear, he was declared outlaw (friedlos) by repeated formal declaration of infamy and put to the justice of the injured clan, which now was allowed to kill him with impunity. His assets were confiscated, and it was forbidden for anyone in the district to accommodate and feed him.

Evidence

If the defendant was present, the taking of evidence followed. The focus was mostly on the testimony of witnesses, which could be provided by both parties. The witnesses had no right to refuse to give evidence, except in the case of close relatives; however, the other side could reject them on account of bias. Under oath, they had to comment on the circumstances whereby the other side had the right to comment on their statements. If the accused was present, he could confess, voluntarily, without using torture. He could also prove his innocence with an oath. The *oath in purgation (Reinigungseid/juramentum purgatorium)*, with which his *compurgators* (*Eideshelfer/coniurator*), mainly respectable persons, would make a vow to his credibility, was in the course of the Late Middle Ages no longer permitted, since it was an apparent source of abuse. If there was neither evidence nor an oath in purgation to determine the guilt or innocence of the suspect, the court could resort to a verdict of divine judgment such as the *Cruentation (Bahrprobe).*

Verdict

The final verdict, based on the last votes of the parties, was either an acquittal or a conviction. In the latter case, the accused was declared outlaw. The revenge actions of the injured clan could only be averted if an *expiation contract (Sühnevertrag)* was successfully concluded. By paying a substantial atonement penalty, the condemned could buy himself out of revenge. An execution by the authorities was only carried out in exceptional cases; for the same reason that it was not possible for the accused to ask the authorities for mercy because the right to inflict punishment was not in the hands of the court, but the injured party. The proceedings before the district court were therefore similar to that in civil proceedings. It was opened up by the claim of the aggrieved party and driven forward by the procedural acts of the parties. The court acted passively in finding the truth.

6.7.2.2.2 The inquisitorial procedure before the Criminal Court

New procedural principles

The Land Peaces led to actions of the authorities for significant breaches of the peace. If the feud was to be contained efficiently, the local community had to take action. Therefore, in many places of the Confederation, the inquisitorial procedure was added to the accusatory proceedings in the 14th century. In this case, the initiation of the proceedings and the taking of evidence took place *ex officio* by the authorities themselves, and the focus was now on material ascertaining of the truth. In addition to curbing the feud, this procedure also served to combat the poverty delinquencies of the people harming the state (*landschädliche* Leute), such as beggars, thieves, and veteran mercenaries. They were travelling in large numbers in the country and considered a plague in the cantons of the Confederation, which for a long time did not enact an efficient policy for poor people.

Origin

Pope Innocent III (1160–1216) introduced the inquisitorial procedure in the church trials at the beginning of the 13th century. In his papal bull *Qualiter et quando* (1215), he urged that church judges should not allow the oath in purgation in trials against fallible clerics and instead should investigate the real truth. Accused clergymen should no longer be able to avoid indictment by aiding and abetting the oath in purgation. The Officiale now had to research for himself what had happened. This procedure was initially incorporated into the criminal procedural law of the northern Italian cities and appeared in the 14th century in the cantons of the Confederation.

The accusatory procedure remained almost everywhere for a long time parallel to the inquisitorial process. In some places, it was formally abolished, as in Basel, or as in Zug, habitually repealed, because it was too ritualised and too cumbersome. Also because the right to indict punishment by the authorities had now become so widespread that they could claim the right to take action for themselves. In the early modern period, it was mostly the city courts as criminal courts, which ruled on capital crimes.

Pre-trial

If someone was apprehended as a beggar or thief, for example, during an officially declared *Chase after Beggars* (*Bettlerjagd)* or someone was denounced for another offence, such as fornication or witchcraft, it was the city council's task to investigate the crime. The accused was locked in the tower, usually a disused part of the city fortification, where deputies of the city court interrogated him or her. In contrast to the accusatory procedure, there was a procedure before the actual trial in which the extraction of a confession (*Vergicht*) was paramount. Without a confession, the accused could not be convicted, because a publicised misjudgement would have seriously called the political power of the authorities in doubt. Therefore, *torture* was used to obtain a confession. The accounts of various confederate cities show that torture has been used since the 14th century.

Interrogation

The first interrogation, the *friendly question (gütliche Frage)*, took place without physical coercion. If it did not lead to a convincing result for the examining deputies, they proceeded to the *painful question (peinlichen Frage),* meaning an interrogation, which used a gradually increased torture. The *executioner* (*Scharfrichter, Nachrichter*) and his servants put thumbscrews on the accused or pulled them up on a rope with their hands tied behind their backs, where they also could hang a stone on their feet. Other torture methods were also used. The deputies decided whether the torture should be increased or repeated, depending on whether they believed the statements of the tortured person or not. Under pain of torture, the abused often admitted offences that they had not committed, such as manifesting suspicion of witchcraft, but also of sodomy and zoophilia, and property crime. Likewise, the tortured often denounced innocent people from their circle of acquaintances as accomplices. The questions and answers of the interrogation were recorded in detail as they formed the basis for the subsequent conviction in the main trial.

If the defendant did not confess to the alleged offence despite torture, the deputies had to release him but could impose obligations. Often he had to swear an *Oath of Truce (Urfehde)*, whereby he promised not to take revenge on the authorities for dungeons and torture in addition to quite often being expelled from the country. In Basel, the released could at least be granted compensation for pain and suffering.

Main Trial

In the main trial following a confession, which was not open to the public, the question of guilt was no longer a focus, but only the severity of penalties. The defendant had to repeat his confession (*Vergicht)*. In the case that he revoked his admission, he was tortured again, or the investigating deputies appeared as witnesses. Thus, in the criminal trial, a defendant neither had the rights of suspected persons nor institutionalised defence options. To withstand torture was for most people improbable. The only salvation was the decision of the court to decide *on mercy instead of right*. This occurred when respected citizens intervened with an intercession to spare the defendant, which was more often the case for town citizens than for external people. Locals were favoured through the right of pardon.

Execution of the death sentence

A death sentence was executed in a remarkable ritual. Since the police force and the prosecution efficiency of the authorities were low until well into the early modern period, the punishment should have the highest possible effect of deterrence. After the population was made aware of the impending spectacle by the ringing of church bells, the condemned was escorted to the execution site by judges and clerics. This was usually at a location that could be seen from afar, just outside the city gates, or at a transition to a new dominion, such as on a hill, on a slope next to traffic routes, or at an important transportation hub.

Thieves were usually hanged and left on the gallows until they were putrefied to deter the public. To raise their infamy, they were often attached head down, or with a dog hanged at the same time. Their bodies were often not buried in the consecrated ground but buried next to the gallows. Less dishonourable was the beheading, which was ordered for open manslaughter, in contrast to a treacherous murder. Foreign murderers, assassins and bandits could be broken on the wheel. With a cartwheel, their limbs were crushed and then "braided" into the spokes of the wheel, and their corpse was left in this position to decay on a vertically pegged wheel axle.

Heretics, witches and moral offenders were burned and their ashes scattered into a river or lake. The executed was deprived of the hope for a bodily resurrection at the Last Judgment. Drowning was a typical style of execution for women. Using *Floating (Schwemmen)*, they were floated on a rope with bound limbs from one river bridge to the next and then pulled out again. So they had at least the possibility to survive.

Hangmen

The hangman performed the execution. Due to the physical contact with the dishonourable lawbreakers, he became, in turn, dishonourable and therefore socially marginalised. He was not allowed, such as in Berne, to visit public taverns and handled tasks in the city for which no one else could be found. Due to the social isolation of the hangman, the office was in many towns handed down from the father to the son. The hangman was not only responsible for torture and executions, but he was also knacker, dog killer and flusher (cloacarius). He also had to drive the lepers out of the city and bury the suicides. Since he knew the anatomy of the human body, he was also in demand as a medical counsel.

6.7.2.2.3 *Poverty Delinquency and Witchcraft*

Historical execution practice has been analysed and statistically evaluated by historical research only for a few sovereignties of the Confederation. The results show that the death penalty was most often handed down for theft and witchcraft. Also, death sentences were delivered for murder and manslaughter, for child murder, adultery and sexual offences, blasphemy and political revolt. The convicts were mostly men except for witchcraft and child murder. The few statistical evaluations of early modern court practice show that executions were not frequent. Most executions took place in the 16th and even more frequently, in the 17th century. In Lucerne, between 1551 and 1798, around three death sentences were carried out each year and about five per year in the Bernese Aargau, whereas there were accumulations in particular times. In the 18th century, the concepts of Enlightenment led to a humanisation of criminal practice in some places, but not everywhere. In the alpine regions of the Confederation, they had almost no influence.

More non-residents were executed for theft than locals were. The harsh reaction to this comparatively trivial offence points to the considerable poverty delinquency of that time. Since the 16th century, the population had grown significantly. This growth led in the countryside to the fragmentation of peasant property into such small units that no longer offered a livelihood. Thus, the proportion of the poor in the rural population increased. Those who did not go into foreign mercenary services sought their livelihood in the city, where the provision for the poor people was already much more institutionalised. However, the urban craftsmen had with guild structures already barricaded against unwanted competition, so that the newcomers had hardly any opportunity to practice a respectable profession, which often left them only begging, prostitution and theft. On the road many "travelling people" ("fahrendes Volk") could be seen. Besides the actual gipsies, there were also deserted or involuntarily unemployed soldiers, migrant crafts- and journeymen, religious refugees and lepers.

Pillory of Sursee. The pillory, in the form of a statue niche and covered with a canopy, is located 1.7m above the ground on the southeastern cornerstone of the town hall. The neck-iron, with which the punished were chained, still hangs in it. Until the 18th century, the pillory was used to exhibit malefactors. Photo: Author.

In wartime and times of economic crisis, the authorities reacted draconically to poverty delinquencies. For example, in many places, the death sentences piled up for theft (and also for witchcraft) in the decades during and after the Thirty Years' War (1618–1648), when many dismissed mercenaries flooded the Confederate territory. Except for this increase, executions were somewhat rare, because the judicial authorities did not lightly pass death sentences.

Milder penalties

In case of theft, the judges could also order a more lenient punishment than execution. In economic good times, first-time market-, field-pilferers or cattle-thieves were branded with a glowing iron and then expelled from the city or the county. Sometimes they had a hand cut off, their noses slit, or their ears cut off. This marked and warned the people about them. Some had to serve their sentences on the galleys of Italy or France. Even prostitutes could be branded. For offences committed verbally such as blasphemy, slander and perjury, the tongue could be cut off or torn out. The courts were free to decide whether to order such "more lenient" penalties or not. The legal norms in the early modern period did not contain defined levels of penalties since the principle of legality in criminal proceedings was unknown. Quite often, the courts themselves doubted the meaning of the threatened death sentences and were content with an exile or mutilation punishment.

Chastisements on the pillory (*Prangerstrafen*) would be pronounced for burglars, fraudsters, counterfeiters, bigamists and other petty criminals. They should expose the faulty and reveal it to the ridicule of others as a deterrent for the public. The neck-iron, which was put around the neck of the fallible for several hours, was often found in a busy location, such as the town hall or the marketplace. The pillory was made in many places in a *Trülle*, a swivelling cage, or in the *fiddle (Halsgeige)*, a wooden, two-piece block in which neck and wrists were confined like in a pair of pliers.

Bell Facilities

The growing insight that poverty could not be fought with the methods of criminal law during the 18th century led to improved public welfare of the poor. Since the Reformation, the cantons issued mandates to regulate the poverty and beggar problem. In these, companies and guilds in the cities were urged to assist their poor members. In the countryside, the parishes were to support them with money and grain. However, in times of continuing bad harvests and inflation, this public welfare was often overwhelmed, so that other measures had to be taken. These included the expulsion of non-domestic people or the instruction of able-bodied workers in the rural community or the municipal bell facilities. Based on English and Dutch models, labour education facilities were opened in the first decades of the 17th century in Zurich, Berne and Basel, but also in Freiburg and St. Gallen. These institutions served to keep the homeless, beggars and petty criminals off the streets. Since the institutionalised had to clean public streets and squares, there was a considerable risk of flight. To banish them, they were put on a metal-iron with a bell attached to it (hence the name). With the suppression of the painful and embarrassing punishments in the second half of the 18th century, real offenders were also admitted to these institutions. During the 19th century, the bell facilities became the penal institution, in which perpetrators should be improved by regular work.

"Flogging" and Bell Workers. The "Abschmeizeten" was a public flogging. In the picture above it is applied to a market thief. In the image below, bell workers (jiggers) can be seen working in the city of Berne. Picture: Stadtbrunnenchronik des Karl Howald (1796–1869). Reproduction with kind permission of the Burgerbibliothek Bern.

Witch trials

As recent research reveals, the late medieval roots of the European witch-hunt lie in the Dauphiné and in present-day western Switzerland, where there existed a functioning inquisition since the heretic trials of the 14th and 15th century. The witch trials immediately followed the heretic trials. The early modern Confederation has an above average number of witch trials in a European comparison. The statistical culmination point is between the late 16th century and the middle of the 17th century. This period includes the Thirty Years' War; several plague epidemics and a significantly deteriorating climate (the "Little Ice Age"). The deterioration in living conditions associated with these factors led to disease, violence, hunger and inflation, and intensified witch-hunts. At times of need, the witches had to serve as "scapegoats", in which the fears and aggressions of the population could be discharged.

There were significant regional differences in the frequency of persecution. More and more trials took place in regions where the blood jurisdiction was split among various local rulers, who were free to decide on life and death, such as in the Vaud and Grisons. In the Vaud, where after the conquest Berne had left the jurisdiction to the local seigneurs, more than 1,600 people were sentenced to death for witchcraft from 1580 to 1653. Neighbourly conflicts, rumours, and accusations became trials that served the authorities to document and enforce their political power. This happened in both the Catholic and the Reformed cantons. Hundreds of people were sentenced to death for witchcraft in the Catholic Freiburg, the neighbouring canton of the Reformed Vaud. Under torture, the accused confessed to alleged habits of witches, like casting of spells, participation in the Witches' Sabbath and pacts with the devil.

Of the approximately 10'000 witch trials that took place in the Confederation's territory, more than half ended with a death sentence. The judicial authorities sometimes doubted the meaning of the death penalty and imposed a milder sanction or acquitted them. Around 95 % of the people involved were women. In the second half of the 17th century, persecution decreased in most cantons. Around 1740, another wave of persecution flared up in today's central Switzerland. After that, there were only a few separate trials in Schwyz, Glarus and Grisons.

Early modern criminal law practice was primarily concerned with the disposal of lawbreakers and the deterrence of the public. Furthermore, the punishment was to atone for the wrong done. Since the various breaches of law were a sin from a religious perspective, the added pain could also be interpreted as anticipated suffering, which meant that with them the penalties to be expected in the hereafter were shortened. The draconian sanctions were thus given a theological meaning. The convicts had been prepared by the priests, which accompanied them on their last walk. If they manifested themselves as repentant sinners at the site of the execution, the punishment had served its purpose not only for the Church but also for the secular authorities. Until the 18th century, the latter's monopoly on the power of the use of force was not yet secured, and therefore was dependent on a demonstration of authority.

7 The beginnings of jurisprudence

There was no academic educational institution for prospective lawyers in today's Switzerland until the 15th century. A legal education was acquired, if at all, at foreign law schools and universities. This explains the reception of the legal material into Swiss law, namely the Roman-canonical law taught there. Also, at the University of Basel, founded in the middle of the 15th century, and the law schools established in various cities of the Confederation in the 16th century, the focus was initially on an education in Roman law. It was done partly in the spirit and with the methods of humanism. In the 17th and 18th century, Switzerland played a vital role in the dissemination of natural law. However, up until the end of the Ancien Regime, due to the predominance of lay judges, local legislation and jurisdiction in most cantons were often largely unaffected by contemporary jurisprudence compared to other countries.

7.1 The early reception of Roman-canonical law

Ecclesiastical and urban schools

After the disintegration of the Roman Empire, higher theoretical learning was only taught in educational institutions of the church. Namely in the cathedral-, collegiate- and convent-schools, which were established from the 8th century onward and which were used to educate the aspiring clergy. The more significant monasteries, following the classical educational ideal of the liberal arts *(artes liberales),* imparted knowledge in the subjects of the *Trivium* (grammar, dialectics, and rhetoric) and the *Quadrivium* (geometry, arithmetic, astronomy, and music). Within the framework of dialectics and rhetoric, some rudimentary legal knowledge was also conveyed. The same applies to the urban *Latin schools*, which were opened from the 13th century onward to educate the citizens. The sons of wealthy families mainly attended the lectures of the schoolmaster, who had been appointed by the City Council, but sometimes there were also scholarships for talented students from destitute families. The Latin schools of Berne and Freiburg were particularly well regarded.

School of Law in Bologna

The founding of law schools in northern Italy in the early 12th century opened a way to acquire a more comprehensive legal education. In 1120, the first law school based on the municipal art school was founded in Bologna.

This academy served to train its municipal officials, but it was also open to international students. The main subject of teaching was initially the Roman legal *Digests* (or *Pandects*), a collection of 50 books, which contained the opinions of Roman jurists. The Digests had been incorporated in the *Corpus Juris Civilis* of the Eastern Roman Empire during the 6th century by order of Emperor Justinian. In Western Europe, they remained unnoticed for centuries. It was only the "renaissance of the 12th century" triggered by scholasticism that aroused interest in the great texts of antiquity and created the methodical prerequisites for digesting and understanding them. Another subject of the lessons in Bologna was the collection of ecclesiastical legal records by the monk Gratian (*Decretum Gratiani*), which he had created in 1140 for teaching purposes. In this collection, Gratian had grouped several thousand ecclesiastical source texts around factual issues and harmonized them employing a dialectical approach. This collection was supplemented in later periods with collections of papal decrees (*Decretales*).

Swiss students

This "new" legal material, together with the teaching methods inherited from scholasticism, attracted a rapid and robust influx of students, including foreigners. The first students from the area of today's Switzerland can be traced back to the end of the 12th century, especially students from Grisons and Ticino, who lived close to northern Italy. In the 13th century, the number of international students increased sharply, because the upswing of the cities and the intensification of trade necessitated an adaptation of the existing law and the development of new legal norms. Besides, the increasingly self-conscious bourgeoisie wanted to participate in education. For the period from 1265 to 1300, 220 students from today's Switzerland can be verified in Bologna. Only about 50 of them were laymen. They were descendants of the city nobility or the upper bourgeoisie and wanted to acquire legal knowledge with the aim to take over municipal offices after their return. They became city scribes, notaries, bailiffs, councillors and mayors. The majority of the remaining students were clerics, often with only the lower ordinations, who wanted to qualify for admission to a cathedral chapter or a canonical monastery.

Their names can be found in the cathedral chapters of Chur, Constance, Basel, Lausanne, Sion and Geneva and in collegiate chapters such as the Grossmünster and the Fraumünster in Zurich, in Beromünster, Bischofszell, Solothurn, Schönenwerd, Rheinfelden, and Zurzach. Around 30 of these clerical students subsequently served as judicial vicars at a bishop's court. In 1273, Albero von Montfort became the first judicial vicar of the Diocese of Chur to be trained in

Bologna and Nicolas de Clarens the first studied judicial vicar of the diocese of Sion in 1304.

The lessons in Bologna were taught separately for the student associations of the locals *(scolares cives)* and those of the foreigners *(scolares forenses)*. After 1230, these two student associations each formed their *universitates*: those of the *citramontani* and those of the *ultramontani*. In the latter group, the students were again organised according to their geographical origin or language groups into *nationes*. The students from today's German-speaking Switzerland belonged to the *natio Teutonicorum* because they came from the same language area as the German students, whereas the western Swiss were part of the Burgundian nation and the Ticino and Italian Grisons part of the Lombard nation.

Bologna as a role model

In the 13th-century law schools in other cities in northern Italy were founded such as in Reggio, Vicenza, Padua, Vercelli, Piacenza, and Siena. Law schools and universities gradually developed in other countries too, first in southern and central France (Toulouse, Montpellier, Avignon, Paris), in Spain (Salamanca, Valencia, and Seville), in England (Oxford and Cambridge), in the 14th century as well in the territory of today's Germany. Notably at French universities (Paris, Orléans), at German academies (Heidelberg, Tübingen, Freiburg i. Br, Leipzig, and Erfurt) and an Austrian (Vienna), numerous students from the Confederation can be identified in the 15th century.

Bologna was a pioneer and model for the emergence of law schools and universities across Europe. The instruction there was the same as in Bologna with the same legal material and the same methods. The political and cultural ideas of Rome formed a common thread, and the Holy Roman Empire was regarded as a successor to the Roman Empire of antiquity (lit. as *translatio imperii)*. The German Emperor, who also ruled northern Italy in the Staufer period, was regarded as the legitimate successor to the Roman Emperor. Based on this concept of continuity, the Corpus Iuris Civilis, the law book of Emperor Justinian, was also considered the law of the Emperor of the Medieval Empire. Accordingly, the Roman law of the Digests was applied as the Imperial law.

Law teachers

The first generation of teachers were the *glossators*. They analysed Roman law with the fundamental theoretical approach of scholasticism. Contradictions were resolved by the formation of syntheses, and these were recorded as commentaries (gloss) next to or in the text. Besides, the glossators created summaries, collections of controversies and works on procedural law. The first documented glossator was Irnerius (before 1100-after 1125), the last Accursius (1183–1263). A subsequent generation of law teachers, the *commentators or consiliators* not only wrote comments on the Digests but also created extensive legal opinions *(consilia)* on the local law of the northern Italian cities and were more interested than the previous generation in the legal reality of their time. Their comments included not only private law, but also the commercial, trial, and criminal law. The most famous consiliators were Bartolus de Saxoferatis (1313–1357) and Baldus de Ubaldis (1327–1400). In addition to Roman law, ecclesiastical law was also researched and taught at the law schools. The *decretists* dealt with the decree of Gratian, the next generation of the *decretalists* with the collections of the since 1234 supplemented papal decretals.

Gateways for scholastic law

Once they returned from their training, clerical lawyers sought to apply the knowledge acquired in their work. Their institutions became the gateway to church law, as well as Roman law, which was applied to resolve legal issues on a subsidiary basis. The following organisations can be mentioned:

- The *ecclesiastical courts* of the dioceses, where judicial vicars had been working since the end of the 13th century. They introduced not only the Roman-canonical proceedings at the officialates but also substantive law terms and legal figures.
- The *arbitration proceeding*, which was carried out by worldly officials, but also by respected and often legally trained church dignitaries. As in the secular arbitration, attempts were initially made to bring the parties to an amicable settlement. If this approach failed, the following arbitration proceeding was based strictly on the wording of the written law, which meant ecclesiastical and Roman law. Thus, scholarly code also entered into the decision.
- The *notary*. In addition to Roman and canonical law, students were also able to learn the *ars notaria* at the universities in northern Italy. As a result, the creation of official documents spread on the one hand from the south, from north Italy to Grisons, Valais, and Geneva and into the estates of Savoy in today's western Switzerland. On the other side, from the north, the notary office of the officialate penetrated the territory of today's Switzerland. According to a papal decretal, a legal notary had to officiate at every ecclesiastical court as public keeper of records and attester. These notaries of the officialate also wrote secular legal documents such as sales contracts, lease- and loan-agreements, donation contracts and testaments. They used forms with a

prescribed text, which was not only in the terminology but also regarding the listed legal institutions based on Roman-canonical law.

- *The Keeper of Records.* Legally trained clergymen offered in the 14th and 15th century their services as free notaries and occasionally also entered the administration of a city. As city clerks, they kept the council and court records as well as the council correspondence, and they issued certificates for the city and for private persons. Following an order of Emperor Sigismund from the year 1439, every town clerk was supposed to be a public notary at the same time, and even small towns often employed a studied notary as a town clerk. He was oftenthe only lawyer in the city administration. Therefore, he was consulted by the Council as a legal adviser and was given the task of recording and improving the municipal law. While editing the city law he also often introduced scholarly law.

The secular students of law, whose number increased in the 14th century, entered after their studies the service of the aristocratic and religious sovereigns and the cities and exercised different offices and functions. From the middle of the 13th century, they often administered the royal estates in the territory of the Confederation as Imperial procurators *(procurator imperii).* They spoke law, settled disputes and collected taxes. Alternatively, they were, as legal experts *(jurisperiti),* Counsellor *(consiliarii)* in the service of noble sovereigns such as the Habsburgs and Savoys or of the cities. A law study qualified in general for the assumption of political offices in the cities. In particular, the towns of Geneva and Basel appointed in the Late Middle Ages lawyers trained as counsellors and keepers of records. In the 15th century, members of the local upper class were selected for most of the offices.

Early reception

The activity of the clerical and secular jurists in the institutions and functions mentioned in the Confederation led to the *early reception* of scholarly law. Terms derived from the Roman-canonical code can be found in notaries' files, lawyers' pleadings, judgments and transcriptions of local law since the middle of the 13th century. Besides the terminology, the substantive Roman law also found its way into local law. E.g., the testament was introduced together with the notary. In 1260, it first appeared in Valais, then in the Vaud and Geneva. In 1283, the citizens of the city of Freiburg were awarded the testamentary capability (Testierfähigkeit) by their town lord, and in Basel, a first will from the year 1294 is verified. The remaining areas of today's German-speaking Switzerland followed suit in the 14th century.

Other examples of legal figures adopted from the Roman law are the distinction between property (*dominium*) and possession (*possessio*), the testament and the acquisitive prescription, guardianship, adoption, cession and debt recognition as well as general concepts such as representation, proxy, and the statute of limitation. It was predominantly introduced in the field of private law because the Roman state law and criminal law were much less suitable for adaptation due to the different constitutional and social conditions.

In many places, Roman law served as a *subsidiary* source of law. If local law contained no legal question or no answer to it, it was derived from the academic counsellors of the Roman legal doctrine. In the wake of the emerging trade and money economy in the urban and courtly area, the learned law proved to be better suited to solving legal problems than the traditional, often out-dated and incomplete town law. As a result, the local city law, land rights, and even the Offnungen were interspersed with Roman-canonical terms and institutions. How intensive this process of reception has been, can hardly be universally assessed, but needs to be seen in a differentiated way for each place in its time. The trend was more intense in western and southern Switzerland than in Alemannic Switzerland and more intense in cities than in rural areas. In the cities of Basel and Schaffhausen, the openness towards the Roman law was very high. In towns with clerical rulers such as St. Gallen, Geneva, Sion and again Basel scholarly lawyers were employed, which shaped the law of these religious sovereigns. Contrary to the previous historical research, the influence of academic law was not marginal in German-speaking Switzerland of the Late Middle Ages. In the 16th century, however, it partially declined.

7.2 The University of Basel and Humanist Jurisprudence

In Basel, which joined the Confederation in 1501, the first university in Switzerland was founded. The law school had an excellent reputation, especially in the time of humanism. Basel remained the only confederate university city until the founding of the University of Zurich in 1833.

Early days

In Basel, there had been a general studies program for the participating clerics during the church Council from 1431 to 1449, so that they could also use their stay for their studies. Both the students and the lecturers were provided with the rights and privileges of the Universities of Paris and Bologna. At this Council-university Lectures on canonical law, which included a good part of the Roman law, were held. After the end of the Council, the citizenry of Basel called for the foundation of its city university as a substitute. Provided with a deed of origination of Pope Pius II, the urban school started its teaching activities in 1460.

The law faculty had a privileged position from the very beginning and was well appointed with six regular chairs at the institution. At first, the lectures were dominated by canonical law and later by Roman law. Following the example of Bologna, the *baccalaureate*, the licentiate, and the doctorate were obtained, in either Roman or canonical law or both. Whoever wanted to complete both doctorate degrees to become *Doctor iuris utriusque*, had to study for ten years.

Because of a lack of local lecturers, many learned Italian lawyers were named as teachers of the law. They taught according to the method and with the literature of Italian commentators. With Erasmus of Rotterdam (1466–1536), who lived temporarily in Basel from 1514 onward, the city became the centre of the Upper Rhine humanist circle until the Reformation. Lawyers followed Erasmus to Basel from different countries, which led to a flourishing period of the law faculty. Worth mentioning are Sebastian Brant (1458–1521), Ulrich Krafft (1455–1516), Johann Ulrich Surgant (1450–1503), Thomas Murner (1475–1537), Claudius Cantiuncula (Claude Chansonnette, 1490–1549), Johannes Sicardus (1499–1552) and Bonifacius Amerbach (1495–1562). Notably, Cantiuncula and Amerbach contributed significantly to the charisma of the Basel Law Faculty in the first half of the 16th century.

Humanist Jurisprudence

During this time a change was underway in the application of Roman law, initiated by French lawyers who were influenced by humanism. Until the Late Middle Ages, based on the work of the glossators and consiliators, Roman law had been conveyed in the form in which Emperor Justinian had it incorporated into the Corpus Juris Civilis. However, the lawyers commissioned by Justinian had partially revised and modified the texts of the ancient Roman authors in their compilation. The northern Italian lawyers had taken no offence at this alienation, but the French did. Inspired by the humanist demand for a return to the sources, they tried to strip off the Justinian transformations and to dig out the original. They used philological methods developed by humanism for this purpose.

Of great importance in the development of the historical-exegetical method was the law school of Bourges, especially the lawyers Andreas Alciatus (1492–1550) and Jacobus Cujatius (1522–1590). These French lawyers opposed the tradition of the *mos italicus* of glossators and commentators and presented the mos gallicus with the aim of making classical Roman law accessible but purged of textual falsifications. They ignored the literature of the commentatory era and focused instead on the classic texts, which they sought to understand as such.

Cantiuncula first applied this new method in Basel. He made significant efforts to tap the Roman sources of law for his students and to teach them legal argumentation by employing these.

The students should not be introduced to jurisprudence by the authorities from the era of glossators and consiliators, but rather by the direct application of the sources. While his successor Sicardus decidedly advocated the mos gallicus, Bonifacius Amerbach represented a middle ground between the old and the new school. He sought a synthesis between the two schools and used commentaries from both. In Basel, this led to a balance between the two adherents in the following period and at other law schools in the Confederation.

Thanks to this flourishing period of humanist jurisprudence, the number of law students at the University of Basel increased markedly after the middle of the 16th century. The students came from the city of Basel and the rest of the Confederation, but also the neighbouring region of the Upper Rhine and southern Germany. Returning to their hometowns, they became notaries or keepers of records in cities, but were also, if the social position of their family allowed it, capable of assuming a political office. In the Confederation of the 16th century, the University of Basel had a significant function for the training of lawyers. However, because of its comparatively peripheral geographical location, it never became a Confederate state university. In the 17th century, the number of law students dropped sharply. The attendance of international students decreased and domestic students, as the students of other law schools in Confederate cities, were often content with a propaedeutic education in codes to work in the administration and commerce. Similarly, foreign lecturers were only rarely designated, and many of them were descendants of the circle of leading Basel families and concurrently practised law as city consultants and appraisers.

7.3 Intensification of scholarly methods in the early modern period

Stagnation

In 1495, the Imperial Chamber Court was established as the supreme court in the Empire. The new court regulations determined that half of the court assessors should be lawyers and that all should take an oath upon taking office that they would apply as their basis of the decision both the scholastic as well as the local law of the principalities, dominions, and courts. The Roman scholastic law was given the same status as the particular local law. The authorities confirmed the process of ascertaining the specific local codes by a learned method. Moreover, the formation of a legally trained class of lawyers at the lower levels of the judicial administration was encouraged. However, in the territory of today's Switzerland, the development was entirely different.

In the Peace Treaty of Basel (1499), prior historical research detected the basis for a de facto separation of the Confederation from the Empire and the starting point of a decreasing reception of scholarly law. The number of students from the territory of the Confederation attending foreign universities decreased from the 16th to the middle of the 18th century. In many places attempts increased to keep learned lawyers out of the institutions of the judicial administration; lawyers and notaries were no longer welcome. In the early modern period, the development of local law continued in various places without any input from the scholarly community. However, this view of prior research is not valid for the entire territory of the Confederation, and simple, mono-causal explanations do not do justice to the actual circumstances. As shown, the Peace Treaty of Basel did not bring about a general exemption from the jurisdiction of the Imperial Chamber Court since it kept its importance for Basel, Schaffhausen, St. Gallen, and the dominions of free imperial abbots and bishops. The Peace Treaty was instead a part of the process of divergence between the Empire and the Confederation, which had already started in the 15th century.

Underlying causes

The fact that there were comparatively few lawyers trained in Roman law in the Confederation of the 17th century did not only have political and legal reasons. Recent research points out that the economic and social developments in the Old Confederation from the second half of the 15th century onwards also prevented the establishment of a legal profession. Until that time, the big cities of the Confederation had European significance as export and trading places. However, a severe economic and market crisis led to drastic changes in the social and economic conditions. The city of Freiburg, for example, experienced after a period of economic prosperity a drastic decline in the textile industry in the second half of the 15th century. On the one hand, the guilds were unable to adapt to the new fashion trends and on the other with the decline of the fair in Geneva; the most important sales channel dried up.

As in other cities, the former merchant families after that devoted themselves to the mercenary services and the administration of the subject territories acquired by the town. There was no longer any need for the further development of debt and commerce law by contemporary jurisprudence. State and administrative law became more relevant for the preparation of patrician sons for prospective political offices. The provincial cantons became economically stronger and politically more important. This increasingly characterised the self-image and image of others of the Confederation, which presented itself as an entity of peasants. Internally the pragmatism of the government of dignitaries dominated in the cantons. No longer the scholastic argument counted, but the pragmatic compromise. This was the breeding ground for the emergence of an aversion against the academic law and its bearers.

Variances at the local level

As with the causes of this phase of stagnation, the location and time of its appearance also need to be differentiated. In cities such as Basel or Geneva, which had significant institutions for legal education from an early period onward, there was never a lack of lawyers. In Basel, the city council decided in criminal cases based on the written appraisals (*Bedenckhen*) of city consultants. The Academy in Geneva had a law school since 1566, where Roman law was taught. From 1711 onwards, only those who had completed a law degree were admitted to the city's *register of lawyers* (*tableau des advocats*). As the jurisprudence of the Officialates shows, the ecclesiastical rulers in the territory of the Confederation were also open to trained lawyers.

In the 17th and 18th century, Basel still received a great deal of scholastic law and merged it with domestic law. During the edition of the Basel city court order of 1719, the author Johann Friedrich Wettstein (1689–1753) not only used the state law of Württemberg from 1610, which was heavily influenced by scholarly law, as a model but also included contemporary academic literature. Even in other cities, the city law was revised with the inclusion of scholarly law. This municipal law always extended to the rural territories dominated by the city. Law schools were opened in Berne and Zurich, but also in other cities, in which legal knowledge on a modest scale was obtained with an academic foundation. In the county of Savoy and the Bailiwick of Chablais scholastic law was subsidiary to local law. These examples show that the "theory of stagnation" advocated by the former doctrine needs to be perceived with certain nuances and relativization.

7.4 Academies and Law Schools

In the early modern time, there existed law schools in various reformed cities of the Confederation besides the University of Basel. Despite their name, these were usually not independent institutions but only provided a few professorial chairs attached to a public educational facility.

With the transition to the new faith, the jurisdiction of the Catholic Church disappeared in the cities of the Reformation, and with it the efforts of the bishops to train the clergy. These cities had to take over the training of pastors themselves. At the suggestion of the reformers, the authorities expanded the existing municipal schools into theological institutes. These were not only responsible for the training of the aspiring clergy but were also accessible by the laity, which opened the way to a broader education. These institutes also established professorial chairs of law over time and provided the sons of the leading families with adequate training for their future role as rulers.

Geneva

With the approval of the Council, the Reformer Johannes Calvin proclaimed in 1559 the establishment of an academy in Geneva, and the first rector was Theodor Beza. The Academy, which had initially appointed four theological and philosophical chairs, became an international college of Calvinism. The outbreak of the Huguenot wars in 1562 made it impossible for French Protestants to study at a French university. Beza, therefore, requested the creation of an additional chair at the Geneva Academy. The first professor of law was Pierre Charpentier (died 1612). The influx of refugees in the wake of the Bartholomew's Night (1572) brought many French law students and several well-known professors to Geneva.

As in Basel, the literary humanist scholars sought the philological analysis and the edition of Roman law. Famous professors of this period were François Hotman (1524–1590), Ennemond de Bonnefoy (1536–1574), Jacques Lect (1556–1611), Denis Godefroy (1549–1622), who published in 1583 a complete edition of the Corpus Juris Civilis, and Jacques Godefroy (1587–1652), who edited the *Codex Theodosianus*.

This edition of the collection of Roman imperial laws, completed in AD 485, made Godefroy famous, and his reputation attracted many foreign law students to Geneva such as French and Germans, as well as Dutch, English, Scandinavians, Poles, and Hungarians. Not only because of the well-known scholars, but also because of its beautiful location and its social life, Geneva became a popular stopover on their educational trip or cavalier tour. In the 18th century, the Geneva Academy, in particular because of the work of Jean-Jacques Burlamaqui (1694–1748), focused on natural law.

Theodor Beza (1519–1605). Beza was born in Vézelay (Burgundy) and died in Geneva. He studied law in Orléans and graduated with a doctorate. After that, he lived off his fortune as a poet in Paris. When Beza converted to the Reformed faith in 1548, part of his property was confiscated, and he had to leave the country. He fled to Lausanne and taught there at the Latin Academy. In 1558, he moved to Geneva and joined Calvin, whose doctrines he defended in many writings. Image: Theodor Beza, Oil on wood 1577, International Museum of the Reformation, Geneva

Jacques Godefroy (1587–1652). Godefroy was born in Geneva. He studied law and history in Paris and Bourges. In 1616 he returned to Geneva. In 1619, he became the professor of law at the Geneva Academy and member of the Council of the Two Hundred. Three years later, he moved to the Council of the Sixty and 1629 in the Minor Council. In 1632, he was appointed as keeper of records, so he gave up teaching; In 1638, he resumed teaching. Image: Wikimedia commons

Lausanne

One year after Berne had conquered the Vaud and introduced the Reformation there, the rulers of Berne established in 1537 an academy in Lausanne. However, legal education was not an issue here at first, because the Bernese sovereigns were able to train their offspring in their city. It was only in 1708 that a chair for natural law and public law was created to combat grievances in the administration of justice. In 1710, Jean Barbeyrac (1674–1744) was appointed, who left after various disappointments in 1717 for the University of Groningen. Even his successors were far from succeeding in establishing systematic legal studies; which was not accomplished until the beginning of the 19th century.

Berne

Building on the urban Latin school, a theological institute opened in Berne in 1528, where initially three professors lectured. In addition to theology, the biblical languages and the liberal arts were taught. Because the institute was housed in an abolished Franciscan monastery, it was called "Kollegium zu Barfüssen" or "the monastery" for short. The school taught not only prospective pastors but also educated patrician sons. To prepare the aspiring members of the government and regulatory experts for their task, the lectures on rhetoric and dialectics also imparted knowledge of the *ius publicum*, such as state and international law. A genuine professorship of law was first established in 1680 with the legally trained theologian Johann Caspar Seelmatter (1644–1715).

Seelmatter had studied with the great expert of natural law Samuel Pufendorf in Heidelberg and taught for three years as an honorary professor in Leiden. In Berne, he started to lecture on the "foundations of law", namely on natural law. International law, as well as public and private law, were initially less relevant. The focus was on the training of lawyers in public law, who could successfully argue with opponents in often occurring legal disputes with other Confederate bodies.

With the syllabus proposed by the Bernese Council of Education in 1722, private law was upgraded. It was explained by the *differentiation method (Differenzienmethode)*. The professor was to read the institutions of Justinian and compare them piece by piece with the prevailing law of 1615. The syllabus was based on the academic program of the *Usus modernus pandectarum*, a contemporary law school with a modern interpretation of Roman law. The Roman scholastic law was practised at that time as a subsidiary law in Berne. Distinguished professors of the 18th century were Sigmund Ludwig von Lerber (1723–1783), who in 1761 edited the "Erneuerte Gerichtssatzung für die Stadt Bern und derselben deutsche Städte und Landschaften", and Gottlieb Walther (1738–1805), an early representative of the *German Historical School* in Switzerland.

In 1787, liberal patricians influenced by the ideas of the Enlightenment established the "Political Institute". It was intended as a bridge between high school and university and should prepare young people for a comprehensive study of jurisprudence. With the invasion of the French in 1798, the institute stopped its operation but resumed in 1805 as an academy with four faculties.

Zurich

In 1523, just a little earlier than in Berne, a theological school, the "Prophezey", was established in Zurich's monastery at the Grossmünster. The first principal was Huldrych Zwingli. After his early death, the other great Zurich reformer, Heinrich Bullinger, took over this office. As in Berne, bourgeois sons, who did not want to prepare for a ministry but for a future political career, got their training at this institute. However, an individual legal education was far from being on the curriculum; the students were taught Latin, logic, ethics, and history. It was not until 1694 that the theologian Hans Heinrich Schweizer (1646–1705) taught natural and international law based on the writings of Samuel Pufendorf. An actual professorship for natural law was in 1731 entrusted to the theologian Hans Jakob Zimmermann (1695–1756). Private law was not taught as a separate subject in Zurich until the end of the 18th century. Anyone who wanted to get a comprehensive legal education had to move to Basel or to a foreign university.

Two works of Zurich scholars from the era of the Ancien Régime stand out: *De Helvetiorum Republica libri duo* (1576) and *Eidgenössisches Stadt- und Landrecht* (1721–1746). The humanist theologian Josias Simler (1530–1576) wrote "De Republica Helvetiorum libri duo". It was the first handbook of the Confederate constitutional law and a favourable description of the history of the Confederation. It contained information of the Tagsatzung, the arbitration courts and the legal structures of the cantons. It was widely used and published in many editions and several translations. The second work was by the Zurich mayor Johann Jacob Leu (1689–1768) and contained an impressive source collection of the particular right of the confederate cantons for his time. Leu placed the (incompletely collected) Confederate law in the context of Roman scholastic law and the natural law. He wanted to show that there is not only a scholarly *ius commune* at the level of the Empire but also a common confederate private law.

Freiburg

In Freiburg, a law school was established in 1763. Since the city soon lacked the financial means for the lectures, it was assigned to the Jesuit Order. From 1775

Tobias Barras (1740–1813) taught various subjects of law until 1798, when the academy building was converted into a military barrack for the French troops.

This overview of the schools of law illustrates that in the cantons of the Confederation – apart from Geneva and Basel – a comprehensive education of law did not develop until the 18th century. In the early modern period, not only the administration of justice but also the further education of particular law was in many cantons a matter of legal practitioners with no scholarly training. The suggestions and methods of contemporary jurisprudence were consequently integrated less into particular law than in other countries.

Johann Jakob Leu (1689–1768). 1707–1709 Leu travelled for study purposes in Germany, the Netherlands, and France. Especially in Marburg, he devoted himself to natural law. In 1709, he entered the Zurich chancery office. In the following years Leu held various posts, in 1759, he became mayor of the city. In 1755, an Interest Rate Commission was established, although as a state institution, but independent of the financial administration, to invest money for the citizens of Zurich abroad. Outwardly, the commission acted as a company named Leu & Cie. and later became Bank Leu. Together with his sons, Leu published from 1747 the twenty-volume "Allgemeine Helvetische, Eydgenössische oder Schweitzerische Lexicon", which was the first to cover the entire territory of Switzerland in those times. Image: Louis Carlen, Rechtsgeschichte der Schweiz, 3rd ed., Berne 1988, p. 145.

Josias Simler (1530–1576). Simler studied theology in Basel and Strasbourg. In 1552, he became a professor of New Testament theology at the Grossmünsterstift in Zurich, and in 1562 professor of Old Testament theology. He wrote works of various kinds, including the first book that dealt extensively with the Alps. His textbook "De Republica Helvetiorum libri duo", which unites constitutional law and history, appeared only after his death. It was translated from Latin into German, French, and Dutch and remained a standard work on the constitution of Switzerland until the 18th century. Image: Leonard Meister, Helvetiens berühmte Männer in Bildnissen von Heinrich Pfenninger, Zürich 1799.

7.5 Natural Law in Switzerland

The concept of natural law as super positive law, independent of the will of a legislator, already existed in Greek and Roman antiquity. Thanks to Christian theology, this concept was preserved in the Middle Ages and the modern era. In the 16th century, the idea developed that natural law originated less from divine revelation but human reason. Traditional law, including the Roman law, now lost its authority. The adherents of rational law set up legal systems by deduction, based on principles that can be justified by reason, not by recourse to traditional rules of law. That led to a large number of new dogmatic approaches to law and a new system of the legal substance.

Protestant Orthodoxy

Starting from England, the Netherlands and France, the Enlightenment reached the Confederation comparatively late. Enlightened reasoning initially resonated in the reformed cities among academically educated clergymen, who sought to revive the theological rationale ossified by Protestant orthodoxy. They were in particular against the *Formula Consensus*, a creed passed in 1675, to which various Reformed churches committed their pastors. Theologians such as Jean-Alphonse Turretini (1671–1737), since 1697 professor at the Geneva Academy, Jean-Frédéric Ostervald (1663–1747), pastor at the Neuchâtel Collégiale, and Samuel Werenfels (1657–1740), a professor at the University of Basel, strove to abolish this creed. They advocated a Christianity that, despite traditional structures, gave ample space to reason. They coined the concept of *Protestant Orthodoxy*, which emphasised the rational and moral ideas of Protestantism to preserve the old legacy for a new era.

European adherents of the Natural Law

Like the theologians, lawyers sought principles derived from reason as the foundation of the legal system. Which legal rules could claim universal validity and consequently be followed by the members of all denominations? This question was of the utmost importance especially during the Thirty Years' War (1618–1648), which had begun as a religious war. In 1625, Hugo Grotius (Huig de Groot, 1583–1645), a Dutch lawyer and diplomat, published in exile in Paris a textbook of international and private law (*De jure belli ac pacis*) which tried to commit the warring parties by principles of the natural law to the observance of rules.

Based on the preparatory work of late Spanish scholastics such as Francisco de Vitoria (1480–1546) and Francisco Suarez (1548–1617) and the Oxford-educated Alberico Gentili (1552–1608), Hugo Grotius established with this work, the modern international law. The natural law of the early modern period, based on reasonably observable principles, first evolved in the Protestant countries. In Germany, the first chair of the natural law was established in 1661 in Heidelberg for Samuel Pufendorf (1632–1694). In his major work, *De iure naturae et gentium* (1672), Pufendorf combined the fundamental principles derived from human nature with philosophical-moral categories and then derived rules for the human coexistence. In the same way, other adherents of the natural law such as Gottfried Wilhelm Leibniz (1646–1716), Christian Thomasius (1655–1728), Richard Cumberland (1631–1718), John Locke (1632–1704) and Baruch Spinoza (1632–1677) worked on philosophical systems that could set standards for human life in society.

First Lectures in the Confederation

In the reformed cities of Switzerland, the professional circles took notice of the publications on natural law by foreign scholars. Johann Caspar Seelmatter held a first public lecture on natural law in 1680 at the Bernese School of Law after he had previously lectured *jus naturae et gentium* for three years in Leiden. Further lectures followed from 1694 in Zurich by Hans Heinrich Schweizer and in Basel from 1706 by Johann Jacob Battier (1664–1720). His father, Simon Battier (1629–1681), had already held private lectures on natural and international law in 1666/67.

In the French and Anglo-American-speaking countries, the concepts on natural law spread thanks to Jean Barbeyrac (1674–1744), Jean-Jacques Burlamaqui (1694–1748) and Emer de Vattel (1714–1767), three scholars of Western Switzerland. Their work was not only the prelude to the emergence of an actual *Ecole romande du droit naturel*, but their translation work also contributed significantly to the dissemination of the concepts of natural law.

Jean Barbeyrac (1674–1744). Barbeyrac attended school in Montpellier (F). When he was twelve years old, his family had to leave France because of the Edict of Nantes. He moved to Lausanne, where Barbeyrac attended the academy. He then studied theology in Geneva, later in Berlin and Frankfurt. In Berlin, he received a parish, but he gave up because of hostility and devoted himself to the study of natural law. In 1710, he was called to Lausanne and in 1711 to Groningen (NL). Image: Wikimedia commons

Barbeyrac

In 1708, the Bernese authorities appointed Barbeyrac to the Lausanne Academy. Barbeyrac was a French religious refugee in Berlin, who had become known by his French translation of the work on natural law by Samuel Pufendorf. In 1706 he had published his major work as *Le droit de la nature et des gens* and in 1707 its short version (*De officio hominis et civis,* 1673) as *Les devoirs de l'homme et du citoyen*. With these translations from Latin, Barbeyrac met the demands of his time since he made the work of the great thinker on natural law accessible in a common language. He caused a reactivation of interest for Pufendorf among the scholars and at the same time the dissemination of his ideas to a broader audience. French was the language of diplomats and elite circles throughout Europe at that time.

Princes, politicians, the educated and the aspiring bourgeoisie read the short version created by Barbeyrac called le petit Pufendorf. That way the concept of the natural law also found its way into the French law faculties, which at the time still focused on Roman law in the tradition of the *mos gallicus*.

Barbeyrac was already very famous at the time of his appointment in Lausanne. However, his teaching career in western Switzerland lasted only briefly. Since the law studies in the *Pays de Vaud* was not a prerequisite for access to the legal profession, just a few students were present in his lectures. Added to this were a minimum salary and ideological disputes. Barbeyrac refused to sign the Formula Consensus as requested by the Bernese authorities. In Groningen, where he started to in 1717, he translated the primary work of Grotius (as *Le droit de guerre et de la paix*, 1724) and various writings of Richard Cumberland.

Even after his departure, natural law continued to be upheld in Vaud. Loys de Bochat (1695–1754), his successor on the chair at the Academy, published in 1726 a dissertation on natural law. His successor, Beat-Philippe Vicat (1715–1770), published in 1782 the *Traité de droit nature* in four-volumes. Fortunato Bartolomeo de Felice (1723–1789), who lived in Yverdon, published several works on the natural law based on the lectures of Burlamaquis and other authors followed. The natural law became a "fashion item" of the French-speaking lawyers during the 18th century and was studied and taught well into the 19th century.

Jean-Jacques Burlamaqui (1694–1748). Burlamaqui was born in Geneva, where he also died. He studied philosophy and law at the Academy of Geneva and in 1716 obtained a lawyer's license. He gave private lessons to young noblemen and took a liking to teaching. He applied in 1720 for the title of honorary professor. In 1723, he became a professor of natural and civil law. He was also politically active: in 1721, he was elected to the Council of Two Hundred, in 1730 to the Council of the Sixty and in 1742 to the Minor Council. Image: Wikimedia commons

Burlamaqui

The Geneva School of Law was also influenced by the natural law in the 18th century. In 1723, Jean-Jacques Burlamaqui was nominated to a chair of the Academy. He had previously successfully given private lessons to young international students and had even attended lectures by Barbeyrac in Groningen. At the academy, he taught natural law based on Pufendorf's work in addition to Roman law. The extraordinarily high level of his teaching established his reputation as a lecturer, and many international students went to the Geneva Academy to attend his lectures. The French, German and English nobles among his listeners spread his writings in their home countries. He published his main work in 1747 as *Principes du droit naturel*. It is characterised less by originality than by clarity and conciseness so that Burlamaqui acted as an intermediary into extended circles.

His thoughts influenced in particular the political reasoning of Europe in the second half of the 18th century, such as the philosopher Jean-Jacques Rousseau; whose writings paved the way for the ideas of revolution. After a translation of his work into English (*The principles of natural law*, 1748), Burlamaqui was also read in England and the United States of America, including the pioneers of the independence movement in the United States. After Burlamaqui had to retire from teaching for health reasons, the natural law lectures in Geneva were continued based on his writings.

Emer de Vattel

Emer de Vattel (1714–1667), a student of Burlamaqui from Neuchâtel, was from the year 1747 onward a Saxon envoy in Berne and wrote, due to a comfortable office, a book on international law (*Le droit des gens*, 1757). It was a smart compilation of other writings on the natural law, especially that of Christian Wolff. Since de Vattel traced the often complex system of thought of the great thinkers of the natural law to some simple principles, his work was widely distributed internationally. It was translated into several languages and used in the science and practice of international law until the second half of the 19th century. For more than one hundred years, the United States Supreme Court had considered it an authoritative statement.

Impact

The writings of the Naturalists were actively read and lively discussed in Switzerland during the second half of the 18th century. However, until the fall of the Ancien Régime, ideas on natural law barely found their way into jurisprudence and legislation. The concept of equality and freedom for all people was theoretically affirmed, but not transferred into the current law. The theory of the social contract was not applied to the existing constitutional system. A revision of the existing private law under the systematics and dogmatic of the method of the natural law did not take place. However, from the ideas of natural law and the eagerly received literature of the Enlightenment philosophers like Rousseau, Voltaire and Montesquieu, the readiness for social change grew, first among the educated and then among the general population. The American Union constitution of 1787 was considered a model for a state order that derived the conditions of human coexistence from natural law. Many hailed the French invasion in 1798, but with the chaotic conditions during the following period of the Helvetic Republic, the disappointment grew quickly and substantially.

Emer de Vattel (1714–1767). De Vattel was the son of a Protestant pastor. He spent his childhood in the Principality of Neuchâtel, which at that time belonged to Prussia. De Vattel first studied philosophy in Basel and then theology in Neuchâtel and Geneva. In Geneva, his interest in law was stirred, probably by attending the lectures of Jean-Jacques Burlamaqui. His professional career led him through the diplomatic service to writing. Picture: Oil on canvas, between 1745 and 1765, unknown painter. Bibliothèque publique et universitaire Neuchâtel (Public and university library of Neuchatel).

Part 3: The Modern Era

8 Constitutional development in the 19th and 20th centuries

The Swiss federal state was founded in 1848. Its formation was preceded by an eventful history of fifty years, beginning with the Helvetic Revolution. The unitary state of the Helvetic Republic, established after this revolution in 1798, collapsed rapidly. In 1803 Napoleon had to use the Act of Mediation to restore the system of mostly sovereign states with weak central authority, in order to preserve the Confederation as a satellite state of France. In 1815, influenced by the powers of the Congress of Vienna, this mainly federal system was based on a federal treaty, which allowed the federal government hardly any authority except in security policy. However, due to early industrialisation and the liberal movement in the following years, there occurred a change in political reasoning. From 1830, cantonal constitutions were issued which more closely corresponded to the principles of the revolutionary period. These constitutions, like the drafts of a national constitution in 1832 and 1833, were crucial preparatory work for the 1848 constitution, which, following the Sonderbund War, was put into effect by the victorious liberal forces against the will of the conservative Catholic cantons.

This long and eventful history explains why the constitutional system of Switzerland, established in 1848, could only be created in this way and not otherwise. The cohesion of the newly created Switzerland was precarious and not only at the beginning of the federal state. By recourse to the late medieval founding myths and the creation of national symbols, the young state should be strengthened and created as *a nation of will*, Switzerland. The national symbols included the national flag and the national anthem, but also the single currency, uniform measures and weights, as well as the national legal codifications. The resistance of the *minoritised* expressed itself in the rejection of the nationwide uniform measures, weights and legal codes. The stubborn fight against their loss of sovereignty was also an attempt to preserve local characteristics - such as the law - and therefore a piece of their historically grown identity. However, the economic necessities associated with industrialisation and the development of the railways made the consolidation of the federal state unavoidable. This consolidation took place with the constitutional revision of 1874, which was enforced against considerable federal resistance.

Massively increased federal powers were instituted with the *custodial regimes* during the two world wars. In the 20th century, however, political rights and fundamental rights were also greatly extended. For the development of constitutional law, the gradual implementation of equality between men and women, social legislation, and new areas of law resulting from the technological advances were essential.

However, Switzerland's cautious approach to the EC and the EU, and its discomfort with the process of European unification demonstrate that the traditional adherence to the local identity persists in the 21st century.

8.1 Helvetic Republic

8.1.1 The Helvetic Revolution and the French invasion

Collapse of the old order

Under the influence of the French Revolution, after 1789, many disadvantaged people wished for a change in the existing constitutional systems in the Confederation. The authorities and the majority of citizens benefiting from the existing constitutional structures - members of ruling families, privileged citizens, clergy and wealthy peasants - rejected changes, and only a minority of these groups sympathised with the revolution. Among the legally disadvantaged people in the city, countryside and subject territories, it festered. Local *revolts* announced the disintegration of the old order. In 1790 and 1791 popular uprisings in the Vaud, Schaffhausen and the Valais were defeated by the authorities. Great attention was paid to the uprising of Stäfa in 1794, with which the Zurich rural population demanded some rights from the authorities of the capital. Everywhere the demands were similar.

In this first phase, the people demanded reforms rather than revolutionary transformations. The rural subjects wanted legal equality with the urban citizens and the abolishment of feudal levies. The politically disadvantaged classes of urban residents asked for participation and the realisation of freedom of trade and commerce. In the peripheral regions of the Confederation, the first constitutional overthrows took place in Geneva. In 1793, based on the French model of a National Assembly, a declaration of *the rights and obligations of the social individual* (Déclaration des droits et des devoirs de l'homme social) was issued and in 1794 a *constitution* (Constitution). In the diocese of Basel, the episcopal subjects proclaimed the *Raurachian Republic* (Raurachische Republik) in 1792 and in Chur a national assembly was formed in 1794 against the oligarchic conditions in the territory of the Three Leagues (Drei Bünden). In 1795, the Prince-Abbot of St. Gallen had to grant greater freedom to his subjects in the

Old Countryside (Alten Landschaft) in a *friendly contract* (Gütlichen Vertrag). Constitutional drafts were also prepared elsewhere.

Zurich and Berne, the power centres of the Confederation, kept their troops constantly alert in the face of these internal revolts and the French threat.

Politics of the Jacobins

France intensified its hegemonic policy, which had been pursued since Louis XIV in the 90s of the 18th century. In order to carry the achievements of the revolution to other countries, but also to tap their resources (public finances, mercenaries), France tried to create a belt of satellite states around its borders. From 1792 onward this policy led to several wars against the coalition of anti-revolutionary European monarchies (Napoleonic Wars).

The Confederation was officially neutral in this European conflict, but it favoured and supported the counterrevolutionary powers. The Peace of Campoformio (1797), which ended the first coalition war after the defeat of Austria, had a substantial impact. The Confederation's importance for France increased on the one hand as a buffer zone against Austria and on the other as a transit country to the sister republic founded in 1797 in northern Italy, the Cisalpine Republic. Therefore, France no longer wanted to recognise the Confederation as a neutral power, but to transform it into another "sister republic". If possible, this should be done with the help of revolutionary-minded patriots from the Confederation. The main actors were the Basel head of the guild Peter Ochs and the Vaud lawyer Frédéric-César de Laharpe. With the help of France, Ochs wanted to enforce the equality of rights demanded by the people and establish a Helvetic Republic and potentially prevent a military intervention by France. Laharpe's goal was to liberate the Vaud from the rule of Berne, which is why since 1796 he had addressed corresponding memoranda to the French Directorate.

Constitutional change

The Helvetic Revolution began in Basel. Once the French troops had occupied the dominions of the Prince-Bishopric of Basel in the Jura in 1797, the Confederation could not stop France anymore. The Tagsatzung was only capable of a final solemn federal summon. In January 1798, the city of Basel granted the rural territories legal equality. As a symbol of the new order, a *liberty tree* was erected in many places.

After that, the revolution gathered speed in the cities of Vaud. Berne sent its troops in order to defend the Vaud, but at the same time, the French army advanced to the frontier to support the Vaud. At the end of January 1798, the *Republic of*

Léman was proclaimed in Lausanne. Berne withdrew its troops in order not to allow France a pretext for an attempt on Old Bernese territory. The Vaud was "liberated" like the Prince-Bishopric of Basel and immediately occupied by the French troops.

Fall of Berne

In other cantons of the Old Confederation changes of power also occurred, such as in Lucerne, where the Patriciate voluntarily abdicated and in Zurich and Schaffhausen. The patrician governments in Berne, Solothurn and Freiburg, however, were determined to preserve the old order. France, therefore, prepared a military intervention and concurrently negotiated with Berne. On March 2, 1798, the attack took place from the west and north. Freiburg and Solothurn surrendered without a fight, and the French troops invaded the Bernese area. At the Battle of Neuenegg, they suffered a defeat on March 5th against the Bernese troops, but on the same day, they beat them at Fraubrunnen and Grauholz to take flight. The Bernese government capitulated and handed over the city to the French general Balthasar von Schauenburg (1748–1831). His soldiers plundered the houses in the capital and dragged the Bernese treasury together with the Bernese bears to Paris.

With the fall of Berne, the demise of the Old Confederation was sealed. The cantons of central Switzerland had to give up their resistance after further, smaller battles. Representatives of the urban bourgeoisie and the rural upper classes took over political power from the patrician families.

8.1.2 The Constitution of the Helvetic Republic of 1798

Unitary state

On April 12, 1798, the "indivisible Helvetic Republic" was proclaimed in Aarau. For the first time in its history, the Confederation received a written constitution valid throughout its territory. This established a unitary state with centralised administration, based on the sovereignty of the people and a representative system according to the model of the French directorate constitution (Direktorialverfassung) of 1795. Peter Ochs drafted the text of the constitution with the intention of submitting it to the cantons and adapting it to their requirements. However, the French Board of Directors changed the draft at its discretion on several important points and put the constitution into effect with military force.

Cantons

The Helvetic Republic initially totalled 22 cantons: Valais, Léman, Freiburg, Berne, Solothurn, Basel, Aargau, Lucerne, Unterwalden, Uri, Bellinzona, Lugano, Grisons, Sargans, Glarus, Appenzell, Thurgau, St. Gallen, Schaffhausen,

Zurich, Zug and Schwyz. Soon, however, there were territorial changes: Berne had to accept a further reduction in size, and as well as the Aargau and the Vaud, the *Oberland* was declared an independent canton. The cantons of central Switzerland were merged into a single canton, *Waldstätten*, since they had adopted the Helvetic Constitution only at military pressure and further resistance was expected. The cantons in the eastern part of the Republic also converted into the cantons *Säntis* and *Linth*.

The cantons were constitutionally no longer sovereign states, but administrative units similar to the French departments. The highest official of the cantonal administration was, comparable to a French prefect, the governor of the Directory. He headed a five-member *administrative chamber*, which led the cantonal administration. Districts, ruled by the district governor and local agents, which led the administration, replaced the former domestic territorial borders.

Directorate

The Helvetic Constitution introduced a strict separation of powers comparable to its model, the French directorate constitution of 1795:

The executive consisted of a board of directors with five members who were bound by the collegiality principle. This should prevent to unite all the power in one person, as happened in France during the reign of Robespierre. The duties of the Board included the enforcement of the laws and, although not compatible with the principle of separation of powers, the election of the President of the Supreme Court.

Parliament

The legislature was divided into two chambers, the Grand Council and the Senate. This division corresponded to both the French model and the American Union constitution of 1787. The cantons were represented in the Grand Council in proportion to their population, and each canton had four delegates in the Senate. The negotiations of the two councils were public, a novelty in the confederate constitutional history. The cantonal representatives were elected by cantonal electors, which in turn were elected by the *active citizens* in municipal assemblies.

Judiciary

The judiciary was based on a written constitution of the courts - again a novelty - with a three-tier, hierarchical organisation: the *district courts*, the *cantonal courts*, and the *Supreme Court of the Helvetic Republic*. In 1800 another judicial authority was created, the municipal *justice of the peace,* who was to bring about the reconciliation between the parties in order to prevent their going to court.

The district courts were established as the first instance, the cantonal courts as a court of appeal for criminal and civil cases, which had been decided by the district courts, and as a first instance for serious criminal cases. To the Supreme Court of the Helvetic Republic, the third instance, each canton could delegate one judge. The Supreme Court had three functions: it was the court of cassation for all criminal and civil cases, the appellate body for serious criminal cases, and the sole authority for judging state crimes such as treason.

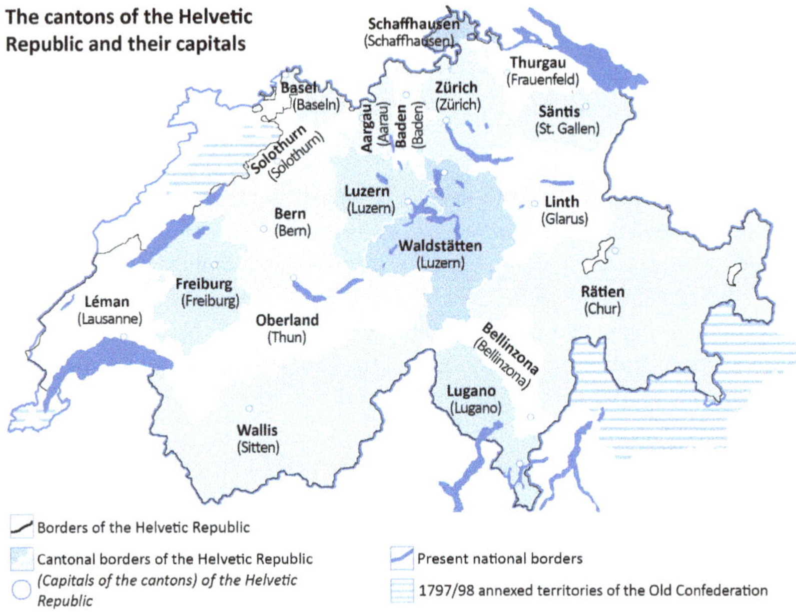

Civil rights and liberties

Following the model of the French Declaration of Human and Civil Rights (1789), the Helvetic Constitution contained a catalogue of civil rights and liberties, including freedom of conscience, freedom of the press and the right of ownership. However, these were not unlimited freedoms. Freedom of conscience could be restricted for police reasons. in exchange for compensation, the state could intervene in the ownership of the property. Land and property were not allowed to be burdened with financial loans that could not be bought off. This last restriction was aimed at relieving feudal burdens. The Constitution did not contain any provisions on freedom of trade and commerce, nor a general legal equality or the granting of political rights to women.

The constitution contained many new provisions, but their implementation demanded further detailed regulations. These were drafted by the Grand Council, which had the initiative right for the legislation. The Senate acted as a kind of "approval authority". It was either able to accept the drafts or reject them and send back for a further revision to the Grand Council. This procedure could be repeated several times. With a waiver of the Grand Council for a new version, the project would be terminated prematurely.

Many of the rights enshrined in the constitution, although the implementation laws were enacted, often failed in their enforcement.

8.1.3 Failure and importance of the Helvetic Republic

Like the Cisalpine Republic in Italy and the Batavian Republic in the Netherlands, the Helvetic Republic rapidly disintegrated. After four coups and a new constitution (1802), this "sister republic" of France was also dissolved.

Reasons for collapse

Many reasons caused the collapse of the Helvetic Republic. To mention are in particular the following:

- An abrupt introduction of something new. The constitutional system of the Helvetic Republic was too strong a break with the past since it lacked bridges of continuity. The intended changes in the economic and social structures were too radical and therefore hardly accepted by the population.
- Political inexperience of the citizens. For the first time, every male citizen could take office in the legislature or the executive branch. However, many of the delegates had no political experience and little expertise. They were unable to meet the requirements of the upcoming complex legislative projects, including the introduction of freedom of trade and commerce, the abolition of feudal burdens and the introduction of a new system of taxation.
- Crippling political conflict in parliament. In parliament, the *Unitarians*, the supporters of the unitary state, and the *federalists*, who wanted to restore sovereignty to the cantons, fought against each other. The population was also divided on this issue.
- Financial difficulties. During the period of the Helvetic Republic, French troops were stationed in the Confederation, whose support had to be paid by the "host country". In many places, all livestock was slaughtered for the food

of the troops. The *requisitions* - in addition to substantial cash benefits - burdened the Confederation heavily.

In order to meet the requirements of the constitution, the feudal levies were no longer collected at the beginning of the Helvetic Republic. At the same time, it was not possible to introduce a new taxation system, and therefore the state had to stop payments at the end of December 1801 and declare bankruptcy. In the meantime large parts of the population were impoverished.

Forerunner of the federal state

Even though the Helvetic Republic failed miserably, various elements of its constitution were implemented with the Federal Constitution of 1848. The principle of sovereignty of the people, the separation of powers, the bicameral parliament, the collegiate government, the Supreme Court and the protection of rights and liberties. Other reform projects, such as the codification of private and criminal law, the replacement of feudal burdens, the introduction of freedom of trade and commerce, and the standardisation of currencies, measures and weights, of post and customs, were realised in the second half of the 19th century. The Helvetic Republic had planted the seeds, which sprouted after 1848. Only then the time was ripe for the previously too bold modernisation of the constitutional and legal system. The Helvetic Republican state disliked by most citizens and forcefully imposed on the Confederation proved to be a key precursor to the constitutional system and legislation of the young federal state.

8.2 Mediation

8.2.1 Napoleon and the Consulta

With the bankruptcy declaration of the Helvetic Republic, its end was predictable. Anticipating a revolt throughout the country, Napoleon withdrew his troops in the fall of 1802. Afterwards three different governments claimed power: one in the French-speaking and two in the German-speaking part of the Confederation. The official Swiss government had retreated to Lausanne, the State Commission resided in Berne, and the Tagsatzung was held in Schwyz. When the Tagsatzung began negotiations with Napoleon's opponents, Austria, England and Russia, Napoleon offered his mediation in the Swiss dispute. With the intention of drafting a new constitution for the Confederation, he called on the Unitarians and the Federalists to send delegates to Paris. About sixty people, mostly Unitarians, travelled to the *Consulta* in December 1802. However, a bitter disappointment awaited the Unitarians, because, at the opening session on December 10th, Napoleon made it clear that he wanted to turn the Confederation into a federalist confederation again: "La nature a fait votre etat fédératif. Vouloir la vaincre, ne peut pas être d'un homme sage" ("Nature has made your state federal. To try to defeat it cannot be a wise man's (action)"). He edited the constitution of the Federation and a commission of four senators, after hearing the cantonal representatives, edited those of the cantons. On February 19th 1803, Napoleon handed over the Mediation Act to the confederate deputies. On March 10, 1803, the Helvetic Republic ended, and both the Helvetic Republics authorities and the Supreme Court judges resigned.

Return to cantonal sovereignty

The Mediation Act consisted of 20 chapters: The Federal Constitution and 19 cantonal constitutions. This structure already demonstrated the minor importance of the central federal power and the much larger power of the cantons, which regained their sovereignty within a federal system that had been lost during the era of the Helvetic Republic.

The Confederation was now a *Federation* of 19 cantons. This included the cantons of the Old Confederation of the 13 cantons: Uri, Schwyz, Unterwalden, Lucerne, Zurich, Glarus, Zug, Berne, Freiburg, Solothurn, Basel, Schaffhausen and Appenzell, and the six new cantons Aargau, Grisons, St. Gallen, Thurgau, Ticino and the Vaud. Most important the cantons were now equal to each other, and thus all subordinate relationships with the Confederation were abolished. Since Napoleon personally guaranteed the continued existence of each of the twenty constitutions, they could only be amended with the consent of France. Therefore, the Confederation - as during the Helvetic Republic - was nothing more than a satellite state of France. In these years, at the height of his power, Napoleon was not interested in any national autonomy and self-determination of the Confederation, but he needed it to stabilise his continental European system of rule.

8.2.2 The Mediation Act

Reintroduction of the Tagsatzung

The Tagsatzung became the joint authority of the Federation again and was responsible for foreign relations of the Confederation, such as trade contracts and customs tariffs as well as raising a federal army in case of war. Decisions were taken by simple majority, except for declarations of war, peace agreements and alliances with foreign powers, which only became valid with the agreement of votes from three-quarters of the cantons. A simple majority was achieved by 13 votes since five cantons of the 19 had a double vote. In contrast to before 1798, the populous cantons with more than 100,000 inhabitants now had more political weight. These were the cantons of Berne, Zurich, Vaud, St. Gallen, Aargau and - mistakenly - Grisons. Since the cantons were often not willing to implement the resolutions of the Tagsatzung, they were more of a character of voluntarily observed concordats. Thus, all-embracing reform efforts in the Confederation had virtually no chance.

Landamman of Switzerland

The three powers barely existed at the federal level. The Tagsatzung could not be considered as a legislature, as it had virtually no competencies in this respect, but depended on the goodwill of the cantons. A court no longer existed at the federal level. Only the executive remained in an insignificant form. Article 13 of the mediation constitution stipulated that the Tagsatzung should be held alternately in the cantons of Freiburg, Berne, Solothurn, Basel, Zurich and Lucerne, the so-called *directorial cantons*. For confessional reasons, these consisted of three Catholic and three Reformed cantons. The head of the respective directorial canton bore the title of *Landamman of Switzerland*. His primary duties included the Presidency of the Tagsatzung and the external representation of Switzerland. For this purpose, a few officials were appointed to his office but had no real executive powers, and as the Kings of Holland and Naples and the Viceroy of Italy, were just Napoleon's extended arm in a vassal state.

Development at the cantonal level

At the cantonal level, the Mediation Act reintroduced the old order. In many places, various rights and liberties granted during the Helvetic Republic were revoked. The principle of legal equality and freedom of establishment were mentioned in the cantonal constitutions, but religious freedom, press freedom or the guarantee of personal freedom and the like were not included. The cantonal constitutions can be divided into three groups: those of the city cantons, the rural cantons and the new cantons.

Front of the cover page of the Mediation Act. The cover page is wrapped in dark blue velvet at the front and back, and the front is decorated. For the decoration, silver threads were used, and for the embroidery they were gilded. The original Mediation Act is located in the Swiss Federal Archives in Bern. Image: Swiss Federal Archives, Deckblatt der Mediationsakte (Cover of Mediation Act), reference code K0#1000/1420#4*.

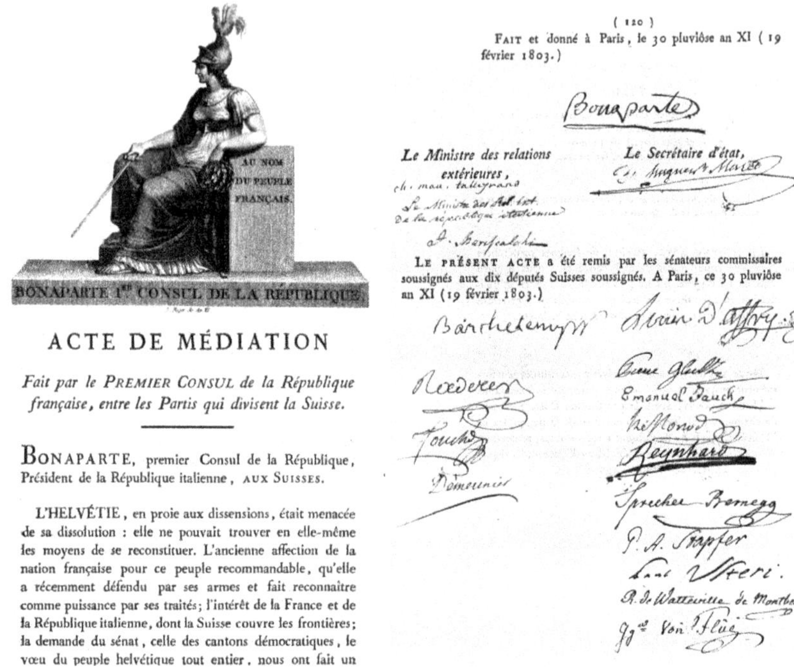

BONAPARTE 1er CONSUL DE LA RÉPUBLIQUE

ACTE DE MÉDIATION

Fait par le PREMIER CONSUL de la République française, entre les Partis qui divisent la Suisse.

BONAPARTE, premier Consul de la République, Président de la République italienne, AUX SUISSES.

L'HELVÉTIE, en proie aux dissensions, était menacée de sa dissolution : elle ne pouvait trouver en elle-même les moyens de se reconstituer. L'ancienne affection de la nation française pour ce peuple recommandable, qu'elle a récemment défendu par ses armes et fait reconnaître comme puissance par ses traités; l'intérêt de la France et de la République italienne, dont la Suisse couvre les frontières; la demande du sénat, celle des cantons démocratiques, le vœu du peuple helvétique tout entier, nous ont fait un

(120)

FAIT et donné à Paris, le 30 pluviôse an XI (19 février 1803.)

Bonaparte

Le Ministre des relations extérieures,

Le Secrétaire d'état,

LE PRÉSENT ACTE a été remis par les sénateurs commissaires soussignés aux dix députés Suisses soussignés. A Paris, ce 30 pluviôse an XI (19 février 1803.)

First and last page of the Mediation Act. Image: Swiss Federal Archives, reference code K0#1000/1420#4*.

In the city cantons, the patricians and the guilds returned to power, and the city assumed the supremacy over the rural territories again. Their supreme body was the Grand Council. Also, there was the Minor Council, which was elected from the ranks of members in the Grand Council. Their judiciary took over the district and appellate courts and the institution of the justice of the peace from the system of the Helvetic Republic. In the rural cantons, the rural community assembly was revived. All men with the right to citizenship could participate, thus helping to shape political life. Economic freedom rights were the least developed there. The six *new cantons* based their organisation on the city cantons.

Like these, they appointed the Grand Council and the Minor Council, district courts and an appellate court, and some even established their independent administrative court. In the new cantons, many reforms of the Helvetic

Republic persisted, such as the principle of separation of powers and ideas on economic rights. In the new cantons, the civil rights and liberties were consolidated in such a way that they were granted even during the subsequent Restoration.

Development of the Commercial Law

In the Federal Constitution, the freedom of trade and commerce and the freedom of establishment were enshrined for Confederates. However, this did not prevent some cantons from imposing restrictions, such as for peddlers and innkeepers, who had often been subject to restrictive regulations.

The replacement of feudal burdens did not succeed during the Mediation period. The constitutions of the rural cantons did not even mention them. In the city cantons and the new cantons, it was made impossible due to the high transfer fees defined in the implementation law.

The number of customs duties increased again compared to the period of the Helvetic Republic. The regulation in the Mediation Act prohibiting the levying of new internal tariffs was interpreted by some cantons to the extent that only new tariffs were banned. All old ones from the past before the Helvetic Republic regained their validity again, with the result that their number also increased again.

Even the standardisation of measures, weights and coins did not succeed, although this reform was discussed several times at the Tagsatzung.

Significance of the Mediation

The Mediation as a constitutional, historical epoch was of great significance because due to the return to federalism the domestic political situation calmed. The federalist state concept was no longer questioned in the following years. The old relationships of subordinates were not revived, and the newly formed cantons endured. They were particularly concerned with the modernisation of the education-, healthcare- and welfare systems and promoted their road transport and forestry.

Nonetheless, the Confederation did not prosper economically, although it was largely spared by the turmoil of the Napoleonic wars by lying in the "slipstream" of European superpower politics. Despite its state of development in the textile industry, the economic upturn failed as a result of the Napoleonic *Continental Blockade* against England. Just as during the period of the Helvetic Republic, there was considerable economic hardship in many parts of the country.

8.3 Restoration

8.3.1 Repeal of the Mediation Act

Influence of Austria

After Napoleon's failed Russian campaign in 1812, Prussia and the German Confederation of the Rhine rose against France. In 1813, Napoleon's troops were defeated in the *Battle of the Nations* in Leipzig, and the end of his rule was conceivable. Napoleon withdrew his troops under pressure from the Allies from the canton of Ticino, where they had been stationed since 1810.

At an extraordinary Tagsatzung in November 1813, the Swiss decided to protect their neutrality and independence and to defend their constitution. However, in December of the same year, allied troops crossed the border to Switzerland. The Austrian Chancellor Prince Metternich declared that Switzerland should regain its independence. In reality, he wanted to replace the French with an Austrian protectorate. He also intended to revive the Old Confederation with its oligarchic, pre-revolutionary structures. The old forces seized the opportunity. In Berne, the patricians returned to power shortly after the arrival of the Austrian troops.

Division between the cantons

In December 1813, the Tagsatzung was called to Zurich. Ten of the old cantons decided to suspend the Mediation Act and to draft a new all-embracing federal constitution as soon as possible. The restorative movement, which attempted to restore constitutional and power structures from before the Helvetic Republic, expanded from Berne to Freiburg, Solothurn and Lucerne. Also in these cantons, the patricians tried to regain their former supremacy. In March 1814, eight conservative cantons (Berne, Lucerne, Freiburg, Solothurn, Uri, Schwyz, Unterwalden and Zug) founded a separate Tagsatzung (Sondertagsatzung) in order to recover the lost subject territories that had meanwhile become cantons. Switzerland was divided into two camps, because the other cantons did not join the restoration movement, but demanded - on the contrary - the consolidation of the Confederation. A war between the two camps threatened to break out.

8.3.2 The "Protracted Tagsatzung" and the Vienna Congress

Principles of a Constitution

In this situation, the three powers allied against France - Austria, Prussia and Russia - intervened in the federal affairs. They prohibited the separate Tagsatzung of the conservative cantons, threatened Switzerland with a renewed, now allied "Mediation" and called on them to draft a new constitution with the 19 cantons as the foundation. The threat was sufficient, and the separate Tagsatzung broke up. In April 1814, the ordinary Tagsatzung was convened with the purpose of achieving an amicable settlement between the cantons. The Russian Czar Alexander I (1777–1825) had been particularly active for this purpose. Faced with conflicting ideas, however, this was a difficult undertaking. The Tagsatzung lasted until August of the following year. It became increasingly clear that the new constitution had to be based on two principles: the first was on the political neutrality since Switzerland could not endure on its own between the various political power blocs, and on the other on a federal authority that was as small as possible.

Throughout the summer of 1814, various bills were drafted, which, however, all failed because of the border conflicts among the cantons. Although Berne accepted the formation of the canton of Vaud, it maintained its claim to Aargau. Only after a renewed intervention by the three powers did a draft of a *Federal Treaty* come about in September, which was supported by almost all cantons. At the same time, it was earmarked to incorporate three new cantons in the Confederation: Neuchâtel, the Valais, which had been an independent republic since 1803 but occupied by France in 1810, and Geneva, which had been under French rule since 1803.

Vienna Congress

The draft had only been possible because it did not deal with the cantonal border disputes. The *Congress of Vienna*, which had been in session since September 1814, would have to take care of this issue. This was a meeting of the restorative powers of Europe, which after Napoleon's fall had the complex task of establishing a new and lasting political order for Europe. France was to be restored within its borders of 1792 and the Congress should decide on the exact borders between France and its neighbouring countries; Switzerland included.

The representatives of Switzerland demanded the recognition of the independence and neutrality of their country. Furthermore, they expressed territorial claims to the Valtellina, to Chiavenna and Bormio and demanded the annexation of the Jura by Berne. The result of the negotiations, however, was disappointing for Switzerland. Although the Congress of Vienna recognised the new cantons of Geneva, Neuchâtel and Valais and granted the Jura and the city of Bienne to the canton of Berne, the additional territorial claims were ignored. The second demand for the recognition of Swiss independence and neutrality was coupled with the adoption of the territorial demarcation decided by the

Congress of Vienna. All cantons took an oath on and enforced this Federal Treaty in August 1815. At the Paris Peace Conference in November 1815, the Allied Powers recognised the independence of Switzerland with its 22 cantons as well as its neutrality.

The neutrality of Switzerland already had a previous history. As early as 1674, during the war between France and the Netherlands, the Tagsatzung had declared its willingness to stay neutral. After the Thirty Years' War, the concept of neutrality had become an internationally accepted option for militarily weak middle states and republics, which wanted to stay out of the conflicts between the great monarchies. Neutrality had also served the Confederation in the subsequent period to defend its sovereignty under international law.

"Restoration"

The Congress of Vienna initiated a phase of a comeback to pre-revolutionary forms of the constitution for some European countries, which was to last until 1830. The philosophical manifesto was provided by the Bernese statesman and journalist Karl Ludwig von Haller (1768–1854), who also coined the name of his epoch with his six-volume work "Restauration der Staatswissenschaft" (1816–1834), which was directed against the Enlightenment.

8.3.3 The Federal Treaty and the Cantonal Constitutions

Content of the Federal Treaty

The Mediation Act had already taken a step backwards in comparison to the progressive constitution of the Helvetic Republic, but with the Federal Treaty of 1815, the elimination of ideas from the Helvetic Republic went even further. The Federal Treaty consisted of 15 somewhat hazily formulated articles. Switzerland now consisted of an association of 22 sovereign cantons. It formed a federation of sovereign states. The purpose of this federation was the assertion of freedom and independence against attacks by foreign powers and the handling of peace and order internally. It was in essence a *defence alliance*. Compared to the Mediation Act, the number of guaranteed rights and liberties had been further curtailed. The only freedom left was the guarantee of partial freedom of trade. The cantons were again able to negotiate directly with foreign countries as before 1798. On the other hand, they were not allowed to enter into separatist pacts (Sonderbünde) with each other. The Tagsatzung as a federal body had few competencies and was mainly responsible for foreign policy and the military. As before 1798, each canton had only one vote, regardless of its population and the deputies had to vote again based on instructions. Between the meetings of the Tagsatzung the canton Zurich was responsible for the federal affairs, whereas Berne and Lucerne alternated as the principal canton in a two-year turn. The institution of the Landamman was abolished.

Cantonal constitutions

The restorative tendency of this period is also reflected in the cantonal constitutions. These were largely based on the constitutional systems before the Helvetic Republic. As during the Mediation period, a distinction was made between the rural cantons, the city cantons and the new cantons. Exceptions were Grisons and the newly added cantons of Valais, Neuchâtel and Geneva. One feature all cantonal constitutions had in common. They contained, like the Federal Treaty, *no* provisions for their *revision*. Therefore, it was not possible to adapt the constitutions to changing circumstances, an inadequacy that would have a substantial impact in the following years. In the judiciary, some elements of the Helvetic Republic survived such as the district and cantonal courts as did the arbitration courts. The prefectural system of the Helvetic Republic was also retained in many cantons.

In the rural cantons, the old constitutional system had already been reintroduced with the Mediation in 1803; there were only a few changes. The cantons lowered the minimum voting age for the rural community assembly to 18, 16 or even 14 years. The city cantons, however, were strongly influenced by the Restoration movement. In some places, the city once again gained political overweight over the rural territories as in the Ancien Régime.

In order to constitutionally guarantee this, particularly in the patrician cantons, the separation of powers was disregarded, and more authority was given to the Minor Council. For example, the Minor Council in Lucerne exercised executive, administrative and judicial powers and was the only body with the right to initiate legislation. The newly established cantons of Aargau, St. Gallen, Ticino, Thurgau and Vaud, during the Mediation period, first attempted to reintroduce their previous constitutions. However, this was met with rejection from the Allied powers, as they opposed the ideas of the French Revolution. The constitutions of these cantons were therefore aligned with those of the city cantons. As in these cantons, an increased *minimum tax qualification* (Wahlzensus) was envisaged for the councillors, and the principle of the separation of powers was negated. Some differences remained such as the equality of rights, which had become more important in these cantons.

8.3.4 Progress in this era

During the Restoration period, some progress had still been achieved. Amongst others, the prohibition of subject territories and the principle of the written constitution were retained from the Helvetic Republic. Also, the remnants of a functioning press system were able to survive. This would become very important for the subsequent constitutional development. With the establishment of a federal war chest, the foundation stone was laid for a Swiss army. In accordance with the central purpose of the federal government, the federal military was vigorously promoted. Further progress has been achieved in the educational sector, where the founding of cantonal schools was promoted. Last but not least, most of the cantons managed to set their finances on a more stable footing.

Since the 1820s, the mechanised textile industry had experienced a boom. The machines required for this purpose were increasingly manufactured in Switzerland and therefore lay the foundations for the Swiss machine industry. Freedom of trade and commerce was in most places kept in the cantonal constitutional law. It was mentioned in the cantonal constitutions of Ticino, St. Gallen, Thurgau, Berne and Lucerne. On the other hand, the guilds in the cantons of Zurich, Schaffhausen, Basel and Solothurn regained their old position of power. No progress had been made in relieving feudal burdens and standardising measures, weights and coins. Finally, at the cantonal level, various civil and criminal code amendments were enacted.

8.4 Regeneration

8.4.1 Liberal trends in the 1820s

Liberal movements and thought leaders

The restorative counter-movement after the political demise of Napoleon could not completely overshadow the liberal political tendencies geared toward implementing the revolutionary postulates. Since the 1820s, liberal sympathisers met in charitable societies, shooting clubs and others to discuss the ideas of the French Revolution and the Helvetic Republic. They publicly criticised the Federal Treaty and demanded a strengthening of the federal power. Of particular importance were the *Helvetic Society* (since 1819) and the *Swiss Archery Association* founded in 1824. The annual federal shooting matches provided the liberal politicians with the opportunity to promote their ideas in front of a large audience. Important statesmen of the Helvetic Republic like Paul Usteri (1768–1831) and Albrecht Rengger (1764–1835) continued to campaign for revolutionary ideas.This public discussion was gradually reflected in the cantonal constitutional law. The principle of the separation of powers was incorporated into the constitutions of the cantons of Solothurn, Ticino, Geneva and Lucerne. The freedom of the press, which had long been recognised in Geneva, was incorporated into the constitutions of Glarus, Zurich, Lucerne and Aargau in 1829.

The Ticino "Riforma"

The canton of Ticino was ahead of its time. A few days before the outbreak of the July Revolution in Paris in 1830, a new constitution came into force meeting the main demands of the Ticinese liberal movement. Stefano Franscini (1796–1857), teacher, school reformer and later Federal Councillor, led the movement. The Ticino constitution of 1830 represented an evolution of the cantonal constitution of 1814, which had been supplemented by democratic and liberal elements. Separation of powers, the reduction of the term of office from 6 to 4 years and the compulsory referendum on constitutional amendments were introduced. Rights and liberties were introduced, such as personal freedom and inviolability of the domicile, freedom of trade and commerce, the right of petition and the freedom of the press. Because it implemented many reform postulates, this constitution was called "Riforma" and became the first regeneration constitution in Switzerland.

8.4.2 The July Revolution of 1830 and its impact on Switzerland

The liberal movement would have been able to influence the constitutional law of Switzerland without external influence, but the July revolution of 1830 in France intensified and accelerated its impact.

July Revolution

In July 1830, the French King Charles X. issued four decrees with the intention of carrying out a restorative coup d'état. Amongst others, he revoked the freedom of the press and dissolved the recently elected, mainly liberal parliament. The French people revolted against these revisions because they also violated the French constitution. After short street riots, Charles X. had to flee. His successor and nephew, the "Citizen King" Louis Philippe, had to take an oath of allegiance to the revised *Charte constitutionnelle* of 1814, which was based on the liberal spirit. Such an oath meant breaking with the principle of the monarchic legitimacy and the indirect recognition of popular sovereignty. As a result of the July Revolution, the liberal bourgeoisie replaced the nobility as the state-forming social class of France.

Popular assemblies

The events in France spread hope and terror in Switzerland. Terror for the strata of society who had exercised political power in the Restoration period and even before the era of the Helvetic Republic and now feared the loss of their position. Hope for the liberal forces, which were waiting for an opportunity to take over power. In the winter of 1830/31, the liberals initiated large popular assemblies in the provincial towns in order to emphasise their claims to the ruling circles, which had been summarized in catalogues *(Memoriale)*. The rural population hoped for better representation in the cantonal political institutions, where the urban population was often over-represented. Under the pressure of the rallies, the members of government either gave in or resigned from their posts. Except for Basel, where armed conflicts finally led to the division of the canton into two half-cantons, the upheavals took place without violence.

The armed actions were usually moderate. The *press* played an important role by criticising the established order and helping mobilise the rural citizens and peasants.

New cantonal constitutions

After the Ticino, ten cantons enacted new constitutions in the first half of 1831, such as Thurgau, Aargau, Lucerne, Zurich, St. Gallen, Freiburg, Vaud, Solothurn, Berne and Schaffhausen. In the other cantons, the regeneration movement did not succeed in taking root.

In the regenerated cantons, the old power structures were put to an end, the people declared sovereign, and the representative democracy was introduced. Liberal personalities such as Kasimir Pfyffer in Lucerne played a critical role in this transformation. Like others, he advocated not only a new cantonal constitution but also a new organisation of the federal government, which was still based on the Federal Treaty of 1815.

Popular assembly in Balsthal on December 22nd, 1831. In Solothurn, Martin Josef Munzinger (called Josef Munzinger, 1791–1855) was a driving force in the regeneration process. In his youth, Munzinger participated in the overthrow of the Solothurn patriciate, which led to a lawsuit for civil disobedience. It was not until 1830 that he became politically active again. At the popular assembly in Balsthal, he proclaimed popular sovereignty and made seventeen demands, including the abolition of tithing. In 1848, he became one of the first seven federal councillors in Switzerland. His son, Walter Munzinger (1830–1873), is the author of the Code of Obligations of 1883 and a co-founder of the Christian Catholic Church. Picture: Burgerbibliothek Bern, Gr.D 194.

Stefano Franscini (1796–1857). Franscini wanted to become a priest, but then left the seminary and took on teaching assignments. He held various political posts and was predominantly involved in popular education and the modernisation of the canton of Ticino. From 1848–57 he served as Federal Councillor of the Department of the Interior. The founding of the Swiss Federal Polytechnic, today's ETH, dates back to his initiative. Image: ETH-Bibliothek Zurich, Bildarchiv Portr_01742/Public Domain Mark.

Kasimir Pfyffer of Altishofen (1794–1875). Pfyffer studied law and philosophy in Tübingen and became a professor of law. He worked as a professor, lawyer and judge. In 1826 started his political career. Pfyffer led the liberal opposition in Lucerne and held various posts. However, he rejected his election to the Federal Council. Picture: Presumably 1860s, photographer unknown. Zentral- & Hochschulbibliothek Luzern (Central & University Library Lucerne), special collection.

8.4.3 Liberal Ideas in the Regeneration Constitutions

Extension of the Rights and Liberties

In the constitutions of the regeneration period, the *rights and liberties* were considerably extended. Freedom of the press, freedom of expression and property rights were now guaranteed. The freedom of establishment, which was of eminent importance for the development of trade, was only valid in those cantons that had joined the Concordat of Freedom of Establishment (Niederlassungskonkordat) of 1819 (Zurich, Berne, Lucerne, Glarus, Freiburg, Solothurn, Aargau, Thurgau, Ticino, Vaud, Neuchâtel, Geneva and Schaffhausen), but continued to be extended and could later also be found in the constitution of Solothurn. The regeneration constitutions also introduced equality of rights and thereby removed the old privileges of class status (Stand) and canton (Ort). Religious freedom, on the other hand, was only granted with great restraint and therefore was often confined to the denomination of the majority of the population.

Popular sovereignty

Important innovations took place in the sphere of democratic rights. In the regenerated cantons, popular sovereignty was established, which led to significant changes for the legislature. New constitutions and constitutional amendments had to be put to the vote of the people, and in the cantonal councils, the rural population should be better represented. The census regulations for the election to the councils were abolished. Therefore the proof of a certain minimum income or minimum assets was no longer required. The opportunity to participate in political life for the peasants and the petty bourgeois was now guaranteed as in the Helvetic Republic. Nevertheless, in many places, the urban population remained overrepresented.

Cantonal authorities

Furthermore, the Grand Council was still stipulated as the cantonal legislature. However, now it constituted the representation of the people, which had become the highest power in the state. The negotiations of the Grand Council had to be held in public. Thus, the public principle - albeit less comprehensively than at the time of the Helvetic Republic - was applied again. The Minor Council was stripped of all its sovereign rights and kept only the leadership of the executive. The power of the councils was also limited by the fact that the courts were free from political dependence based on the separation of powers. The councils could no longer intervene in the court activity. The judiciary remained organised in two tiers in the cantons. The first instance was the district courts (named differently such as Bezirks-, Distrikts- or Amtsgerichte) and the higher cantonal instance, the high- or appellate courts. The institution of the justice of the peace was also retained. Special commercial courts were introduced in Berne and Zurich.

8.4.4 Development at the federal level

In contrast to the cantonal level, the regeneration movement at the federal level did not succeed. Because only half of the cantons had adopted a new constitution, the Liberals could only hope for a chance majority of the decisions at the Tagsatzung. They could not even advance old postulates such as the unification of the currencies. Also, the political balance of power in the cantons repeatedly changed in the 1830s. Glarus, Grisons and Geneva moved to the liberal camp, Lucerne, Schwyz and Freiburg, however, returned to conservatism, as well as temporarily Zurich. Another obstacle to the realisation of liberal ideas was the division of the liberal movement into a moderate and radical orientation. The moderate group sought to create a unified national economic sphere on a federal basis, whereas the *Radicals* wanted to enforce freedom and democracy within the framework of a nationally centralised state.

Constitutional drafts

At the Tagsatzung of 1832, a small majority of 13 and a half cantons decided to draft a new federal constitution. In the same year, the commission set up under the chairmanship of the Geneva professor and politician Pellegrino Rossi (1787–1848) presented a *bill.* This envisaged a middle ground between a confederation of states and a centralised state. The federal authority should be strengthened, and the cantons should at the same time get ample space of freedom. As the legislative branch, a Tagsatzung consisting of 44 cantonal deputies and as an executive a permanently sitting Federal Council should be set up. A federal court was designated as the highest court for civil and criminal cases. Lucerne was proposed as the capital of Switzerland. The federal powers should be greatly expanded, and the freedom of trade and establishment, as well as free movement within Switzerland, ensured. The bill already contained various elements of the later Federal Constitution of 1848 but did not receive a favourable reception. A new – much more conservative – bill from 1833 could not prevail either. At the federal level, the reorganisation in the 1830s did not succeed like at the Vienna Congress of 1815, the special interests of various cantons impeded a countrywide solution.

8.5 The Federal Constitution of 1848

8.5.1 Confessional tensions of the 1840s

In the 1840s confessional tensions led to an aggravated conflict between the liberal and conservative forces. While at the beginning of the regeneration movement differences between the cities and the countryside were paramount, it was now the conflict between the Catholic-conservative party and the liberals or radicals, who were closely linked with the Reformed denomination. The conservatives wanted to preserve tradition, so they fought for federalism and a strong position of the church in society. The radicals, on the other hand, wanted to force Switzerland to redesign and further democratise the country. They championed the nation-state and economic freedom. The Jesuits, who were active in the educational system of the Catholic cantons of Freiburg, Schwyz and Valais, were a thorn in their side; they regarded them as the "Pope's combat troops" and as the greatest opponents of the ideas of the Enlightenment and liberalism.

Appointment of the Jesuits to Lucerne

In various cantons, the tensions grew noticeably. Lucerne changed from a liberal canton to one governed by Conservatives in 1841, effectively becoming the capital of Catholic Switzerland. The decisive factors for the change were the elections for the Constitutional Council, in which the Catholic-Conservative Party emerged victoriously. In order to strengthen the influence of the church on the state, the government called the Jesuits to Lucerne in 1844. They were to lead the seminary and the theological school and provide pastoral care.

Convents Dispute of Aargau

In the largely liberal and reformed canton of Aargau, a constitutional revision was carried out in 1841. This brought a change in the distribution of the seats in the Grand Council. Reformists and Catholics had previously held an equal number of seats, but at the request of the Liberals from then on they should be distributed according to party strength. Although the vast majority of the population adopted the bill, there was rioting in the countryside. The Liberals blamed the eight Catholic monasteries in the cantonal territory for these riots. They were abolished at the request of the Liberals by the Grand Council, which led to protests at home and abroad. The conservative cantons Uri, Schwyz, Unterwalden, Freiburg and Zug, demanded that a special Tagsatzung should be called. The latter decided with a majority of the cantons that the abolition of the monasteries would not be compatible with the Federal Treaty and invited Aargau to reverse them. However, the canton of

Aargau only partly complied with the order by allowing four nunneries to open again.

Also in the Valais in 1844, as in Lucerne, the political situation changed. The Catholic Conservative Party won the majority in the Grand Council, subsequently revoked the freedom of the press, and prohibited reformed home worship services. The radicals tried to undo this but to no avail.

Campaigns of Free Corps

The struggle of the confessions led to bloody conflicts. In response to the appointment of the Jesuits to Lucerne, a first campaign of Free Corps of Liberal armed forces was formed at the end of 1844, and a second one in March 1845. They ousted the conservative government of Lucerne and wanted to drive the Jesuits out of the city. Although armed contingents from Berne, Solothurn, Aargau and Basel Land supported the volunteer insurgents, their campaigns failed both times.

8.5.2 The Sonderbund War

Sonderbund

Alarmed by the campaigns of the Free Corps, the Catholic cantons Uri, Schwyz, Unterwalden, Lucerne, Zug, Wallis and Freiburg entered in December 1845 into a separate pact (Sonderbund) as a defensive alliance against liberal attacks. At the Tagsatzung of 1846, the opponents of the Sonderbund demanded its dissolution, as it violated the Federal Treaty of 1815. But just ten cantons voted for the dissolution. Only after the radical-liberal take-overs in Geneva and St. Gallen was it possible to form a majority against the Sonderbund.

Guillaume Henri Dufour (1787–1875), General of the Sonderbund opponents. Dufour not only worked as a general but also as a cartographer, engineer and politician. He was the first to create a detailed topographical map of Switzerland and was a co-founder of the International Committee of the Red Cross. During the Sonderbund war, as a general of the Swiss army, Dufour was careful not to unnecessarily endanger the lives of his opponents and facilitated a subsequent reconciliation. The Federal Assembly transferred the supreme command of the Swiss army to him even after 1848 three times, which is why he is the first general of modern Switzerland. Image: Photography, ca. 1848, HelveticArchives, GS-FOTO-PORT-DUFOUR_GUILLAUME-1/Artist: Jean de Humnicki.

Military Campaign

The radicals gained further political strength. In addition to the dissolution of the Sonderbund, they also called for a revision of the Federal Treaty in order to strengthen the federal government and to extend the economic and trading areas beyond the cantonal borders. Their conviction that the Federal Treaty of 1815 no longer satisfied the interests of the Swiss economy found more and more supporters. The proponents of a comprehensive revision of the federal government increased. The cantons allied in the Sonderbund, however, were against a federal reform, as they feared a weakening of their political position. The gap between the parties deepened. At the Tagsatzung of 1847, another attempt was made to resolve the conflict through negotiations. Despite intensive negotiations, there was no agreement. The representatives of the Sonderbund Cantons left the conference venue after reading out a protest note. The Tagsatzung decided on the dissolution of the Sonderbund by military force and commissioned General Guillaume-Henri Dufour. He was provided with a federal army of 100,000 men. The troops of the Sonderbund Cantons consisted of only 35,000 men, who were also significantly less trained. After a few weeks campaign and a bloody battle at Meierskappel close to Lucerne, the federal troops occupied the city of Lucerne on November 24th, 1847. The war council of the Sonderbund fled the city. The last canton to surrender was Valais. The dissolution of the Sonderbund ended the last civil war in Switzerland. The victory of the liberal forces also opened the way for the revision of the Federal Treaty of 1815.

Johann Ulrich von Salis-Soglio (1790–1874), Commander-in-Chief of the Sonderbund troops. Salis-Soglio belonged to a noble family from Grisons. His military career also took him abroad. In 1841, he was appointed colonel in the Swiss army and as such with the suppression of the popular uprising in Valais. In 1848 he took over, even though reformed, the supreme command of the Catholic Sonderbund troops. After the defeat, he fled abroad. He was charged with treason but never convicted. After six years he returned to Switzerland and lived in seclusion in Chur. Picture: Rätisches Museum Chur, Inv. No. H1965.63.

8.5.3 The formation of the Federal Constitution

Revolution of 1848

The events in Switzerland were noticed in other European countries. The conservative powers France, Prussia, Austria and Russia tried to influence the Tagsatzung and prevent a revision of the Federal Treaty; they even threatened military intervention. However, the Tagsatzung did not stop the project. When revolutionary revolts erupted in Paris at the beginning of 1848 and these spread to all of France and the other countries governed by Conservatives (Revolution of 1848), the governments of these countries were so absorbed in their domestic problems that they could not interfere further with Swiss politics. The turmoil swept among others King Louis Philippe and Prince Metternich out of their offices.

Constitutional Commission

In February 1848, a commission for drafting a new federal constitution started its work. Except for the cantons of Neuchâtel and Appenzell-Innerrhoden governed by Conservatives, all the other cantons were represented. The commission members consisted mostly of radicals and moderate liberals. In April, the Commission already presented its first draft. With this quick procedure, the radical and liberal forces wanted to exploit their supremacy after the Sonderbund War as well as the political discord of the conservative forces at the federal level. Moreover, the European powers should be faced with accomplished facts. In its preparatory work on the constitutional draft, the commission oriented itself on the cantonal regeneration constitutions and the constitutional drafts of 1832 and 1833. And without openly declaring this intent, also considered the radical-democratic ideals of the French Revolution.

Enactment of the Constitution

At the end of June 1848, the representatives of 13 cantons voted in favour of adopting the draft. In the subsequent cantonal referendums, 15 cantons and one half-canton, which together comprised more than 7/8 of the Swiss population, adopted the draft with large majorities. Even Lucerne agreed to the draft, but only because those who did not vote were counted as adopters. The Grand Council of the Canton of Freiburg ignored the cantonal population and adopted the constitution "in the name of the people". In addition to Ticino, the Catholic-conservative cantons of Uri, Schwyz, Unterwalden, Zug, Appenzell Innerrhoden and Wallis voted against the new constitution. In September, the Tagsatzung declared the Federal Constitution as unanimously accepted, but the cantons Uri, Schwyz, Unterwalden and Appenzell Innerrhoden abstained from the vote. The Tagsatzung was dissolved, and the institutions of the new state were established. On November 6, 1848, the Federal Assembly met for the first time in Berne. Ten days later it elected the Federal Council and the federal judges and decided on Berne as the federal seat.

For the first time after 1798, Switzerland succeeded in giving itself a constitution without foreign pressure. The Catholic population of the cantons of Freiburg and Valais, as well as the central Swiss cantons, perceived the creation of the liberal state as a bitter defeat. These cantons effectively withdrew from federal politics for the following decades. Conservative Catholics sent only a few representatives to parliament in the first decades after 1848, and only in 1892, was Josef Zemp (1834–1908), as the first Catholic-conservative politician, elected Federal Councillor.

8.5.4 The content of the Federal Constitution

Federal state

The constitution of 1848 laid the foundation of today's constitution. The Confederation now became a federal state and representative democracy. This was the result of the previous development. The Federal Treaty of 1815, which had created more than a pure confederation, was consolidated in the following years by a network of concordats between the cantons. These concordats were by no means simply considered contracts between sovereign states. Also, after 1815, a national identity had gradually developed, so that the alliance of the federal state in 1848 was more the result of a consolidation process instead of an abrupt change.

Federal Assembly

The separation of powers was institutionalised at the federal level by determining the powers of the executive, legislative and judicial authorities. On the issue of the structure of the future legislature, two camps had formed in the Constitutional Commission. The small cantons did not want to renounce their historical right to the same number of representatives, whereas the big ones, on the other hand, demanded that the cantons be represented in parliament in proportion to their population. These contradictory demands were met with the creation of a bicameral parliament modelled on the United States Union constitution of 1787 and the Helvetic Constitution. The physician and philosopher Ignaz Paul Vital

Troxler (1780–1866) had already proposed this model. The *National Council* (Nationalrat) was the representative of the entire people. In it, the cantons were represented according to their strength, as they should send one representative as per 20,000 inhabitants. The members of the National Council should be elected by a majority vote. In the *Council of States* (Ständerat), the successor of the Tagsatzung, each canton could delegate two and each half-canton one representative. The Council of States was intended as a counterweight to the National Council, which was dominated by the populous cantons. Both chambers deliberated separately, and submissions only became law after the approval of both councils. An exception to the bicameral system was that on particular matters, such as the election of the executive or the judiciary, both councils had to meet and vote simultaneously as the *United Federal Assembly* (Bundesversammlung). The concept of a bicameral parliament made a significant contribution to the political acceptance of the new constitution because it ensured the political representation of linguistic and denominational minorities at the federal level.

Federal Council

The structuring of the executive was simpler. From the draft constitution of 1832, which provided for an executive modelled on the Directory of the Helvetic Republic, the institution of the *Federal Council* was adopted, but with seven rather than five members, for a better representation of the cantons. Each Federal Councillor headed a department of the Federal Administration. In the beginning, the Federal Council elections were held every three years, later every four years, with the option for re-election. The Federal Council acted according to the *principle of collegiality* so that important resolutions required the approval of the entire Federal Council. The Federal Council was chaired by the Federal President with the function of a primus inter pares, which had to perform representative tasks in addition to directing the government's meetings. The United Federal Assembly elected him for a year based on the length of service. A stronger position of the Federal President had been rejected in the Constitutional Commission because a move towards a monarchy should be prevented.

Federal Court

In the judiciary, the newly created *Federal Court* was the highest instance in criminal and civil law matters. The constitutional jurisdiction, however, was in the hands of the Federal Assembly. The court had no permanent seat, only met at times and had only limited competencies. In criminal matters, it was only responsible for high treason, riots or acts of violence against federal authorities. With the creation of the Federal Court, the three-tier judicial organisation of the

Helvetic Republic was revived: the first instance was occupied by the local- or district courts, the second by the cantonal or higher courts and the third by the Federal Court.

Rights and Liberties

In the area of civil rights and liberties, the Federal Constitution followed the standard established in the cantonal regeneration constitutions. Some rights, however, were limited in scope. Equality of rights was guaranteed, but only for "Swiss citizens of Christian denomination". The same was true of the freedom of establishment, which could be denied to poor people. Settlers (Niedergelassene) were equal to the cantonal inhabitants and were free in the "commercial practice", but had no voting rights in community matters and also no share in community and corporation goods. Because of the resistance of some cantons, broader freedom of trade and commerce could not be realised. However, the constitution guaranteed the free import, export and transit of goods across the cantonal borders and obliged the cantons to treat all settlers from outside the cantons, performing a trade, in the same manner. The lack of comprehensive freedom of trade and commerce at the federal level was, of course, of little relevance, as this right was already enshrined in most cantonal constitutions. The Federal Constitution also did not recognise religious freedom without limitations. It guaranteed the freedom of worship, but only for the recognised Christian denominations. Furthermore, an article contained a prohibition of the Jesuits, and another one forbade the clergy to be elected into the Federal Parliament. In these articles, the confessional conflicts of the previous years had an impact. The women were completely deprived of political rights. Other, only partially guaranteed liberties were universal suffrage, press freedom, freedom of association and the right of petition.

Economic Policy Competencies

With the Constitution, the Confederation was given the task of establishing a framework for the free development of the economy and the removal of trade barriers. With the transfer of customs, it was given the power to lift the cantonal tariffs and to replace them with entry, transit and exit duties at the Swiss external borders, which was then, after 1848, easy to implement. The standardisation of measures, weights and coins, postulated since the Helvetic Republic, proved to be more difficult. In 1835, only 12 cantons joined a concordat that ruled on this topic. The creation of national private law, another basic condition for the free development of the economy, came about only against considerable resistance.

8.6 The constitutional Revision of 1874

8.6.1 Initial revision efforts in the young federal state

After 1848

The first years of the state system established in 1848 served mainly to introduce the constitution and to enact the necessary implementation laws. The Customs Law of 1849 introduced a single customs tariff. The currency issue also advanced, since the French coin standard could prevail, so in 1850 the national currency of the *Swiss franc* was introduced. On the other hand, the standardisation of weights and measures did not succeed. The implementation of a law in 1851, which declared the metric system compulsory for all cantons, failed because of the resistance of western and southern Switzerland. In 1868, another law permitted the concomitant use of the French and English measures and weights.

For the young federal state, *railway construction* became a major domestic issue. It was disputed whether this should be done by private companies or under state leadership. The proponents of private railroads prevailed in 1852 in the early years.

Draft bill for Revision of 1866

In 1864, the preparatory work for a first constitutional revision began. The reason was a trade agreement concluded with France, which granted all French citizens the freedom of establishment and trade. The Swiss Jews, who according to the Federal Constitution had neither the right to equality nor the freedom of establishment, were, therefore, worse off than the French. The draft bill for revision combined the removal of these discriminatory restrictions with other concerns, including the standardisation of measures and weights and further federal competencies. In total, the people and cantons had to vote on nine draft bills for revision. However, in 1866, only the equality of Swiss Jews for the right of establishment was adopted in the plebiscite.

Alfred Escher (1819–1882). Escher was a lawyer and from 1844 until 1847 private lecturer at the University of Zurich. In 1844, at the age of 25, he was elected to the Zurich Grand Council, of which he remained a member until 1882. From 1848–1855 he was a cantonal councillor and from 1848–1882 a national councillor, where he campaigned as a liberal for a federal state. Escher was a vehement promoter of railway construction but lobbied in the National Council for the private construction of the railway. In 1853, he was a co-founder of the Swiss Northeast Railway and in 1856, for the purpose of financing railway construction, co-founder of the Swiss Kreditanstalt (now Credit Suisse). Escher was also active in the planning and construction of the Gotthard line. From 1871 to 1778, he was director of the Gotthard railway company. Escher's display of power was very pronounced and earned him the title of "Federal Baron". Image: ETH-Bibliothek Zurich, Bildarchiv; Portr_05342/Public Domain Mark.

8.6.2 The constitutional Revisions of 1872 and 1874

Democratic Movement

Unachieved goals in 1866 and other reasons led to a renewed revision of the Federal Constitution. The fact that popular rights were only modestly established enabled strong personalities to accumulate a great deal of political power. This was also evident in the cantons, for example in Zurich, where the politician and industrialist Alfred Escher simultaneously held several political offices. An opposition movement formed in Zurich against Escher's power, which was able to assert itself. In 1869, Zurich enacted a democratic constitution. In other cantons, opposition increased as well, and the *democratic movement* finally won new political rights such as the *optional referendum*, the *legislative initiative* as well as the *popular election* of the cantonal government and the Council of States. Soon, the demand for more popular rights was also raised at the federal level.

Kulturkampf

Another reason for a comprehensive revision was renewed religious turmoil. After the Sonderbund War, the relationship between the Catholic population and the largely radical-liberal federal state was strained. From the 1860s, frictions increased and at the height of the Kulturkampf at the beginning of the 1870s, intense arguments ensued.

Anton Philipp von Segesser (1817–1888). Segesser grew up in Lucerne and studied law in Heidelberg, Bonn, and Berlin. In 1841, he passed the Lucerne bar exam. Segesser wrote several important legal, historical works and contributed articles for conservative magazines. Although Catholic, he was against the appointment of Jesuits to Lucerne and the Pope's infallibility dogma; but he remained faithful to his religion. Segesser held various posts: he was a member of the city Grand Cantonal Councillor, State councillor and National Councillor. As National Councillor, he represented the conservative line and fought the federal revision of 1874. Segesser was also in other areas more conservative. He opposed the construction of the Gotthard Railway. Image: Date of recording/name of photographer unknown; Zentral- & Hochschulbibliothek Luzern ZHB (Central & University Library Lucerne ZHB), special collection.

Key reasons were ecclesiastical statements. In 1864, Pope Pius IX condemned in his encyclical "Quanta cura", with a supplemented list, the *Syllabus errorum,* which contained eighty items of "errors" in contemporary politics, science and society, such as the individual freedom of belief, Protestantism, the separation of church and state, civil marriage and divorce. Later in 1870, the first Vatican Council passed the ecclesiastical *Infallibility Dogma*, which meant that under certain circumstances, the Pope was able to declare ecclesiastical doctrines infallible. Liberals, Protestants, but also enlightened Catholics were indignant. They feared for the loyalty of faithful Catholics to the state, so the demands for the expansion of federal competencies in religious matters, and complete secularisation of the state became stronger. In the liberal-governed cantons, another split occurred in the Catholic Church that led to the establishment of independent parishes, which merged in 1876 into the Christian Catholic Church of Switzerland. After fierce clashes between the Roman Catholic Church and the state in several cantons, the Federal Council broke off diplomatic relations with the Holy See. A central mediator during the Kulturkampf was Lucerne's Anton Philipp von Segesser, who, while representing the conservative line in the National Council, tried not to provoke liberalism and contributed much to the consensus and integration of the Catholic cantons into the new federal state.

Swiss Lawyers Association

The Swiss Lawyers Association, founded in 1861, campaigned vehemently for a revision of the constitution. With a petition in 1868, it demanded the reorganisation of the Federal Supreme Court and the unification of the law on a nationwide level. However, this required the creation of appropriate constitutional competencies. In 1872, the draft of a comprehensive revision of the constitution was submitted to the people. Forty of the 114 provisions of the constitution should be changed and 14 deleted; 21 new ones should be added. The intention was a transfer of the power of legislation for all private and criminal law, including procedural law to the Federal Government. The people and the cantons rejected the draft bill. Only nine cantons supported the revision. Among the thirteen rejecting cantons were also the Protestant, radically governed cantons of Geneva, Neuchâtel and Vaud.

In the same year, the preparatory work on the constitutional revision was resumed. In order to avoid another defeat, the liberal forces organised themselves and founded the *People's Association* (Volksverein – the forerunner of the later political party FDP). The new draft bill was based on the bill of

1872. In order to accommodate the federalist circles, it contained less centralist regulations, whereas due to the turmoil caused by the Kulturkampf, many points concentrated on the relationship between church and state. In a second attempt, the goal was achieved, although all Catholic-conservative cantons rejected the revision. In May 1874, the Federal Assembly enacted the revised constitution.

Innovations

The revised constitution brought about changes and innovations in various areas. First, the extended freedom of establishment, which was necessary for the economy. Then freedom of trade and commerce was finally guaranteed in an expanded form. In order to curb child labour and to improve working conditions in the factories, the federal government obtained a legislative competence, which in 1877 led to the factory law.

In terms of ecclesiastical issues, the new constitution instituted comprehensive freedom of worship for all religious communities as well as the freedom of faith and conscience for all inhabitants. However, it also contained various new restrictions of the Roman Catholic Church. In addition to a tightening of the Jesuit ban, the establishment of new orders and monasteries was prohibited and the founding of dioceses subject to obligatory approval by the federal government. Important spheres of public life were secularised, and the churches had to accept a significant reduction in their powers. The right to enact marriage and responsibilities in the area of elementary schooling, civil status and burial were transferred to the state.

There were also important amendments for the federal government and the cantons. As compensation for the cession of cantonal competences, the optional referendum for the enactment of federal laws or generally binding federal decrees was introduced. The Federal government also obtained the power to issue a national Code of Obligations. It did not receive any further competencies to harmonise legal rights. Concerning criminal law, detention because of debts, corporal punishment and the death penalty were prohibited. Furthermore, the federal court was also reorganised. It now met continuously and was given a permanent seat in Lausanne. Since its competencies were greatly expanded, the number of judges had to be increased as well. In addition, the *constitutional complaint* was introduced, with which private persons were given the possibility to reach the federal court in conflicts with cantonal authorities. Overall, the revision of 1874 led to considerable enforcement of the federal government over the cantons.

8.7 The development from 1874 to 1999

8.7.1 The expansion of federal competencies

Until 1999, there was no other total revision of the Federal Constitution, but it went through 104 partial revisions. The federal government obtained increasing powers, which led to the expansion – or further development – of the federal law.

Implementation of the revision program

Until 1890, the federal government worked on the implementation of the revision program of 1874. The Catholics and the federalist circles of western Switzerland, which used the newly introduced optional legislative referendum, often opposed the bills drawn up for this purpose. They rejected the introduction of a compulsory substitute tax for the exemption from military service (1876), a banknote monopoly for the federation (1880) and a federal school secretary (1882) successfully. The death penalty had to be re-admitted in 1879.

Social-, Environmental-, Intellectual Property- and Private Law

Other draft bills were more successful. Due to the increasing industrialisation of Switzerland, the awareness grew that federal regulations in labour and social security law were preferable to the cantonal laws. In 1877, the federal government obtained the competence for a factory law and in 1890 the competencies for the establishment of a health and accident insurance. These regulations were the start of federal social legislation. However, their creation and strengthening encountered quite strong resistance and delays. Thus, the implementing legislation on the health and accident insurance was at first rejected in 1900. The constitutional revision of 1874 had assigned to the federal government also the superintendence over hydraulic engineering and forest police in the high mountains. The Forest Police Act of 1876, based on this competence, was the start of federal environmental legislation. Based on a competence also created in 1874, copyright law was passed in 1883, and in 1888, a patent law and a federal law on industrial designs followed. Thus, the federal government also became gradually responsible for intellectual property law.

The transfer of the competence for private law proceeded sluggishly. After an attempt to create a federal competence for private law had failed in 1872, a second attempt with restricted competencies for the law of obligations, trade and exchange was attempted in 1874. The Code of Obligations (OR), which was based on it, came into force in 1883. The federal government received the competence to create a civil code and a penal code only in 1898. These national codifications were of great symbolic value. They strongly increased the reputation of the federal government and, together with the labour and railway law, created the conditions for the transfer of further national competencies. In 1872, when the Second Railway Act was enacted, the federal government did not yet have the appropriate competence. The rapid technological development in the 20th century then led to a rethinking; legislation in this area was increasingly understood as an original federal responsibility.

Macro-Economic and Cyclical Policy

In 1874, the Federal Constitution (BV/FC) had guaranteed in Art. 31 freedom of trade and commerce throughout the Confederation, an old demand of economic liberalism, since the Federal Constitution of 1848 had still contained numerous restrictions.

However, based on its power as a Custodian Regime (Vollmachtenregime), the Federal Council largely suspended the freedom of trade and commerce during the First World War and at the beginning of the Second World War. Since there was no legitimacy in the constitution, in 1939, it submitted to Parliament the draft bill of a new macroeconomic article, which, was never voted on because of the war. Only through the initiative of The Ring of the Independents (Landesring der Unabhängigen - political party 1936–1999, LdU or Adl) and the Social Democratic Party was progress achieved in 1943. The Social Democrats demanded the introduction of a right to work and a state-controlled planned economy.

After consultation with the commercial associations, the Federal Council opposed this demand with a revised version of the draft bill in 1939. The federal government would receive additional powers in the field of macroeconomic and cyclical policy. In the partially reworded Art. 31, 32 and 34 aFC, the freedom of trade and commerce had been secured with the condition that measures of state control may be applied. Such measures were provided in Art. 31bis aFC, such as the preservation of vital economic sectors and professions as well as a "healthy peasantry and efficient agriculture". Furthermore, measures for the protection of economically threatened regions of the country and the control of economically or socially harmful effects of cartels were introduced. However, cartels were not prohibited in principle. Collective agreements and other joint arrangements by employers' and workers' organisations to promote labour peace could be declared as generally binding (Art. 34ter aFC), which provided the constitution with a *corporatist* element. The people adopted the provisions in 1947. And so, the economic policy of the federal state was now also constitutionally anchored. An economic policy, which until then could hardly be characterised as a *laisser faire* policy, despite the freedom of trade and commerce. In 1978, the federal government was also required to ensure balanced economic development (Art. $31^{quinquies}$ aFC). In 1981, further tasks such as consumer protection (Art. $31^{sexties}$ aFC) and in 1986, tenant protection (Art. $34^{septies}$ aFC) were transferred to the federal government.

Debt brake and Competition law

In order to do justice to these and the other new remits, the federal government increasingly ran into debt. This led to uncontrolled growth of federal spending, and the federal budget ran a deficit in most years. In order to bring it under control again, the federal government was requested to balance the budget in 1995 (Art. 88 aFC).

In the 1990s, as a result of new developments in international business law and the Swiss membership of the WTO, the federal government was forced to allow increasingly more competition in the economy. Like other countries, the federal government exercised restraint in dismantling state support measures in individual areas, such as the national economic supply and agriculture. Instead of measures such as price support and export subsidies, direct payments were introduced. The revised antitrust law of 1995 tightened the cartel law. Agreements restricting competition should now be prevented in principle. Similarly, the merger of market-dominating companies was now subject to a reporting obligation and – in the case of indications of a dominant market position – to an authorisation obligation. The revision of the antitrust law in 2004 introduced the possibility for direct sanction by the Competition Commission. *Leniency* (*Kronzeugenregelung*) should also provide incentives for companies to exit a cartel and cooperate with the competition authorities.

8.7.2 Increase of political rights

Popular Initiative

After the introduction of the optional referendum, the constitutional law was subject to further modifications in the sphere of political rights. The Federal Constitution of 1874 already introduced the possibility for a constitutional revision, however only by way of federal legislation and in the form of a total revision. In 1884, three prominent conservative national councillors submitted a motion that should implement various political demands through a partial revision of the constitution. The Federal Council needed until 1890 to present to Parliament *the right of initiative to partial revision* of the Constitution. In this proposal, the government pointed out, that the partial revision by way of a popular initiative was already provided for in most cantonal constitutions. The radical-liberal majority in the National Council demonstrated limited enthusiasm because they were aware that this would reduce the political power of the parliament over the people. The political minorities applied this law, finally adopted in 1891, to get attention for their concerns. Although most of the popular initiatives subsequently failed, many political concerns were addressed in the form of counter-proposals by Parliament.

Proportional Representation

Both the constitution of 1848 and that of 1874 provided for the majority principle in elections to the National Council. However, since the 1860s, the introduction of a *proportional electoral system* had been discussed in the cantons and introduced in some of them. In 1900, a coalition of representatives of the Catholic-conservative and Social-Democratic parties submitted a popular initiative. They aimed to break the supremacy of the Liberals and Radicals in Parliament, who were over-represented there due to the majority electoral system. The initiative was rejected, as was a second, similar initiative in 1910. Only the third initiative was successful since more and more cantons had meanwhile changed the electoral procedure. Its adoption in 1918 led to the result, that in the election for the National Council in 1919 the Liberals lost 46 of 101 seats, the Social Democrats won 21 seats, and for the first time the Peasants, Trade and Citizens Party (BGB, a forerunner of the later SVP) won 28 seats right away, while the Catholic conservatives stagnated. The introduction of the proportional representation right also influenced the composition of the judicial offices in the Federal Court and the composition of the Federal Council. The parties were now entitled to appropriate seats in proportion to their strength in the National Council. In 1919, the Catholic Conservatives received a second Federal Council seat, in 1929 a representative of the BGB was elected and in 1943 a Social Democrat. From 1959 until 2003, the *Magic Formula* (Zauberformel) applied to the election of the Federal Council: 2 CVP (Christian People's Party), 2 FDP (Liberal Democratic Party), 2 SP (Social Democratic Party) and 1 SVP (Swiss People's Party) representatives, but in 2003, the CVP lost a seat to the SVP.

State Treaty Referendum

In 1921, the State Treaty Referendum was introduced as another political right, which had previously been included in some cantonal constitutions. Foreign treaties that were to be concluded indefinitely or for at least 15 years had to be presented to the people if required by 30,000 voters or eight cantons. The treaties concluded by the Federal Council and the Federal Assembly with foreign countries had always been a thorn in the side of the Democrats and Federalists. Already in 1909, when the Federal Council had entered into a second Gotthard

Treaty with Germany and Italy, which was very unfavourable for Switzerland, a committee from the Vaud region launched an initiative. However, the new constitutional provisions were so narrowly worded, that after 1921, only a few and unimportant state treaties were subject to the referendum. Other important agreements, such as the Free Trade Agreement with the European Economic Community (1972), were submitted to the referendum by the Federal Council without a legal basis. In 1977, Art. 89 par. 3–5 aFC specified which agreements should be subordinated to the State Treaty Referendum.

It was only in 1971 that the general *women's suffrage* was introduced and in 1981, the equality of men and women enshrined in the constitution (Article 4 (2) aFC).

8.7.3 The Custodian Regime during the two World Wars

Custodian Decree of 1914

On July 31, 1914, one day before the German declaration of war on Russia, the Federal Council mobilised the army. On August 3, the Federal Assembly elected former Corps Commander Ulrich Wille (1848–1925) as General and adopted the "Federal Decree on Measures for the Protection of the Country and Maintaining Neutrality" submitted by the Federal Council. In retrospect, this Custodian Decree had far-reaching consequences. The Constitution and democracy were essentially suspended in the following years. In order to respond to major crises, it was considered necessary to eliminate the ordinary legislative procedure and to give the government far-reaching legislative and executive powers, as in other countries. The Federal Decree stated Switzerland's firm commitment to maintaining neutrality in the coming warlike events, and the Federal Council was tasked to proclaim this neutrality to the belligerent states. Article 3 gave the Federal Council unrestricted powers to carry out all measures necessary to assert the security, integrity and neutrality of Switzerland and to safeguard the economic interests of the country.

According to Art. 4, the Federal Council was granted unlimited credit for this purpose. The only obligation of the Federal Council was to give an account of the use of its custodian powers to the Federal Assembly at its next meeting. This transfer of extraordinary powers to the Federal Council was not new. After 1848, it had already been implemented several times during domestic political unrest and wars in neighbouring countries. Of course, the scope and duration of the Custodian Regime were new for Switzerland. As the rest of Europe, Switzerland was also expecting a short war when it broke out in 1914. However, the war and consequently the Swiss Custodian Regime would last many years.

Orientation for the Federal Councillors at the border. In 1918, Gustave Ador, Felix Calonder, Camille Decoppet, Robert Haab, Giuseppe Motta, Eduard Müller and Edmund Schulthess were members of the Federal Council. Picture: Swiss Federal Archives; CH-BAR#E27#1000/721#14094 #463*/CC-BY-SA 3.0/CH.

Ulrich Wille (1848–1925), Swiss General from 1914–1918. Wille completed a law degree in Zurich, Halle and Heidelberg. In 1870, he was drafted into the service, and a year later, he decided on a military career. This with interruptions, since he rubbed many the wrong ways with his dominating leadership style by drill and discipline. From 1903, he taught military science at the Federal Polytechnic in Zurich, in 1914, the Federal Council elected him as General. When the national strike began in 1918, Wille had the cities of Berne and Zurich occupied by infantry and cavalry divisions. Picture: Swiss Federal Archives; CH-BAR #E27#1000/721#14095#1124*/CC-BY-SA 3.0/CH.

Troops marching on the Bubenbergplatz in Berne during the national strike in 1918. Picture: Swiss Federal Archives; CH-BAR#E27#1000/721#14095 #5461*/CC-BY-SA 3.0/CH.

Impact of the Custodian Decree

The Custodian Decree centralised the political power on an unprecedented scale at the Federal Council and the administration. This although there was no constitutional basis, such as in the form of an emergency article. Without having to involve the Parliament and the people, the Federal Council and the administration were able to issue emergency decrees and measures. Therefore, they also intervened in the competencies of the cantons and the constitutional rights of the citizens. For example, the freedom of trade and commerce had largely been removed. The Federal Council made intensive use of its custodial powers. Due to the war and the generally submissive spirit to authorities in politics and society, there was initially little resistance against these measures. The different sympathies for the opponents of the war – German-speaking Switzerland sympathised with the Central Powers, while French-Speaking Switzerland supported the Entente – led to the result that in 1916 the acceptance of the Custodian Regime began to crumble in western Switzerland.

The rift between western and German Switzerland grew larger until part of the Swiss-German press distanced itself from the Central Powers in 1917. Despite the growing popular resistance, the Federal Council continued to issue around 1000 emergency decrees until the beginning of 1919. These decrees not only concerned internal security and external relations but also deeply interfered with the national economy and the legal system. The administration also held great power. Some edicts were issued by individual departments or even by individual department sections. Publication was often avoided so that a clear overview of the measures taken was missing. Nonetheless, the authoritarian regime of the government and administration did not prevent an economic and social crisis. Commerce and domestic trade were down. The population was confronted with inflation, rationing and unemployment. Many people found themselves in economic destitution and relied on public aid. The soldiers received minimal pay for their military service so that many families had to survive without the income of the father. Social tensions between the working class and the bourgeoisie led to a national strike in 1918, during which the strikers faced a massive deployment of the army. Only with difficulty, could a civil war be prevented.

Emergency law of the interwar period

After the end of the First World War, the Parliament succeeded in 1919 to repeal the Custodial Powers, despite the resistance of the Federal Council. However, not all emergency decrees had been rescinded. In the interwar period, for more than half of the laws enacted up to 1939 the right of the referendum was revoked, using the *Urgency Clause* (Art. 89 aFC). Faced with the global economic crisis, unemployment and the rise of fascist groups (*Frontism)* in Switzerland, a normalisation of the political conditions were out of the question, on the contrary, emergency law was adopted to a large extent.

Custodian Decree of 1939

On August 30, 1939, shortly before the German troops attacked Poland, the Federal Assembly issued a second Custodian Decree. In terms of content, this was largely identical to that of 1914. At least the Federal Council was obliged to report to Parliament in the June and December sessions and to submit important measures to the parliamentary commissions for review before their adoption. The Parliament was also able to decide on the continuation of the Custodian Regime after each year. By 1945, several hundred decrees had been issued. Again, the rights of citizens had been widely restricted, and the constitutional powers of the cantons were overridden. On the contrary, the cantons became the law enforcement bodies of federal law.

Refugee Policy

As the investigations of the Independent Expert Commission "Switzerland - World War II" (*Bergier Commission*) have illustrated, the Federal Council made no use of its powers to suspend the Federal Law on the Residence and Establishment of Foreigners (ANAG) of 1931. This granted asylum only to politically persecuted people in Switzerland. In a circular issued in August 1942, the Federal Council even specified that refugees for reasons of race, namely Jews, did not count as political refugees and that they had to be turned away at the national borders. Although the Federal Council already knew at this time about the deportations of Jews. It is estimated that around 20,000 people were turned away at the Swiss borders. Only in July 1944, when the massacres of the Hungarian Jews became known, were the Jews recognised as political refugees. Around 60,000 civilians were protected from persecution by the Nazi regime or fascist Italy until the end of the war, as well as 104,000 foreign military personnel, who could claim protection under the Hague Conventions.

Economic relations with the Axis Powers

As part of the Custodian Regime, the recovery provision of Art. 934 ZGB was not amended to prevent the sale of stolen artefacts belonging to German Jews in Switzerland. After the USA entered the war in late 1941, the Swiss franc was one of the only free convertible currencies. The German authorities acquired with *Nazi gold* and *looted art* Swiss francs, in order to buy raw materials in other neutral countries. Switzerland was an important gold-, art- and foreign exchange-hub for Germany. Swiss banks granted loans to German companies and provided other financial services. Switzerland also allowed Germany and its allies the rail transport of goods and weapons through the Alpine passes. On the other hand, the Axis powers were important export destinations for Switzerland. Between 1940 and 1944, 84 % of Switzerland's arms and munitions exports went to Germany. The authorities were able to rely on the applicable neutrality law. According to the prevailing doctrine and practice, neutral states were not obliged to break off their economic relations with belligerent states. The public supported the concessions of the Federal Council to Nazi Germany, as well as the Custodian Regime in general because both were afraid of German occupation and wanted to prevent the economic burden of the refugees.

Law and Court Practice

The Custodian Regime did not encounter strong criticism among the jurists. One of the few exceptions was the Professor of Public Law in Zurich, Zaccaria

Giacometti (1893–1970), who sharply denounced the practice of the Federal Council. On the other hand, apart from a few exceptions, the Swiss jurists distanced themselves from the National Socialist ideology. In speeches, essays and book reviews, jurists such as Fritz Fleiner (1867–1937), August Egger (1875–1954) and Dietrich Schindler sen. (1890–1948) opposed the German constitutional development and the accompanying National Socialist legal theory. This was not the case in Germany, where the academic jurists played a considerable role in the development of the National Socialist injustice state. The cantonal courts and the federal court refused to become vicarious agents of the expropriation and robbery policy of the Nazi regime. Concerning Swiss *public policy*, they prohibited the execution of German judgments with Nazi and racist content. From 1935, the Federal Supreme Court held in many decisions that Nazi racial legislation was contrary to Swiss public policy, but the executive disregarded these decisions.

The Custodian Regime was abolished at the end of 1945 by resolution of the Federal Assembly. However, many Custodial Decrees remained in force and only at the end of 1952 were the last ones repealed.

8.7.4 The development of the protection of fundamental rights

Recognition of unwritten fundamental rights

The Federal Constitution of 1874 explicitly guaranteed ten fundamental rights. Since the need to expand and secure individual freedom rose after the Second World War, the existing protection of fundamental rights was increasingly seen as incomplete. In the 1950s, however, a change in the constitution was politically out of the question, which is why another way was taken: the extension of the protection of fundamental rights by the courts. In 1959, the Federal Supreme Court recognised the right to property as an unwritten fundamental right, 1961 freedom of expression, 1963 personal freedom including the right to life, 1965 freedom of speech, 1970 freedom of assembly, and finally in 1995 the right to livelihood. Moreover, in 1992 a civilian alternative service was introduced for conscientious objectors of the military service. In the 1970s, political conscientious objectors were still severely punished by military justice.

Accession to the ECHR

In 1974, Switzerland acceded to the European Convention on Human Rights (ECHR), which contained a list of fundamental rights created by the European states in 1953 after the horrors of the Second World War. In order to be able to accede, Switzerland first had to introduce women's suffrage (1971) and abolish the prohibition of Jesuits and convents (1973). The provisions of the ECHR came with the ratification in addition to those of the Federal Constitution and were considered directly applicable. Swiss constitutional law was undergoing further substantive development. The individual could now appeal to the ECHR with a constitutional complaint against a negative judgement of the Federal Court and move his case on to the European Commission for Human Rights in Strasbourg. The latter was merged in 1998 with the *European Court of Human Rights*. The application of the ECHR in Switzerland has strengthened the fundamental right to personal freedom and led to the rectification of the judicial organisation in order to enhance the independence of the courts and ensure a fair trial.

Other conventions

Switzerland also ratified other human rights conventions, such as the International Convention on the Elimination of All Forms of Racial Discrimination of 1965, the two UN Human Rights Pacts of 1966, the UN Convention against Torture and the UN Convention on the Rights of the Child of 1989.

Because of this fragmentation, the status of fundamental rights protection became increasingly confusing. In addition to the old fundamental rights guaranteed in the constitution, there were the "unwritten" ones, which the Federal Court had recognised, as well as those resulting from Switzerland's international obligations. With the total revision of the Federal Constitution of 1999, the fundamental rights and procedural guarantees were therefore summarised in a new, detailed catalogue (Article 7-36 FC).

8.7.5 The rapprochement with the European Union

EC and EFTA

As in the case of fundamental rights protection, Swiss law has also focused on international developments in other areas. Of particular importance was the relationship between Switzerland and the European Community (EC) and (from 1993 onward) the European Union (EU). The Treaty of Rome created the European Economic Community (EEC) in 1957, which became the EC in 1967 and the EU with the Maastricht Treaty of 1993. Switzerland was reluctant to join the EEC or the EC and rejected the unified foreign economic policy, agricultural policy and the long-term goal of a European federal state. Instead, it supported the establishment of the European Free Trade Association (EFTA). Founded in 1960, this less ambitious organisation dismantled the barriers of trade between its members but left them free to pursue an economic policy towards third countries and did not pursue broader political goals. In the following years, however, the EC had greater appeal despite internal crises. Other countries, including various former EFTA states, joined the six founding states. Switzerland sought to safeguard access to the ever-growing EC market by concluding bilateral and sectorial contracts.

EEA

In 1985, the EC decided to remove all remaining barriers to trade and traffic among its members until 1992. For the EFTA countries, the question arose as to how they could prevent the impending isolation faced with an increasingly powerful and harmonious EC. For this purpose, the creation of a European Economic Area (EEA) with the Member States of the EC was sought. It was intended to realise the free movement of goods, services, capital and people and to provide a basis for cooperation in research and development, environmental protection and social and educational policy. The EEA entered into force in 1994 – though without Switzerland, because after a heated referendum campaign EEA membership was rejected by the people in December 1992. Among the many reasons for this result, one key reason was that the petition for accession to the EC – submitted by the Federal Council a few months before the vote – puzzled the population. Given the impending isolation of Switzerland, the Federal Council decided to autonomously establish thepart of EU legislation that was also binding for the EEA countries. The Council also started negotiations with the EU in 1994 to limit the economic disadvantages of Switzerland's absence in the European single market. The negotiations resulted in a series of bilateral treaties.

8.8 The constitutional Revision of 1999

First revision efforts

The 1999 constitutional revision was preceded by decades of effort. Following parliamentary initiatives, the Swiss Federal Department of Justice and Police (FDJP) set up a task force in 1967 chaired by the former Federal Councillor Friedrich Traugott Wahlen (1899–1985) with the task of preparing a total revision of the constitution and collecting relevant suggestions for this task. The final report was published in 1973. In a second phase in 1974, the FDJP commissioned a group of experts to draw up a draft for a new constitution. Federal Councillor Kurt Furgler took over the chair. The Commission presented its draft Constitution in 1977, which, however, was rejected in the subsequent consultation because of the intended new redistribution of competences in the state.

Reduction of the Revision scope

Since a far-reaching substantive revision turned out to be politically impossible, it was decided to focus on a purely formal revision. In 1987, the Federal Assembly agreed to revise the Federal Constitution. The Federal Council was instructed to update the existing written and unwritten constitutional law, to organise it systematically and to standardise the density and language of the text. The strategy pursued by Federal Councillor Arnold Koller consisted of removing the substantive reform projects from the formal revision project and pursuing them separately (*constitutional reform in the modular system*) so as not to jeopardise the revision project with politically potentially controversial substantive reforms. In 1995, the Federal Council presented a revised draft constitution, which was based on the politically feasible. The Federal Assembly adopted it in 1998 – 150 years after the founding of the modern formal state – and in 1999 by the people. The revised constitution entered into force in early 2000.

Friedrich Traugott Wahlen (1899–1985). Wahlen studied agronomy at the ETH in Zurich. As the head of the agricultural production and accounting section of the Swiss Federal Food Administration, he drafted a plan for self-sufficiency in Switzerland during the war. Based on the so-called cultivation battle during the Second World War. Admittedly, Wahlen doubled the acreage, but not Switzerland's self-sufficiency. However, he gained an excellent reputation. In 1942, he was elected to the Council of States and in 1958 to the Federal Council, where he remained until 1965. Picture: https://www.admin.ch/gov/de/start/bundesrat/mitglieder-des-bundesrates/friedrich-traugott-wahlen.html

Kurt Furgler (1924–2008). Furgler studied law in Freiburg, Zurich and Geneva. He was a lawyer in St. Gallen. Furgler held various political offices; in 1971, he became Federal Councilor. In this office, he led the expert commission, which was to prepare the total revision of the Federal Constitution. Furgler also initiated the revision of family law as well as the constitutional article for the equality of men and women and, consequently, the revision of the marriage law. Image: www.dodis.ch/~temp-cache/public/portrait/12000/dodis-P12150-F2.jpg.

Arnold Koller (b. 1933). Koller first studied economics in St. Gallen and then law in Freiburg. In 1980, he became a professor at the University of St. Gallen. From 1986 until 1999, he was Federal Councillor. Initially, Koller headed the military department, from 1989 the judiciary and police department. As head of this department, he was responsible for the total revision of the Federal Constitution in 1999. Picture: Official portrait of a member of the Swiss Federal Council, www.ejpd.admin.ch/ejpd/en/home/about-us/dv/firehere_dv/brk.html.

Formal and material modifications

According to the chosen strategy, the the focus of the new constitution were *formal* modifications. It should give a complete picture of the so far written and unwritten constitutional law. Some provisions were reformulated, gaps were closed, and open questions were clarified. Various regulations of the old Federal Constitution, such as the articles on the subjects, the emigration agencies and the bribe collection fees, had become obsolete and were therefore removed.

As a new purpose of the federal state, the Federal Constitution of 2000 mentions equal opportunities of all (Art. 2 FC). The Federal government and the cantons should work to ensure that every person can participate in social security schemes, receives the necessary care for health, and can find work, accommodation, and education. Families, children and adolescents should be protected and promoted (Articles 11, 41 and 67 FC). Another new objective has been the commitment to sustainable development and the preservation of natural resources (preamble, Art. 2 and 73 ff. FC).

The new constitution explicitly stipulates previously "unwritten" fundamental rights, such as those recognised by the Federal Supreme Court after 1874 or resulting from international agreements. It clarifies the liberal competition rules (Art. 26 f and 94 es.) and contains the political rights of the citizen, in particular, the initiative and referendum in unchanged form, but more clearly presented (Art. 136,142 FC).

The relationship between the Federal government and the cantons as well as their rights and obligations are regulated in Articles 3, 42, 49 and 55 FC. Both sides commit themselves to mutual consideration and cooperation. The Federal government should observe the autonomy of the cantons, and the cantons should participate in the decision-making process and the foreign policy decisions of the Federal government. The relations of the federation to the municipalities (Gemeinden) are also mentioned. According to Art. 50 FC, municipal autonomy is guaranteed in accordance with cantonal law. In its actions, the federal government has to take into account the possible effects on the municipalities. It should consider the special situation of cities, agglomerations and mountain regions.

Finally, the new constitution also contains a catalogue of the competencies of the Federal government and the cantons (Article 54 et seq.).

8.9 The development after 1999

In 2000, the reform of the Judiciary as an accompanying reform project of the new Federal Constitution succeeded. In 2001, a *debt brake* was introduced (Article 126 FC) and in 2003 a reform of the popular rights. Other revisions concerned the UN accession (2002), the financial equalisation (2004) and the competencies in the sphere of education (2006). The revision of the antitrust law envisaged by the Federal Council failed in 2014 in the parliament.

Revisions on the basis of popular initiatives

The political tool of the popular initiative was increasingly utilised after 1999. On the one hand, it helped to advance the concerns of the population, but also to give a sharper political profile to parties and other interest groups. It can be stated that in the last years' popular initiatives – unlike in the past – can count on success even without broad political support if they pick up the mood of the population at the right time. Side effects of the increase of successful popular initiatives are increased incompatibilities with international law.

Initiatives have repeatedly been successful in topics concerning immigrants ("Prohibition of Minaret Construction", 2009; "Expulsion of Criminal Foreigners", 2010; "Against Mass Immigration", 2014, and on issues related to sexual offences against children ("Lifelong custody for unreachable, extremely dangerous sexual and violent offenders", 2003, "For the criminalization of pornographic offences against children", 2008, "Paedophiles should not work with children", 2013). Less successful were popular initiatives aimed at the redistribution of wealth ("Against the rip-off", 2013; "Ending the tax privileges for millionaires", 2014; "Tax the Millionaire's inheritances for our AHV", 2015).

In the field of healthcare, a number of initiatives related to medical advances have been adopted (Complementary Medicine, 2008, Human research, 2009, Primary health care, 2013, Reproductive medicine and human genetic engineering, 2014), but initiatives related to health insurance have been repeatedly rejected ("Health must remain affordable", 2003; "For a Social Health Insurance Fund", 2007; "For Quality and Efficiency in Health Insurance", 2008; "For a Public Health Insurance Fund", 2014).

The people decided in a very pragmatic way on initiatives that related to the labour law: voting against shorter working hours in 2002, six weeks holidays in 2012, for capping managers' incomes in 2013, and for setting a minimum wage in 2014.

An on-going theme was the revision of the first and second pillar of old-age pension schemes. Both should be adapted to the demographic development and the longer life expectancy of the people. However, the people only adopted the initiative for the increase of the pension age for women from 62 to 63 years in 2001 and 63 to 64 years in 2005. In 2004, the 11th pension scheme revision was rejected, as well as in 2008 the initiative "For a flexible Pension-Age" and the change of the minimum conversion rate in the BVG in 2010.

8.10 The relationship with the EU

Bilateral agreements

In 1999, Switzerland signed a first set of bilateral agreements that the population then adopted in a referendum vote in 2000. They concerned land- and air-transport and movement of persons, research, public procurement, technical approval procedures and agriculture. A second set of bilateral agreements was signed in 2004 and enacted the following year. These enabled Switzerland to participate in EU systems in the spheres of asylum, migration and crime (Schengen, Dublin). The adoption of the bilateral agreements led to a loss of national legislative and administrative autonomy in the legal areas affected by those. The 1999 agreement on the free movement of persons, which was gradually extended, resulted in a high level of immigration of persons from EU Member States. An expression of popular unease was the adoption of the popular initiative "Against Mass Immigration" in February 2014, which put the free movement agreement with the EU in jeopardy.

9 Legislation of the Helvetic Republic in the 19th century

9.1 Civil and Criminal Legislation in the Helvetic Republic

9.1.1 Civil legislation

Freedom and equality of all human beings – this was the maxim that natural law, the Enlightenment and the French Revolution had written on their banner. They demanded the recognition of the legal capacity of all people regardless of their state, religion or nation. Then again, at that time philosophers and lawyers meant by "people" only the male part of humanity; equality between men and women was of no concern for most of them. The provisions made by the French revolutionary law for the legal improvement of women were only briefly in force. The postulates of the Enlightenment included the right to free property. That should be not only free of all restrictions and duties, but also freely available, and usable. These demands were raised in France and Switzerland in the second half of the 18th century against the backdrop of numerous legal and actual inequalities: parts of the peasantry, non-residents and foreigners, Jews, illegitimate and all women were in the Ancien Régime consistently disadvantaged before the law.

Constitutional postulates

The Helvetic Constitution of 1798 established a series of provisions for the private law system. However, unlike the French *Déclaration des droits de l 'homme et du citoyen* of 1789, which served in part as a model, it did not state any general legal equality. Article 5 said that the natural freedom of individuals is inalienable and finds its limits only in the freedom of others. According to Art. 6, freedom of conscience was unlimited; all services were allowed as long as they did not disturb the public order. Private property should be able to be confiscated by the state only in urgent cases and for fair compensation (Article 9). Land should not be burdened with loans, interest or easement from which one cannot be bought free (Article 13). Article 48 of the Constitution established the applicable laws of the cantons as a provisional guideline for the courts and held out the prospect of a single private law applicable to the entire territory of the Helvetic Republic. The intention was to replace the fragmented statute law of cities and rural regions with a unified civil law codification.

Unity of Private Law

As in France, in some cantons of the Old Confederation, namely in Berne, Zurich, and Basel, there had already been efforts in the Ancien Régime to standardise private law. At the end of the 18th century, the law of the principal city was occasionally enacted with the claim to apply throughout the sovereignty as the subsidiary law to the locally administered rights. However, this was only partially achieved because the subject territories of the city cantons had primarily retained their legislative autonomy. If necessary, the rural subjects had to submit their statutes to the City Council of the principal city for approval. The Helvetic Grand Council should now create legal unity for the entire territory of the unitary state by passing a civil law, thereby transforming the substantive concerns of the constitution into statutory law. It should become the basis of the jurisprudence of the newly created Supreme Court of the Helvetic Republic, which like the lower courts suffered under the fragmentation of law. At the end of 1798, the Helvetic Grand Council set up a legislative commission at the request of the Directorate. This issue did not progress beyond initial planning because its members were overwhelmed with other, more urgent tasks. Under the impact of a renewed federalism, the commission ceased its work in 1801, since the national legal entity was no longer politically opportune.

In anticipation of these unsuccessful attempts of codification, various individual laws were enacted as early as 1798. As in France, this meant that spheres of code that needed to be reformed were first to be subject to a temporary regulation.

Replacement of feudal burdens

A first matter was the replacement of *feudal burdens*. Among them was the obligation of the rural population to do corvée labour and pay taxes in kind or money. These had their origin in the medieval feudal and judiciary system and in church tithes. If they had not been abolished in the Late Middle Ages or early modern period, they had lost considerable importance until the 18th century. The actual *serfdom* existed at the beginning of the Helvetic Republic only in some provincial regions, especially in Thurgau. Under the influence of the Enlightenment and the French Revolution, Solothurn (1785), Basel (1790), the Prince-Abbot of St. Gallen (1795), and Schaffhausen (1798) had released their subjects from bondage. Elsewhere it was long gone. It only consisted of a kind of taxpayer duties. The perception that they had once been the remuneration for landlords and judicial sovereigns in exchange for the lending of estates or the personal protection by the Landlord was long ago lost. The tithes due to the ecclesiastical and secular authorities were considered as materially onerous. Since only the rural population owed them, they were also regarded as unfair. The Helvetic Grand Council, which consisted of a pretty sizable proportion of peasants, quickly issued a *tithing law*, which abolished the minor tithe and tithe for newly broken agricultural land (Neubruchzehnten) without compensation and declared the Grand tithe to be replaced. The farmers should be able to buy themselves off against the amount of a twentyfold annual tax. However, this law was not implemented for economic and political reasons until the end of the Helvetic Republic.

Therefore, the replacement of the tithes became a task of the cantons after 1803. In cantonal constitutions, private-law codifications and individual laws, the principle of the redemption of land burdens and tithes as well as the actual modalities were determined. By 1850, the replacement had taken place in most places. However, the farmers had to indebt themselves to finance the redemption money. Therefore, the liquidation of the remaining feudal rights was accelerated in the middle of the 19th century, partly by reducing the replacement code or by entirely abolishing the obligation to repay.

Rights of the Illegitimate

The second area of regulation was the improvement of the illegitimate. For the protection of marriage and to contain extra-marital sexuality, children born out of wedlock had been legally disadvantaged, especially since the Reformation. They had no full citizenship and were both actively and passively incapable of inheriting. Sometimes this harsh private law principle was undermined by official exemptions. In various rights, children born out of wedlock were granted an active right of inheritance, at least toward the mother, or a passive right of heritage in favour of their legitimate children. After being presented with a series of requests for legitimation, the Grand Council passed a law in late 1798 on *the statutory eradication of the blight of illegitimate birth, with limited equality in civil rights*. This law granted extramarital born descendants full political rights as well as the active and passive testament ability. Out of consideration for the legal inheritance rights of the relatives born out of wedlock, however, no intestate rights were granted to them.

Rights of Foreigners

In many places of the Confederation, foreigners – means non-citizens - were excluded from the guilds and other urban associations (Gesellschaften) until the time of the Helvetic Republic. Thus, they could not exercise free trade or commerce. They were also not allowed to acquire landed property because this was often only accessible to the citizens. Elsewhere, the citizens or the community just had a *right of withdrawal*, with which they could prevent the sale of land to an outsider. The Helvetic Republic was not only based on a unified and indivisible state territory, but also on uniform citizenship for all Swiss. That resulted in the requirement to lift restrictions on freedom of establishment and freedom of trade and commerce. In various laws, the Grand Council tried to equalise the outsiders with the locals. The Law on the Establishment and the Legal Capacity of Foreigners of 1798 granted foreigners the right of establishment, purchase of land and the free exercise of trade, art, and science, provided that they did not belong to a power hostile to France or the Helvetic Republic.

Improvements for the Jews

The Helvetic Republic also made efforts for a legal improvement of the Jews. These had been expelled from many parts of the Confederation in the early modern period. By resolution of the Tagsatzung in 1774, their settlement had been limited to the villages of Endingen and Lengnau (near Zurzach). Through the payment of the so-called *Jewish Customs* (Judenzoll), they were able to acquire letters of shelter (Schirmbriefe) which enabled them to practice free trade, but not to exercise a craft or to purchase real estate. A decision of the Grand Council in mid-1798 forbade the levying of the poll tax on Jews for the future. Shortly after that, the directorate put the Jews on equal standing with the foreigners. However, equality with the (other) Swiss failed due to the anti-Semitic sentiments of the peasant's majority in the Grand Council.

Marriage law

Unlike the French constitution of 1791, the Helvetic Constitution contained no provision on the legal nature of marriage. Like the French constitutional law, the Helvetian councillors no longer regarded marriage as a religious relationship, but as a *civil contract*, which was reflected in the laws passed by them. In these new regulations, the jurisdiction of the matrimonial law was assigned to the ordinary district courts. The authority of the Catholic diocese and the Protestant courts was de facto repealed. That led to considerable resistance in the Catholic cantons of Switzerland, since the sacramental character of marriage, in particular, was called into question. Thus ecclesiastical jurisdiction was reinstituted in eastern Switzerland soon after. A draft of a substantive state matrimonial law was not put into force so that the previous marriage law - and in the Catholic places the church law - continued to be applied. The marriage was performed as before in front of the pastor. On the other hand, civil records were now introduced in the municipalities, in which marriages were also to be registered.

The prohibitions on marriages between members of different denominations, which still existed in many cantons, were now abolished as well as the collection of *marriage enrolment monies* (Einzugsgelder), which until then had to be paid by women when they married men from another village.

With the collapse of the Helvetic Republic, the ideals for freedom and equality became politically inopportune for quite some time and were only gradually revived in the law of the Federation. The laws passed by the Helvetic councillors were repealed. The rights of Jews and foreigners were again restricted and many communities reintroduced marriage enrolment monies and moving rights.

9.1.2 Criminal Law

The Helvetic Republic was not welcomed by most of the people in Switzerland. The Helvetic authorities were confronted with opponents of constitutionalism, troublemakers, and rebels, revolts of local people, coups d'états, unrest among compulsorily recruited troops and desertion. As in France during the Revolution, in a first phase of the Helvetic Republic, special police powers were conferred on the Directorate, which was also used to take political hostages. First penal laws of 1798 earmarked the death penalty for counterrevolutionary acts, refusal of military service and mutiny. Military courts appointed by the authorities repeatedly issued death sentences.

Criminal Code

The martial courts were already abolished in 1799. That was not because the political situation had calmed down, but because the criminal norms had been incorporated into the *Criminal Code of the Helvetic Republic* issued on May 4th, 1799. It represented an almost literal, albeit a lousy copy of the French *Code pénal* of 1791. The criminal code was like its model a modern criminal law, influenced by the ideas of the Enlightenment and therefore a novelty for the territory of the Confederation. It contained two parts.

The first section describes the punishments. The *death penalty* was to be done by decapitation, without any torture and the cruel implementation of the criminal law was therefore no longer permitted. The prison sentence was intended in different degrees of severities and durations. The *chaining punishment* (*Kettenstrafe*) was the most severe penalty and possible for a long time (restriction: not life-long). The condemned had to drag an iron ball attached to an anklet and do heavy public labour. Women were punished without chaining in the *penitentiary*. In the *cane house* (Stockhaus) the convicts were in solitary confinement and only received water and bread. They were also used for work, but these were less exhausting, and the convicts had a third of the pay for better nutrition, and a third was retained for the period after their release. The *detention* corresponded to that of the cane house; however, the convicted were not in solitary confinement and the duration of the sentence was not allowed to exceed six years. All penalties were preceded by a display at the pole of infamy. That lasted between two and six hours, depending on the type of sentence.

In the special section of the code, all sorts of offences were listed, among them notably numerous, the crimes against the state, which were fitted with draconian threats of punishment. This way, the young republic sought to secure its existence.

Reasons for resistance

The Criminal Code faced resistance for many reasons. The judge's commitment to a precise level of penalties was unfamiliar to criminal law practice and was perceived as being inapplicable. Until then the pillory punishment only applied for dishonest offences, and the various punitive norms for political crimes enabled real state terror. Besides, the appropriate penal institutions were missing for the multiple forms of imprisonment. The existing bell works (Schellenwerk) in several Swiss cities since the early 17th century had only been set up for the correction of petty criminals. The lack of acceptance soon made revisions of the law necessary. Given this far-reaching state powers, it was perceived as detrimental that the Helvetic Constitution, unlike the French Declaration of Human Rights, did not contain any criminal procedural rights.

In 1799, the Helvetic Senate discussed regulations for the legal protection of citizens in criminal proceedings. As early as 1798, torture had been abolished for the entire territory of the Helvetic Republic, and in 1800, it was stipulated that any physical or psychological methods of coercion to obtain a confession were inadmissible.

Like the civil law, criminal law became obsolete with the demise of the Helvetic Republic. Criminal justice became once again a cantonal competence. That did not mean that the criminal law of the Helvetic Republic was dropped entirely. Some cantons put the Criminal Code into force or used it as a template for their legislation. The institutions aimed at the humanisation of the criminal law practice were adopted into cantonal legal practice with some delays.

9.2 The cantonal codifications

9.2.1 The constitutional situation

The heydays of cantonal codifications

The Mediation Act of 1803 mostly restored the constitutional situation of the Ancien Régime. The legislative powers, in particular, the competence to issue substantive and formal private and criminal law, were handed back to the cantons. Thus, the law prevailing before the Helvetic Republic was again applicable, unless the cantons determined otherwise. Federal decrees were limited to inter-cantonal and international issues. The first cantonal private and criminal law codes were issued during the restoration period. The regeneration period introduced a boost, not only for the cantonal constitutional development. From 1830 onward, political life was defined in many cantons by the belief in progress, and the codifications were deemed as suitable to promote it, for instance by establishing equality and economic welfare of the country. The first decades of the young federal state after 1848 fundamentally did not change anything in the cantonal competence.

The missing constitutional unity until the middle of the 19th century was expressed in the fact that the cantonal legislation was firmly based on foreign models. There was not one cantonal code that could have gained stronger influence than just toward its neighbouring cantons. There was also a lack of a Swiss legal doctrine from which a codification could have emerged. Only the Private Law Code of Zurich adopted between 1853 and 1855 gained supraregional importance.

Rural cantons with community assemblies

The heyday of the cantonal codification process lasted until about 1870. Until then, most cantons had adopted a private law and criminal code, and numerous other projects and individual rules were added. However, most of the rural cantons with a community assembly (Uri, Schwyz, Unterwalden, Zug and both Appenzell) had less intensive legislative activity compared to the cities. In these cantons, only brief laws - if any - were adopted. In a few cantons, the practice of jurisprudence was even continued by the traditional customary law until the enactment of federal regulations. The reason for this situation was not the absence of economic necessities. In the first half of the 19th century, for example, Appenzell already had established a flourishing textile industry. But in a direct democracy, persuading the citizens takes time. That is shown by the example of Glarus, where the draft bills of the codification had been rejected by the rural community "with a loud cheer" in the 1840s and only got accepted two decades later.

Legislative activity in the cantons slowed down in the 1880s as laws on a federal level started emerging.

9.2.2 The economic situation

Industrialisation

The cantonal codifications of the 19th century were not only an expression of political self-confidence, and a means to achieve socio-political goals, they were also answers to the accelerating economic change since the 1820s. Whereas at the beginning of the century the bourgeoisie and traders, such as innkeepers, butchers, and millers, demanded political self-determination and freedom of ownership, now the increasing industrialisation made a comprehensive and swift modernisation of private law necessary. While in the Ancien Régime the spinners and weavers were still working in their own home, the mechanisation shifted this labour to the factories.

"La Douane", Faoug. Former customs station on the cantonal border between Freiburg and Vaud Photo: Author.

From this textile industry emerged the machinery industry, which in a short time had developed into an export industry of international importance. Between 1817 and 1849, the trading volume doubled. Industrialisation demanded that the internal cantonal particularism was overcome through legislation and that legal security and legal unity be created, at least in the cantonal legal sphere.

The merchants perceived the approximately 400 municipal, cantonal and private customs duties as a barrier to trade. The Federal Constitution of 1848 finally abolished them. With this measure, but also with the unification of the currency, the postal and the telegraph services, the Federal Constitution created the conditions for the second wave of industrialisation. In addition to the textile, machine and watch industry, the food and chemical industries emerged, followed by the banking and insurance industries.

After the opening of the "Spanish Bread Railway" in 1847 from Zurich to Baden, Switzerland was seized by railway fever. Until 1870 a dense railway network was built. With the construction of the railways, the industry benefited from improved traffic conditions, which promoted imports and exports. Therefore, a uniform and new debt and commercial law became an urgent desideratum. That, in turn, favoured national legal harmonisation. Entirely new regulations had to be installed for the transport, liability and intellectual property law, often under much time pressure. The rapid growth of industry and the service sector led to the emergence of factory workers and salaried employees and resulted in a decline of the peasant population. The number of people employed in the industry increased rapidly. Land liberation facilitated the migration of day labourers and small peasants from the countryside to the factories, a process favoured by the increasing import of food.

9.2.3 The scientific situation

Law studies at German universities

From the early 16th century until the middle of the 18th century, only a few students from the Confederation visited a foreign university. The gradual political termination of the Holy Empire led to an intensification of scientific exchange. In the same period, education at the local law schools was modest in many places. From the second half of the 18th century, the number of Swiss studying at foreign faculties increased. Inspired by the spirit of the Enlightenment, again attempts were made to establish a close connection to the flourishing science activities at international universities. At the turn of the 19th century, it became common practice for aspiring lawyers to deepen their knowledge acquired at the local law school for one or more semesters at prestigious international law faculties. In addition to the reputation of the respective department, the status of individual professors of law was also essential for the choice of the place to study.

Numerous Swiss moved to Bonn or Berlin to attend the classes of Friedrich Carl von Savigny (1779–1861), the founder of the *Historical School of Jurisprudence*. Others moved to Heidelberg, where Anton Friedrich Justus Thibaut (1772–1840) taught, a proponent of legal unification and in the *codification dispute* an opponent of Savigny, who rejected it. Tübingen and Göttingen were also acclaimed places to study, as were Strasbourg and Vienna. Although the study period was sometimes idled away for the cultivation of the

Burschenherrlichkeit, many of those attending the lectures of these luminaries of Roman law were influenced in their later work as judges or advocates. In the second half of the 19th century, it was the great *Pandectists* who commanded a sweeping power of appeal. Even students from French-speaking Switzerland often studied at German academies, but also at French universities such as Besançon and Chambéry.

Influence of German Jurisprudence

These study visits at international, primarily German, law faculties had a considerable influence on the codification process of the cantonal private law. The majority of law editors of cantonal private law books had studied at German law faculties and were influenced by the academic program and the individual teachings of the lecturers there. They were open to the learned Roman law, but also the indigenous legal traditions in the cantonal codifications, as suggested by the representatives of the German Historical School of Jurisprudence, such as Savigny. Occasionally, regulations in the draft bill were written off directly from the textbooks of the former lecturers. For example, Peter Conradin von Planta (1815–1902), editor of the Grisons Civil Code of 1862, took over the rules of unjustified enrichment directly from pandect textbook of Thibaut, whose lectures he had attended as a young student.

The strong influence of German jurisprudence in the 19th century was not only noticeable in private law, but also for the successive emergence of the science of public law in Switzerland. In their publications on the history of state and law, scientists inspired by the German Historical School of Jurisprudence, such as Johann Kaspar Bluntschli (1808–1881), Philip Anton von Segesser (1817–1888) or Johann Jakob Blumer (1819–1875), presented the applicable law in its historical development. Therefore its historical background could legitimise constitutional law. Other authors and law professors such as Wilhelm Snell (1789–1851), Simon Emperor (1828–1898), Paul Usteri (1768–1831), Heinrich Zschokke (1771–1848) and Gustav Vogt (1829–1901), however, were oriented toward the natural-liberal law. Based on the theories of Immanuel Kant and Auguste Compte, they increasingly distinguished the (public) law from politics. The law contained in the constitutions, statutes, and regulations was consequently understood as a separate text corpus, which was accessible by scientific research and theory formation. In the young federal state, teaching in public law also had a political function. When federal law was taught to students, the new state was also firmly established in their minds.

The Universities of Zurich and Berne

The founding of universities was part of the policy agenda during the Regeneration period. Whereas the former high schools were predominantly the educational centre of the patricians, the new democratic rulers wanted to make the college or university an instrument for a broad popular education. In 1833, a university was founded in Zurich, and 1834 another in Berne. In 1835, the University of Basel was reorganised, following the German model. Since there were no domestic lecturers, the positions for Pandects were often given to young German scholars of Roman law. For example in Zurich to Theodor Mommsen (1817–1903), Heinrich Dernburg (1829–1907) and Ferdinand Regelsperger (1831–1911), in Berne to Julius Baron (1834–1898) and Philipp Lothmar (1850–1922), and in Basel to Rudolf v. Jhering (1818–1892) and Bernhard Windscheid (1817–1892). Although some of them only briefly stayed at a Swiss university and then left for a German academy, there nevertheless emerged an uninterrupted chain of Romanists whose teachings had a significant influence on the cantonal and later also on the Swiss private-law practice.

The ranks of lawyers

In the 19th century, the ranks of learned lawyers were established in Switzerland. The administration of justice was no longer, as in the Ancien Régime, a domain of untrained, politically selected practitioners. Instead, it was placed in the hands of university-trained specialists and so experienced a boost in professionalism. The jurists of the 19th century were not only crucial as lawyers, judges and law editors, but also often participated in other spheres of public life, such as representatives of the cantonal legislature or executive, and from 1848 as members of the Federal Assembly, some even as Federal Councillors. They also held prominent positions in the economy or made notable military careers in the second half of the 19th century.

9.2.4 The codifications of the private law

Classification

According to a structure established by Aloys von Orelli and adopted by Eugen Huber and others, the cantonal codes of private law created in the 19th century can be divided into three groups:

- a group influenced by the *French Civil Code* of 1804 in western and southern Switzerland;

- the cantons of Berne, Lucerne, Solothurn, and Aargau influenced by the *Austrian General Civil Code* (ABGB) of 1811;
- a group around *Zurich with its private law book* (PGB) of 1853–1855, inspired by the German Historical School of Jurisprudence, and those cantons of eastern and central Switzerland that imitated it.

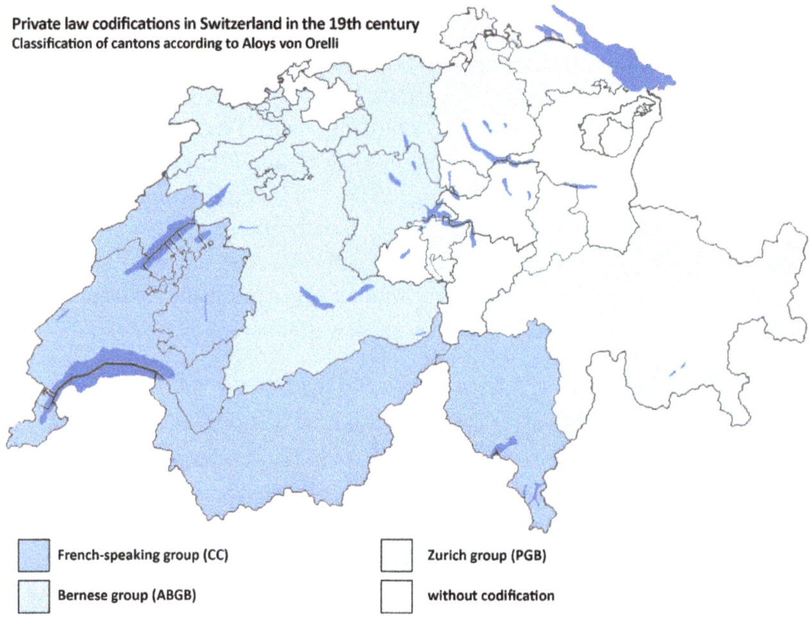

This classification is useful for a first orientation, but at the same time inaccurate. Because there are many similarities, which were not due to the use of the same templates, but due to the geographical proximity, the same linguistic origin or the historically related, legal developments. Besides, the cantons often used the same model very differently, and some codes were based not only on one but several templates. Finally, various cantons did not adopt a private-law change for different reasons. These reservations need to be kept in mind in the following presentation.

9.2.4.1 *The French-speaking group*

For the French-speaking cantons of western Switzerland, the linguistic proximity naturally suggested a reception of the French Civil Code. The excellent acceptance of the Civil Code in the European academic circles was another advantage. This code, in which Napoleon had been actively involved for the edition, was considered a successful fusion of traditional customary law, Roman law, and natural law principles. The ideas of the rationalistic natural law and the political agenda of the revolution - equality, freedom of the person and ownership - were realised as exemplary.

The old city republic of Geneva was politically part of France when the Civil Code was passed in 1804. When Geneva entered the Confederation in 1815, following the collapse of the Napoleonic rule, the Civil Code was retained. Projects to create their own legal code petered out, which is why the Civil Code remained in force until 1912. Only some modifications in individual laws in the area of family, inheritance and real estate rights were added. The Bernese Jura, the former Prince-Bishopric of Basel, had also been a part of France since 1799, in which the Civil Code was applied. After the Congress of Vienna had awarded the territory to Berne in 1815, the Civil Code remained valid until the enactment of the Federal Civil Code (ZGB). In the canton of Vaud on the other hand, work on a separate code was started immediately after the canton was founded in 1803, and in 1821 Switzerland's first modern codification of civil law was adopted there. In its fundamental conception, its structure and in essential parts, it followed the model of the French Civil Code in marriage, family, inheritance and real estate law and it also adopted the customary law of Vaud. The Code of Neuchâtel of 1854/1855 also closely followed the French model.

More independent was the Valais Civil Code of 1855, edited by Bernard Etienne Cropt (1798–1896). As in other Catholic cantons, the right to marry was still defined by church law, and until 1874, the right to divorce was barred. The canton of Ticino, like the Vaud, was founded during the Mediation period. The newly won sovereignty expressed itself in the establishment of a codification agenda. However, a Civil Code (Codice civile) was only enacted in 1838. It drew inspiration from the French Civil Code and the Austrian General Civil Code (ABGB) as well as the civil code of the Italian city Parma. The most original civil code in this group was the one of Freiburg dating back to 1850, edited by the Mayor of Morat, Samuel Frédéric Balthasar Chaillet (1775–1843). Chaillet first took the Vaudois code as a model in his editorial work, but increasingly deviated from it. The solutions he introduced were similar to the ABGB and the contemporary drafts of the Dutch Civil Law Book (Burgerlijk Wetboek).

9.2.4.2 *The Bernese Group*

Berne

Proceeding as the French-speaking cantons was out of the question for the canton of Berne. The patricians had governed Berne again at the time of the Restoration, so the code of Napoleon, who had defeated the old Berne in 1798 could not serve as a model. Instead of the French Civil Code, Samuel Ludwig Schnell used the recently published Austrian General Civil Code (ABGB) as a starting point. It was recognised as a successful accomplishment of the natural law in the sense of Immanuel Kant. That met Schnell's expectations, who was a staunch supporter of Kant since his studies in Tübingen, as was the editor of the ABGB, Franz von Zeiller (1751–1828). In his editorial work, he also took into account the Bernese Court Statute from 1761, the Bernese marriage court statute of 1787, the jurisdiction of the Bernese Court of Appeal and the Roman law according to the concept of the modern Pandects (usus modernus pandectarum).

The court statute of 1761, a revision of the court statutes of 1539 and 1614, consisted of four parts: family law, inheritance law, property law and the code of obligations. The inheritance law was wholly regulated, whereas the other three parts, especially the code of obligations, were patchy and unsystematic and the personal rights were completely missing. Schnell picked the absent regulations from the ABGB and also based the draft on its structural outline. Thus, a successful combination of scholarly and customary local law was achieved. The latter also included some legal figures of the Roman law, especially since David von Fellenberg (1587–1628) had adopted them in a revision in 1614.

Piece by piece the new law came into force between 1826 and 1831. It was concise, precise, and simple to understand because academic terminology had been omitted deliberately. In addition to elements of the liberal natural law, it still contained marriage bans and discriminatory provisions for the illegitimate amongst others and thus reversed essential achievements of the Helvetic Republic.

Berne Ludwig Samuel Schnell (1775–1848). Schnell completed a law degree in Tübingen. In 1805, he became a professor at the Bernese Academy and after its conversion to a university in 1834, university professor. Although somewhat liberal, the patrician government appointed him to the editorial board for the redrafting of various laws. He wrote the "Code of Civil Procedure in civil matters" and the "Civil Code for the City and Republic of Berne with commentary." Image:Staatsarchiv des Kantons Bern (State Archives of the Canton Berne), T.B. Personen 634.1.

Solothurn Johann Baptist Reinert (1790–1853). Reinert studied law and philosophy in Berlin before he worked as a lawyer and as a judge. Reinert was also politically active. In 1814, he participated in the uprising against the patricians, which earned him a short stay in exile. From 1827, Reinert held various political offices. First, he was member of the Grand Council for 14 years, then a member of the state council for 13 years. With his liberal but moderate mindset, he was instrumental in shaping the first democratic cantonal constitution. Various cantonal laws originated from his pen, including the Solothurn Civil Code. Image: Zentralbibliothek Solothurn (Central Library Solothurn), h 56.

Lucerne, Solothurn, Aargau

The Bernese Civil Code was the first modern civil code in German-speaking Switzerland. Kasimir Pfyffer (1794–1875) took it as a model for the editing of a civil code for the canton of Lucerne. Pfyffer had attended lectures of Thibaut as a student in Heidelberg and was like Schnell, a supporter of Kant. The law, which gradually came into force from 1832 to 1839, contains traditional legal material from Lucerne, such as matrimonial property law, inheritance law and mortgage law, in addition to provisions of the ABGB and the Bernese Civil Code. The Civil Code for the canton of Solothurn (1841–1847), edited by Johann Baptist Reinert (1790–1853), combined old Solothurn law with provisions of the ABGB in the form of the Bernese Civil Code and regulations from the French Civil Code. The Civil Code of the Canton of Aargau (1828/1856) was influenced in its earlier parts by the ABGB and the Vaudois Civil Code, and in its later parts by the Zurich Civil Code (PGB). The law books of the Bernese Group are therefore regarded as successful combinations of old cantonal law with elements of the modern natural law codification.

9.2.4.3 The Zurich Group

Zurich

In contrast to the civil law books of French-speaking Switzerland and those of the Bernese group, which are based to varying degrees on foreign codifications, the Private Law Code for the canton of Zurich, which was adopted from 1854 to 1856, was the first to select an independent route. That was related to the academic career of the two law editors Friedrich Ludwig Keller (1799–1860) and Johann Kaspar Bluntschli (1808–1881). Both first studied at the Political Institute in Zurich, then in Bonn and Berlin with von Savigny, who could persuade them on the merits of the German Historical School. However, unlike the latter, they did not reject the idea of codification but only adopted his concept that modern law should evolve from the traditional, proven law. Therefore, instead of a different codification, Keller and Bluntschli chose as a starting point the existing law of Zurich, which for the most part dated back to before 1798.

In Zurich, a revision of the private law was on the agenda of the government since the Mediation period. However, this only became a matter of prime concern for the liberal state of the Regeneration period, when the press and numerous petitions from the population requested the modernisation and simplification of the existing cantonal private law. Given the boom in trade and industry, the old Zurich law no longer met the demands of the economy. Legislative work, however, was delayed considerably. Keller, initially appointed as a law editor, had to resign for political reasons from his mandate in 1839. Alfred Escher (1819–1882), a dominant figure in Zurich politics in the middle of the 19th century, blocked the draft bills submitted by his successor Bluntschli for eight years due to personal and political reasons.

Model for Eugen Huber

Bluntschli's approach as a law editor was in many respects a role model for Eugen Huber in his work on the draft of the Swiss Civil Code. Through his education and his teaching and research activities at the young University of Zurich, Blunschli was familiar with both the traditional Zurich law and the Roman law dealt with by contemporary Pandects. In his 1838/39 published "Staats- und Rechtsgeschichte der Stadt und der Landschaft Zürich" he had reviewed the old Zurich law. Based on the social and economic needs, he made use of his partial drafts both of this treatise and the Roman law. For the person, family and inheritance law, he relied on domestic private law and had already adopted certain standardisations in the Ancien Régime. In these substantive matters, which concerned all citizens, public acceptance was particularly important.

On the issues in the property law, he started with the Zurich law but aligned it to the contemporary requirements of trade and transportation. He developed a code of obligations as well as commercial and company law, based primarily on scholarly Roman law and on modern commercial law, as it had developed in other European countries at the time. The labour law provided provisions for the protection of the working class. The Zurich Private Law Code (PGB) therefore represents a synthesis between traditional Zurich law, scholarly Roman law, and the modern commercial law. It was also adapted to the requirements of the location and time and in language and the level of complexity to the current needs of the lay jurisdiction. That made it the forerunner and model of the Swiss Civil Code (ZGB).

Zurich Friedrich Ludwig Keller (1799–1860). Keller was first active in Zurich, as a professor, as a judge, and as a politician. He was the co-founder of the University of Zurich. In 1842 Keller gave up his political career and moved to Germany. He taught Roman law at the Universities of Halle and Berlin, where he also became politically active again. In 1853 he was admitted to the Prussian nobility but was heavily indebted as a landowner. Picture: Austrian National Library, PORT_00016798_01.

Zurich Johann Kaspar Bluntschli (1808–1881). Bluntschli completed his law studies in Berlin and Bonn as a Doctor of both rights. At the age of 25, he began teaching Roman law at the University of Zurich, later also German law and legal history. Bluntschli was both member of the Grand Council of and the State Council of Zurich. He was also a deputy at the Tagsatzung. After an unsuccessful election campaign to become mayor, he gave up all his political offices and left Zurich. He first moved to Munich, then to Heidelberg, where he received a professorship in political science. Politically, he could no longer gain a foothold, but he enjoyed great prestige as a legal historian, law editor (including the Zurich private law) and promoter of international law. Image: Heidelberg University Library, Sig. P_0315 Kasten_40.

Glarus Johann Jakob Blumer (1819–1875). After his law studies in Lausanne, Zurich, Bonn, and Berlin, Blumer became a member of the Civil Court and then of the Appellate Court. In 1874, he became the first permanent president of the Federal Supreme Court. Politically Blumer started as a municipal councillor, then worked as a district councillor. In 1848, he was elected to the Council of States, where he campaigned for the creation of the Federal state. Besides writing critical legal works, Blumer also devised the civil and criminal code of Glarus. Picture: Landesarchiv des Kantons Glarus (State Archives of the Canton of Glarus), Photo collection.

Nidwalden Karl von Deschwanden (1823–1889). Von Deschwanden studied law in Zurich and was influenced by Friedrich Ludwig Keller and Johann Caspar Bluntschli. He worked as a lawyer and as a judge in various courts. As a liberal politician, he campaigned for the Federal state, for the total revision of the cantonal constitution and the humanisation of criminal law. Von Deschwanden wrote numerous legal, historical essays and various law decrees of Nidwalden, including the Civil Code of Nidwalden. Image: Staatsarchiv Nidwalden (Nidwalden State Archives), P 32-6, estate Dr. med. Robert Durrer.

Eastern and Central Switzerland

The Zurich Private Law Code (PGB) exerted considerable influence on the codification activity in the cantons of eastern and central Switzerland. Its adoption was an impetus and a model for their codification work. The private law code for the canton of Schaffhausen of 1864/1865 took over almost literally the provisions of the Zurich PGB. The personal and family law of the canton Zug of 1862 was an adaptation of the Zurich law, as well as that of the Canton of Thurgau from 1860. The inheritance law of 1859 for the canton Nidwalden, designed by Karl von Deschwanden (1823–1889), oriented itself on the traditional, local legal rights, whereas the personal and family law of 1853 was based on the Lucerne Civil Code. The Civil Code of 1869/1874 for the Canton of Glarus was written by Johann Jakob Blumer, who in addition to the traditional right of Glarus used the Zurich PGB as a template for the wording and systematics.

The Civil Code for the canton of Grisons from 1862 was even more independent. The author Peter Conradin von Planta (1815–1902) utilised not only the traditional cantonal law and the Zurich PGB but also the General Prussian Land Law of 1794, the Austrian ABGB and the French Civil Code. His selection was guided less by theoretical legal considerations than by a focus on political acceptance. In this point, as well as in the effort to make the text clear and concise, it resembled the authors of the Zurich and Glarus texts as well as the Berne and Solothurn codes.

Peter Conradin of Planta (1815–1902). Von Planta studied law in Leipzig and Heidelberg. After three years as a lawyer, he became a journalist. He subsequently published several magazines, to promote a new federal constitution, but had to discontinue them for financial reasons. After that, von Planta worked as a keeper of records and in various courts. He held several political offices, such as National and State Councillor. Planta wrote outstanding historical works, especially on subjects from his homeland. He also wrote poetry and dramas, which earned him little praise. He was highly acclaimed for his edition of the Criminal Code, the Code of Civil Procedure and the Civil Code of the canton of Grisons. For the latter, he received the honorary doctorate of the University of Zurich. Picture: Oil painting by Ernst Schweizer, Rätisches Museum Chur, Inv.H1969.851.

9.2.4.4 The Cantons without codification

Different motives

In various cantons of the Zurich group, there existed just enough political perseverance for the codification of separate spheres of the private law. In other cantons, not even that was the case. In the cantons Uri, Schwyz, Obwalden, Basel-Land and Appenzell-Innerrhoden, there was no need for codification in the 19th century. They were satisfied with a collection of land rights, some of which dated back to the early modern times. In Basel-Stadt, St. Gallen and Appenzell-Ausserrhoden there were codification efforts and some bills were also drafted, but they were never enacted for different reasons. For example, the draft for a Basel Civil Code prepared by the law professor Andreas Heusler (1834–1921) was presented to the public in 1865. Expecting the immediate codification of a Swiss Federal Code of Obligations, the Legislative Commission of the Grand Council stopped its deliberations on the draft in 1870.

* * * * *

Cantonal codifications of the private law

French-speaking group	
Bernese Jura	Continuation of the Code civil until 1912
Geneva	Continuing the Code civil + individual laws
Vaud	1821
Neuchâtel	until 1857 part of Prussia, 1854–1855 own codification
Valais	1855
Freiburg	1850
Ticino	1838
Bernese group	
Berne	1826–1831
Lucerne	1832–1839
Solothurn	1841–1847
Aargau	1855
Zurich group	
Zurich	1854–1856
Schaffhausen	1864–1865
Thurgau	partial codification 1860
Nidwalden	partial codifications 1853–1859
Zug	partial codifications 1861–1876
Glarus	partial codifications 1869–1874
Grisons	1862

* * * * *

9.2.5 The Codification of the Criminal Law

In the 19th century, the majority of the cantons had a private law, as well as a criminal code and a civil and criminal procedural code. Especially in French-speaking Switzerland, the cantonal commercial law was independently codified. Quite often the same lawyers who had edited the cantonal private law drafts were also concerned with the other rules. Johann Jakob Blumer, for example, was the first academic lawyer in his canton to compile the Code of Civil Procedure of 1860, the Criminal Law of 1867, and the Criminal Procedure Code of 1871. The Glarus Factory Law of 1864, which was very progressive in its time, also originated from his pen.

1803–1830

With the demise of the Helvetic unitary state, the question arose for the cantons on which legal basis they wanted to place their criminal law. Berne, Vaud, Solothurn, Thurgau, Lucerne, and Basel decided to keep the Penal Code of the Helvetic Republic for their territory. Freiburg adopted a modified version of the *Carolina* (Constitutio Criminalis Carolina). Neuchâtel and Schwyz also used this old law from the Holy Empire for a while. By contrast, newly formed cantons in the period of Mediation quickly enacted their criminal codes as an expression of their new self-confidence as a state, such as Aargau (1803), St. Gallen (1807) and Ticino (1816) and then followed by the 'old' cantons Basel-Stadt (1821) and Lucerne (1827). In the first phase, the cantonal legislation of the criminal law was influenced by the French Penal Code (code pénal) of 1791, the Austrian Penal Code of 1803 and by the Bavarian Penal Code of 1813, drafted by Anselm v. Feuerbach (1775–1833). The scope of sanctioning was now, unlike in the earlier city and land rights, tied to circumscribed criminal provisions to exclude arbitrariness in the sentences.

The prison sentence was included in a qualified and a tempered form like in the Code of the Helvetic Republic. Death sentences were often threatened but rarely executed. The draconian French Penal Code of 1810, co-edited by Napoleon, found no acceptance in the cantons. An exception was Geneva, which at the time of the adoption was still part of France, and where French law continued to be formally applied until 1874 even after the entering of the Confederation (1815), albeit with numerous mitigating and modernising revisions.

1830–1848

The Regeneration triggered the second wave of cantonal criminal code amendments. The new constitutions of different cantons required the adoption of a new criminal law, the abolition of torture, the restriction of the death penalty, the presumption of innocence and the protection of the rights of the accused in criminal proceedings. To comply with the constitutional law, besides the codifications of substantive law, also codes of criminal procedure were issued in various cantons. The prison sentence came into focus as the principal sanction. To alleviate the criminal law practice, the penalty for criminal offences was lowered and the number of political crimes reduced. For these, the death penalty was not anymore foreseen. The Swiss-German law books were in this phase partly inspired by the contemporary draft bills for criminal laws in Baden, Württemberg, Bavaria, and Hanover.

1848–1870

From 1848 to 1870, 16 cantonal criminal codes were issued. Some cantons in Central Switzerland, such as Obwalden, Schwyz, and Glarus, for the first time in history, released a Criminal Code (StGB), other cantons such as Aargau, Schaffhausen and Lucerne revised an earlier code. The contemporary Swiss criminal jurisprudence lamented the strong somewhat unreflected penchant of the cantonal legislatures on the German and French legislation but praised the effort for brevity and general understanding. As a fundamental model served the Prussian Penal Code of 1851, which had been influenced by the French Penal Code of 1810. As the German-speaking cantons were more inclined to follow German law, while the French-speaking cantons were more inclined to follow the French, there was a *rapprochement* between the two groups. The criminal concepts and criminal offences were formulated in many places by German criminal science. The cantonal criminal law thus benefited from the progress of the German doctrine.

Mutual influences between the cantonal law books were also quite common. In particular, the Basel Criminal Code of 1846 and the Lucerne Criminal Code of 1861 served as the primary templates. After the Federal Constitution of 1848 had prohibited the death penalty for political offences, some cantons banned the death penalty entirely, for example Freiburg in 1849. However, in many places, corporal punishment was still a penalty as was the chaining penalty as a modified form of imprisonment.

After 1870

Most of the cantonal codes adopted after 1870 were revisions of earlier laws. They were mostly influenced by the Penal Law of the German Empire from the year 1871, which was enacted during the unification of the North German Confederation with the southern German states. Akin to its template, the

Prussian Penal Code, it was strongly motivated by the idea of retaliation of criminal acts.

Notwithstanding the fact, that the federal legislation had already provided for separate criminal provisions since 1848, and since the 1860s efforts were made to create a constitutional basis for a national criminal code, criminal codes in the cantons were still issued at high cadence. The federal competence adopted in a referendum in 1898 made the end of the cantonal penal codes foreseeable. The last canton to release a criminal code was Appenzell-Innerhoden in 1899. Uri and Nidwalden did not even codify their criminal law. Criminal justice there was based on older land-right books, on separate statutes and customary court practice until the adoption of the Swiss Federal Criminal Code.

9.3 The cantonal procedural and judiciary law

During the 19th century, most of the cantons adopted codes of civil and criminal procedure. As with the codifications of substantive law, the legislative wave first began in western and southern Switzerland and then spread to northern and eastern Switzerland. The need for legislation was particularly urgent in those cantons that were newly formed after the Helvetic Republic. Although less extensive than in substantive law, the law editors oriented themselves on foreign codifications and French and German jurisprudence.

Civil proceedings

The French-speaking cantons and Ticino took over individual institutes and procedural principles from the French Code of civil proceedings (Code de procédure civile) (1806), such as the institution of the justice of peace and the trade magistrate (Gewerberichter), the principles of public and oral procedure, the negotiation maxim and the principle of free evaluation of evidence. The codification movement began with the Code of civil proceedings (Code de procédure civile) of Geneva (1819). Its editor, Pierre-François Bellot (1776–1836), influenced by the ideas of Jeremy Bentham (1748–1832), tried to achieve a simple, swift, and cheap trial.

The first German-Swiss trial law was the Code of Civil Procedure of Berne (1821). The editor and head of the Legislative Commission, Samuel Ludwig Schnell, drafted further substantive law a few years later. As in other cantons, the same legal scholar was entrusted with the editing of both substantive and procedural law. As with the functional civil law, Schnell started with the Bernese court statute of 1761. In the sphere of procedural law, this ordinance had been significantly influenced by the doctrine of the ordinary civil proceedings.

The ordinary civil proceedings were developed in the 17th and 18th centuries by Roman-canonical law and the judicial decrees of the Imperial Chamber Court. It distinguished itself by a non-public and written form of procedure. The negotiating and contingency maxims were further elements as well as a tie to firm rules of evidence. The procedural codes issued in other German-Swiss cantons also borrowed from the ordinary civil proceedings. Since many cantons had not established their doctrines of proceedings, in many places the academic literature on the ordinary civil proceedings was used to supplement local procedural rules. In most cases, the cantons changed foreign doctrines according to their needs. Contrary to the ideas of the ordinary civil proceedings in many places, the spoken word and publicity of the procedure were retained, and the firm rule of evidence renounced.

Judiciary

In the sphere of the judiciary, essential changes took place during the Regeneration period. In the countryside, jurisdiction was sometimes still in the hands of the bailiffs. The blood jurisdiction was in the hands of the Minor Council of the city. For separate spheres such as the marriage law, there were independent judicial authorities. A group of lawyers in Zurich associated with Friedrich Ludwig Keller (the "*young lawyers*") called for a reorganisation of the judicial system in the sense of the separation of powers. The courts should be protected from tutelage by the administration and the influence of the executive. Therefore, the strict separation of the executive power and the judiciary was demanded, whereas the judge was often allowed to take on a parliamentary mandate. In the regenerated cantons, this was achieved through constitutional changes and organisational laws. To enable a court ruling of two instances at the cantonal level, cantonal *high courts (Obergerichte)* were created. In addition to serving as the appellate instance, these often also served as cassation courts for the civil and penal sentences passed by the lower district courts. The law also allowed them the supervision of the judges of peace, the lower courts, as well as the lawyers and notaries.

Reformed criminal proceedings

The cantonal criminal procedure law had been influenced since the regeneration period by the French *Code de l'instruction publique* (1808) and by the discussion about the *reformed criminal proceedings*. Since the 18th-century foreign criminal jurisprudence had denounced the deficiencies of inquisitorial proceedings as the examining magistrate had far too extensive competencies. The pre-trial he carried out was an essential part of the criminal proceedings and was designed to urge a confession. The subsequent primary hearing was only about the repetition of the admission and the determination of the punishment. The evidence collected by the examining magistrate was not re-examined by the court. The judges were also not independent of the Executive, and they could intervene in the criminal proceedings at any time for political reasons. The representatives of the reformed criminal proceedings advocated the strict separation of powers and the upgrading of the main proceedings. They called for an initial hearing open to the public and conducted orally, a reassessment of the evidence at the main trial, the examination of exonerating evidence and the involvement of legally non-trained laypersons to ensure the independence of the case law.

The people should be represented in the form of *jurors*, especially in the case of severe criminal cases and political offences. Jury courts were already in use in England since the 18th century. The Code de l'instruction public issued by Napoleon knew a mixed system after the inquisitorial preliminary proceedings followed the main accusatory procedure. In this, the *public prosecutor* (ministère public) represented the indictment; this authority was not subordinate to the judiciary, but the executive. The main hearing was public, oral and focused on the immediacy of the considered evidence.

The introduction of the reformed criminal proceedings in Switzerland first took place in the regenerated cantons: In Zurich with the law on the criminal justice of 1831, in Solothurn with the law on criminal proceedings of 1832 or in Lucerne with the law on criminal procedure in 1836. At the same time, the rights of the accused were strengthened in many places, in particular by recognition of the presumption of innocence and the right to a regular judge. Furthermore, it was also regulated how long and under what conditions an accused person could be taken into custody. These guarantees of legal protection reflected a greater awareness of the personal freedom of citizens while the Liberalism movement tried to limit the state power.

With the introduction of the reformed criminal proceedings, the coercion of confessions and torture were abolished. It was now forbidden to inflict pain to coerce a confession. From 1874 onwards, the Federal Constitution prohibited physical punishments. In some places, as a substitute for torture, penalties for lies and disobedience were introduced to make stubborn accused talk. However, the criminal proceedings in Switzerland were not reformed in one fell swoop, and some cantons took their time until the middle of the 19th century. For example, in 1851, the canton of Berne issued a code of criminal procedure based on the French model. As a means to "democratise" the judiciary, juries for severe criminal cases had been set up in the cantons. The first ones were installed in 1844 in Geneva and 1846 in Vaud. Federal Juries (Bundesassisen) were introduced in 1849 for federal criminal justice. It was also intended to ensure the publicity, spoken word, and immediacy of the criminal proceedings.

The cantonal civil and criminal procedure codes were revised since the middle of the 19th century at intervals of 20 to 30 years. A more significant need for revision resulted from the introduction of federal private and criminal code amendments. The jurisprudence remained in the hands of the collegial courts; in the lower courts, the assessors were still mostly legally untrained laymen. The cantonal Grand Council appointed the Presidents of the Court, while the people elected the assessors.

Transition to the independent lawyer

In most cantons, at the beginning of the 19th century, the transition from the judge-advocate to the independent lawyer as the representative of individual party interests took place. Several cantons introduced a *patent system* as early as the Mediation period, which made the admission to the profession of lawyer subject to state-stipulated conditions. State training and examination regulations should ensure the professional qualifications of lawyers. The legal education now had to be proven by studying at a law school or university or by legal practice. As a result, the reputation of the studied lawyers increased, and at the same time, advocacy was established as a profession. In the professionalisation of lawyers, however, there were significant variances in time. After the Helvetic Republic some smaller cantons, such as Schaffhausen and the two Appenzell, issued an actual prohibition of "trained" lawyers and continued to hold on to the system of the judge-advocate for quite some time. In Appenzell-Innerrhoden this ban remained until the introduction of the freedom of trade and commerce in 1874.

In 1876 and 1878 the Swiss Lawyers Association tried to unify the cantonal training regulations, but it failed with this concern against the resistance of federalists. Against the background of the cantonal fragmentation, a federal rule of the law was considered unnecessary. Instead, cantonal lawyers' associations were founded in the following years. It was believed that these were better suited to protect professional interests. It was not until 1898 that the Swiss Bar Association was founded. It aimed to promote the reputation of the legal profession and the collegiality among professional colleagues. National uniform regulation of the professional license was not even reached in the 20th century. Finally, the Federal Law on the Free Movement of Lawyers, which entered into force in 2002, laid down the professional and organisational prerequisites for being registered as a lawyer in the cantonal professional register, fulfilling the requirement for inter-cantonal freedom of movement.

10 National legal unification

10.1 The Code of Obligations of 1883

Trade barriers

Until 1848, the currency, postal, customs, measures and weight system in Switzerland was a matter for the cantons and municipalities. The legacy of the Ancien Régime included several currencies, different measures and weights, and around 400 private, municipal and cantonal customs duties, such as road and bridge fees as well as locally different consumption fees on different products. In some places, the postal service was privately owned, which had an impact on domestic as well as foreign trade. However, with the advancement of industrialisation, was perceived as a barrier to trade. It could be cheaper for a freight-forwarder to handle goods transports from St. Gallen to Geneva through France or Germany instead of Switzerland. The Tagsatzung repeatedly discussed measures to unify domestic transportation after 1803. The stimulation of the interior economy became even more urgent with the founding of the South German Customs Union 1829 and the German Customs Union 1834 because these complicated the Swiss export considerably. Starting in the Restoration Period, *inter-cantonal concordats* were concluded, to remove trade barriers for some limited geographical regions. Building on these efforts, the Federal Constitution of 1848 created the basis for the abolition of internal tariffs (Article 23 es.) and the standardisation of postal services, currency, measures, and weights (Article 33 es.). The implementation of these postulates was complicated and was only enacted with delays. The dispute how the cantons should be compensated for lost customs revenue was particularly heated. As domestic and foreign trade intensified, the question soon arose as to whether a *national trade law* should be established.

Cantonal Trade Law

Up till then, the cantonal trade law was regulated in different ways. In Geneva and the Bernese Jura, the French Code of Commerce (Code de commerce) of 1807 was applied. Freiburg adopted in 1850 its commercial code, which was similar in structure and content to the French model. In Vaud, Neuchâtel, Valais, and Ticino, only the *rights to bills of exchange* (*Wechselrecht*) was codified on the model of the Code of Commerce. Various Swiss-German Cantons also had independent exchange regulations. They regulated commercial and company law in their private law. The scope of the regulation was very different. For example, while the "Civil Code for the Canton of Berne" contained only a few company law standards, the private law code for the canton of Zurich contained a comprehensive regulation of the trade law.

Demand for national trade law

The extension of the rail network since the middle of the 19th century made the transport of goods and trade beyond the cantonal borders ordinary. The voices calling for a national commercial law increased. In the context of rapid economic development and accelerated social change, the cantonal laws were perceived as too small-scale and also as too static and too patchy. The cantonal laws did not at all or only insufficiently regulate new legal problems in the financial area, such as shareholders-, securities-, transport- or liability-law. Besides, the cantonal fragmentation of trading rights made it difficult for practising lawyers to apply the law.

Draft of trade law

Initially, attempts were made to standardise the *exchange law*. In 1854, thirteen cantons met at the invitation of Berne for a conference. They decided to introduce an *exchange system* by way of the concordat and instructed the Basel councilman and lawyer Emmanuel Burckhardt-Fürstenberger (1819–1867) to prepare a draft. This draft, based on the model of the *General German Exchange System* of 1847, was submitted to the cantons for approval, but only six of the 13 cantons passed the relevant exchange laws. The next impetus came in 1861 from the draft for a *General German Commercial Code* (ADHGB), which had been commissioned by the German Federation. Thus, Switzerland faced the question of whether to follow suit and reach such an agreement, especially as the expansion of the railways and the development of the telegraph system intensified trade relations. In 1862, the Federal Council commissioned the Bernese law professor Walter Munzinger (1830–1873) to draw up a draft for a national trade law, including the bill of exchange law. He presented his draft in 1863.

During the consultations of the cantonal concordat, however, a controversy emerged whether a separate law had to be enacted for the trade law. The principle of an independent codification, as adopted by French law with the separation into a Civil Code and a Code of Commerce, was considered obsolete. Munzinger and Bluntschli instead propagated the *Code Unique* and therefore the integration of commercial law into a code of obligations, as was the case in the Zurich Code of 1854/56, which Bluntschli had designed. Under the leadership of Berne, the German-speaking cantons, in particular, supported this integration by referring to similar efforts in Germany. The cantons of western Switzerland, on the other hand, rejected them based on their dualistic codification tradition. After lengthy discussions and delays, the concept of unity finally prevailed. Inspired by a petition from the Swiss Lawyers Association, the Federal Council commissioned Walter Munzinger in 1868 to expand his draft for the commercial law into a Code of Obligations.

Opposition

The *if* and *how* of national legal unity remained highly controversial. Domestic private law – starting with the exchange law, trade- or obligations-law, and later also the whole civil law – was only established in the young federal state after a long and tenacious struggle between the various political forces. The business community urged the unification and the practising lawyers involved in commercial law, but also by the Swiss Lawyers' Association, an association of trained lawyers founded in Lucerne in 1861, whose primary aim was to promote legal harmonisation. With petitions, the organisation tried to motivate the federal authorities to act. *Opposition* against these efforts came from those cantons that were less industrialised and saw no advantage in giving up their cantonal sovereignty and their right to independently enact private law. Those cantons with provincial community assemblies also feared that the loss of the legislative power would degrade their provincial community assembly to a mere electoral body.

The cantons of western Switzerland, who in the first decades after 1848 were willing to transfer only as many competencies to the federal government as necessary, wanted to protect their industry, out of fear that private-law legislation could become the vehicle and instrument of a national economic policy and would enable the Swiss-German industry to expand into their region. Moreover, they wanted to maintain the orientation of their legal culture towards France. The cantonal codes of western Switzerland, influenced by French law should retain their basic individualistic structure and be preserved from a "relapse" into cooperative arrangements as they appeared in the Swiss-German codifications. The lawyers from the French-speaking part of Switzerland did not have any interest in standardisation because they feared being cut off from the high standards of French civil law jurisprudence.

Swiss Lawyers Association

The views about the methods of legal harmonisation were also divided within the Swiss Lawyers Association. A group of young lawyers, to which Walter Munzinger and later also Eugen Huber belonged, pressed for legal unity, to achieve higher legal security and at the same time to strengthen the national identity. However, an older generation of distinguished cantonal codifiers and legal scholars rejected the unification, including Johannes Schnell (1812–1889), Andreas Heusler (1834–1921) and Philip Anton von Segesser (1817–1888). They represented a conservative-antiquarian version of the German Historical School of Jurisprudence, and they were above all concerned with the research and care of cantonal law. After the lawyer's day of 1868, which passed a petition to the Federal Council for the unification of the law by a majority, some of them left the association. The *Journal of Swiss Law* – published by the organisation – subsequently entered a state of crisis.

The resistance, motivated by many different views, could only be mitigated by lawyers entrusted with national legislative work by considering the law of the various parts of the country in their drafts. The situation was defused in 1874 by the introduction of the *optional referendum* on federal regulations. This legal institution, which had first found its way into cantonal law in the 1860s as part of the democratic movement, enabled the voters to control and, if necessary, prevent federal law. That made it easier for some of the opponents to agree to the unification of the law because with the referendum the democratic rights were broadened. National legal unity was established at a later stage in Switzerland than in other European countries. Unlike in states with a monarchical constitution, where the law could be passed "from above", Switzerland had to find a political majority for the national law from the very beginning.

Walter Munzinger (1830–1873). Munzinger completed a law degree in Paris, Berlin, and Berne, where he received his doctorate in 1855. From 1863 until his death he was a professor at the University of Berne. Although a specialist in French civil law, he oriented his preparatory work for the Swiss Code of Obligations under the German law. Following the example of his father (Josef Munzinger), Munzinger became politically active at an early age. As early as the age of 17, he took part in the Sonderbund War on the side of the Liberals. He was elected to the Bernese City Council and the National Council. Munzinger's liberal spirit also affected his faith. He campaigned for a liberal church and against the "rule of Rome" and became the co-founder of the Christian Catholic Church, which does not recognise the primacy of the pope. Image: Stadtarchiv Olten (City Archives Olten), Sig. PA-117-001.

Heinrich Fick (1822–1895). Fick was born in Kassel (DE). He studied law in Marburg, Vienna, and Berlin. The fact that Fick advocated the Prussian Empire made it impossible for him to pursue both a professional and a political career in his homeland. He received neither a professorship nor the bar patent, and when he was elected mayor of Marfurt, the Electoral Prince refused his approval. The call of the University of Zurich in 1851 suited him, and he moved to Switzerland. Fick worked for 31 years as a professor of Roman law, trade and exchange law and from 1875 he also taught at the Polytechnic, today's ETH. Image: UZH Archives, Sig. AB.1.0254.

Draft of Code of Obligations

Munzinger's draft for a Code of Obligations in 1869 was based on the draft of the exchange law by Burckhardt-Fürstenberger and his draft of the trade law of 1864. He also oriented himself on the *Draft of Dresden* from 1866, a selection of the Code of Obligations for the German federal states, on the French Civil Code and the Zurich Code. The latter had in turn been a role model for the Draft of Dresden. The close contact between German and Swiss private law jurisprudence led in this epoch to mutual influence of the law projects. According to the Federal Council's mandate, the trade law was now part of the Code of Obligations, which applied to all citizens and not, as in western Switzerland, only to merchants. Thus, private law became "commercialised" and subjected to the logic and rules of trade.

Constitutional Foundation

While the federal authorities at the beginning of the 1860s had still assumed, that a concordat could establish a standard commercial law, a constitutional foundation was now the goal. When they linked the project with other issues and at the same time set a basis for the national codification of all private law and also of criminal law, the number of opponents increased. The people rejected the constitutional revision of 1872. For the second attempt in 1874, the template was slimmed down and found in this form a popular majority. In Article 64 aFC, the Confederation got the competence to legislate "on all legal relationships relating to trade and moveable transportation (i.e. Code of Obligations, including the trade and exchange law)." That was equivalent to about one-third of the private law. The rest remained under cantonal legislative power for the time being. Since Walter Munzinger had died unexpectedly and far too early in 1873, the draft for the Code of Obligations (OR) was revised by the Zurich law professor Heinrich Fick (1822–1895) and then consulted and linguistically corrected by a commission of experts. In 1881, the law was adopted by the Federal Assembly and put into effect in early 1883. In the following years, the OR had an impact far beyond the national borders. It influenced the legislative work on the German BGB, as well as those in Italy and Turkey.

10.2 The Civil Code of 1912

"System and History"

After 1874, efforts were made to establish a legal entity in other domains of private law. In particular, the Swiss Lawyers Association repeatedly urged to continue the work of codification, since the juxtaposition of the national obligations and trade law and the "rest" of cantonal civil law proved to be impractical. The association's board was commissioned to draw up a conditional compilation of the civil law of all cantons. This preliminary scientific work for a national civil code was assigned in 1884 to the association's president Eugen Huber (1849–1923). Huber submitted his work successively in the years 1886 to 1893 under the title "System und Geschichte des schweizerischen Privatrechts". In four volumes with a total of 3,157 pages, he presented the individual institutes of civil law following the applicable law of all cantons. It was a masterpiece with which he established his reputation as an outstanding legal scholar. In 1892, before the final volume was completed, the Federal Council commissioned Huber to prepare a draft civil code, even though the federal government had no constitutional competence for it. In the same year, Huber was named professor at the University of Berne, and the local proximity to the federal politics would be of great use to him in the future.

Presentation of the drafts by Huber

By 1898, Huber had presented three partial drafts: on the effects of marriage, on the right to inheritance, and the mortgage. At the same time, the Federal Council took the necessary steps to establish federal competence. In a bold double strategy, he wanted to obtain these not only for the civil law but also for the criminal law. The amended article 64 aFC and a new article 64bis aFC were approved by the people and the cantons with a substantial majority. Given the fact that in 1872 a vast majority had opposed precisely this legal unification, the excellent performance was a result that surprised even the Federal Council itself. However, as a concession to federalism, it was enshrined in constitutional law that the cantons were responsible for the organisation of the courts, the judicial process, and the jurisdiction.

The partial drafts of the Civil Code were discussed by a small commission of experts, then reworked by Eugen Huber and finally summarised in a preliminary draft by the Swiss Federal Department of Justice and Police (1900).

For the latter, Huber wrote explanations in three supplemental volumes. The preliminary draft was handed out for consultation and from 1901 to 1903 discussed by a sizeable expert commission. To support their work politically as broadly as possible, it was ensured that this commission represented the diverse parts of the country, various spheres of law and different interest groups. The committees of the Council of States and the National Council discussed the template from 1904 to 1907. At the end of 1907, the final vote took place in parliament, and the Federal Councils unanimously ratified the law. Since the referendum was not called for, the Swiss Civil Code (ZGB) came into force in early 1912.

Incorporation of the Code of Obligations

In the course of preliminary work on the Swiss Civil Code (ZGB), the question arose whether the Code of Obligations (OR) should be integrated into it or not. In most other European codifications, the code of obligations was an integral part of the codification of private law. A commission set up in 1901 by the Federal Department of Justice and Police proposed that the OR should be incorporated into the Civil Code, but that specific legislation should regulate the trade law. With an interim solution, a slightly revised version of the titles 1 to 23 of the OR came into force simultaneously with the ZGB. The adaptation of titles 24 to 33 was postponed, and after further delays, they were not enacted until 1937. From then on, the entire OR formed the content of the fifth part of the ZGB, but formally remained an independent decree with its particular classification and article numbering.

Procedure by Eugen Huber

That the Civil Code could enter into force is undoubtedly the merit of Eugen Huber, who stuck to this project for many years with perseverance and determination. His goal was accomplished thanks to a double strategy, such as the close contact with decision-makers and the public and the inclusion of existing legal institutions in his draft. In the crucial stages of the legislative process, Huber sought direct access to the respective head of the relevant department and members of parliament. He made sure that the codification of civil law was preferred to that of criminal law. He had two staunch advocates and supporters in the highest federal bodies, in particular, with the Minister of Justice Ernst Brenner (1856–1911), and Federal Councillor since 1897, as well as with Virgile Rossel (1858–1912), professor of civil law in Berne and from 1896 National Councillor.

Huber also had close contacts with several lawyers who were members of parliament and the expert commissions. In numerous essays and lectures, he tried to win over the general public and the various interest groups for the project. In his drafts, Huber attempted to satisfy both the "conservative" and the "progressive tendency" in private law. To win the federalist forces – which were against the unification – for his project, he also incorporated cantonal, proven legal figures in the ZGB. Especially the Zurich PGB proved to be a prolific source. Huber attempted to meet new social and economic needs by creating different legal forms, especially in personal marriage law, testamentary inheritance law, and the private law order of commercial activities. He met the demands of trade and industry with extensive freedom of contract, but he also sought to compensate for the social differences accompanied by the industrialisation by improving the position of the socially disadvantaged. The ZGB should be based on an underlying social model rather than one-sidedly favouring members of a class or social group. However, several of his proposals to protect the socially disadvantaged were dropped in subsequent deliberations.

To increase the acceptance in the public and at the courts of the first instance, where mostly laymen were active, Huber tried to use a simple and descriptive language. The ZGB should be a "popular" codification, one that all citizens could understand, even those without legal knowledge. Therefore, he accepted legal inaccuracies and omissions, and he rejected a learned legal terminology, a general part, and strict systematic order. In this point, Huber's draft differed from the codification work on the German Civil Code, which aimed at completeness without omissions but finally resulted in an outcome that was only understandable for lawyers.

Eugen Huber (1849–1923). Huber studied law in Zurich, Geneva, and Berlin. After completing his studies, he worked as a journalist and then as an editor. Because of disagreements, he gave up this job and accepted one as a judge. In 1881, he was appointed to the University of Basel, and in 1888, he answered a call to Halle (DE). After receiving the commission for a preliminary draft of Swiss civil law from the Federal Council, in 1892 he moved to the University of Berne. Huber was a "workaholic", at 5 a.m. his working day started. His wife supported him as much as possible in his work on the preliminary draft of the ZGB, and she did a lot of "background work". Colleagues described her as the "mother of the Civil Code". After her death in 1910, Huber wrote her a letter every day for seven years. Huber was also politically active; in 1902, he was elected to the National Council, where he remained until 1911. Painting: University of Berne, Juristische Bibliothek, painter and date of origin unknown.

Model and Sources

Huber mainly used as models and sources of the ZGB the Zurich PGB and cantonal codifications influenced by it, as well as the older law books of the Bernese group. He took over various institutes in the area of matrimonial, inheritance and custodianship law from the private law of the central Swiss cantons. Other regulations, for example in the sphere of marriage, were derived from federal law. Huber was very pragmatic. The controversial issue of the time, whether a proposal came from the learned Roman law or the established German law, was not essential for him. He instead let himself be guided by whether a proposed solution would be accepted. To enhance this, he also drew from the scholarly Pandects law, the civil codes of the French-speaking cantons influenced by the French Civil Code and the draft of the German Civil Code.

Legacy

When the ZGB came into force, it was considered the most modern private law code of its time. It received widespread acclaim and served as a model for the codification work of those countries that had newly formed after the upheavals following World War I. With the demise of the Austro-Hungarian dual monarchy, Tsarist Russia, and the Ottoman Empire the political map of Europe was redrawn. Countries such as Austria, Hungary, Greece, Yugoslavia, Czechoslovakia, Romania and Poland had to revise their old law or issue new private law. In addition to the German Civil Code (BGB), the Swiss Civil Code (ZGB) was always taken into account in these revision and codification work.

The Civil Code and the Code of Obligations also became the godfather of the Chinese Civil Code of 1929, which incorporated much of it, especially from the law of matrimonial property and the law of obligations. This codification has been in force since 1945 as the civil code of Taiwan.

The Principality of *Liechtenstein* directly took over the property law in 1922 and 1926 the person and company law of the Civil Code. The princes of Liechtenstein had resided in Vienna throughout the 19th century. In 1812, the Austrian Civil Code and Austrian Criminal Law had been incorporated in Liechtenstein in full by royal decree. This direct reference to Austrian law became obsolete with the collapse of the Habsburg monarchy. From 1919, Liechtenstein oriented itself along the political and legal methods of Switzerland, which included the reception of parts of the private law.

Turkey, which emerged as a successor state from the Ottoman Empire in 1923, took over the Swiss Civil Code and the Code of Obligations in its entirety in 1926. Mustafa Kemal (Atatürk, 1881–1938) established the Turkish Republic on the Western European model as a secular nation-state. He had to commit himself to the victorious powers of World War I to reorganise the previously mostly Islamic legal and judicial system. Since the French Civil Code was considered out-dated and the German Civil Code as too complicated, the Turkish Minister of Justice, Mahmut Esat Bozkurt (1892–1943), suggested that it be based on Swiss law. Bozkurt was familiar with it due to his studies at the University of Freiburg, where he had graduated in 1919 with a doctorate. However, numerous changes were required in the personal, marriage and children's rights of the Turkish Civil Code to reconcile the foreign law with family structures shaped by Islamic traditions and a well-developed domestic legal culture. From 1926 onward, the law faculties of Istanbul and Ankara lectured from the Swiss legal literature.

Revisions

At the time of its creation, the ZGB and the OR primarily aimed to harmonise private law at the national level. The intention was also not to allow the social and economic differences that existed at the time to flow into the codification and to place everyone on an equal footing in the legal order. In the following decades, there was an increased need for protection: In those areas where there was a one-sided dependency among the contracting parties, the weaker should be protected, such as in the labour and tenant law. With these regulations, the initially intended equality was partially repealed.

In the first decades after its entry into force, the ZGB and the OR needed only a few revisions. However, this changed after World War II and even more so from the 1970s onwards. The reviews followed in shorter time intervals and more often in the OR than in the ZGB. Quite often, a pending problem was not solved with a revision of the corresponding codifications, but rather with a particular law. Recent research mentions the concurrence of the subject matter of the regulation to the public law (such as the Federal Law on farming land rights of 1991, the Data Protection Act of 1992 and the Equal Treatment Act of 1995), but also the increased consideration of foreign and international law (such as the Federal Law on Package Travel and the Product Liability Act of 1993 or the Consumer Credit Act of 2001, all of which are based on EU directives).

In other cases, it was important not to burden the codifications with socio-politically contentious issues such as the Partnership Act, the Sterilization Act and the Transplantation Act (all 2004). However, it was not attempted to seek a solution to every problem via a dedicated law. The reintroduction of condominium ownership (1963), the adoption law (1972), the marriage, matrimonial and inheritance law (1988), the divorce law (1998) and the custodianship law

(2013) had been revised within the ZGB. In these critical areas of human life, the Civil Code already contained regulations that needed to be adjusted to the times.

De-Codification

Special legislation on private law had existed since the middle of the 19th century. It dealt with areas related to technical achievements. In the area of the "classical" private law, however, the flood of individual rules can be understood as an expression of a partial de-codification. The accelerated social and technological change brought forth new regulatory needs for which the codifications from the 19th century did not contain any points of reference. Instead of fitting the new regulatory matter into an existing codification, it was easier to issue a special law. However, with the outsourcing of regulatory issues from the codifications, the systematic legal unity initially intended was effectively reversed. Fewer and fewer spheres of life were regulated by the ZGB and OR and by the contract types they provided. The concept of equality of legal entities also eroded. The scarcity of agricultural land and the change to a service-based society shifted farmers and consumers as legal subjects into a particular focus. The special legislation adopted for their protection exempted – in addition to employees and tenants – other groups of persons from the fundamentally egalitarian private law of codification. The ZGB and OR thus act as historical monuments which could not keep up with the development over time.

* * * * *

Timeline on the origin of the Swiss Code of Obligations and the Civil Code

1854	Conference of 13 cantons to create a standard exchange law
1857	Draft of a Swiss Exchange Order, written by Emmanuel Burckhardt-Fürstenberger
1861	Foundation of the Swiss Lawyers Association
1861	Draft of the "General German Commercial Code" (ADHGB)
1862	Federal Council commissions Walter Munzinger to draft a national trade law
1863	Draft of Walter Munzinger without a constitutional basis
1866	Dresden Draft (Code of Obligations for the states of the German federal government)
1868	Petition of the Swiss Lawyers Association to the Federal Council for legal harmonisation
1868	Federal Council commissions Walter Munzinger to draft a Code of Obligations

1869	Entry into force of the General German Commercial Code
1869	Submission of the draft by Walter Munzinger for a Swiss Code of Obligations (OR)
1872	First referendum for a constitutional revision to create a national private and criminal law; rejection
1873	Death of Walter Munzinger, Commission to Heinrich Fick
1874	Second referendum: Adoption of the constitutional competence of the Confederation for a Code of Obligations, adoption of the optional referendum
1881	Entry into force of the Swiss Code of Obligations
1884	Commission to Eugen Huber for a comparative compilation of cantonal civil rights
1886–1893	Eugen Huber presents four volumes of his work "System and History of Swiss Private Law".
1892	Federal Council commission to Eugen Huber for a draft Civil Code
1898	Acceptance of the constitutional competence of the federal government for the creation of a Swiss Civil Code (ZGB)
1898	Eugen Huber presents three partial drafts of a Civil Code
1900	Preliminary draft of the Federal Justice Department for a Swiss Civil Code
1901–1903	Consultation of the preliminary draft and consultation with an expert commission
1904–1907	Consultation of the initial draft in the parliamentary committees
1907	Final vote in the National Council and Council of States, adoption of the Swiss Civil Code
1912	Entry into force of the Swiss Civil Code and the revised Code of Obligations

* * * * *

10.3 The Criminal Code of 1942

First efforts to unify the law

As with private law, first attempts to establish legal unity at the national level for the criminal law originated in the middle of the 19th century. While discussing the Federal Constitution of 1848, the canton Solothurn proposed to transfer the legislation on crimes and their punishment as well as the criminal proceedings to the federal government. However, a vast majority rejected the request. In the constitution of 1848, only the basis for a national jurisdiction on political offences was created. In addition to this federal jurisdiction, the constitution introduced the prohibition of the death sentence for political crimes, the prohibition of corporal punishment and the ban of exile of Swiss citizens, but the main body of criminal law remained under cantonal jurisdiction. In 1851, the federal government issued a first military penal code and in 1853 regulated the federal criminal jurisdiction. The Federal Criminal Court was responsible for offences against the Confederation (treason, etc.), against internal security (rebellion, electoral fraud, etc.) and foreign states, and also for crimes of and against federal officials.

After 1848, legal practitioners and academics objected the apparent discrepancies between the individual cantonal criminal codes and complained about the different degrees of modernity of the cantonal criminal law regulations. Several cantons were behind in the modernisation of the penal system. The Zurich law professor Heinrich Pfenninger (1846–1896) wrote: "It is certain that a great evil is the existence of 20 different penal codes in the territory of Switzerland. The habitual criminal who "works" in various Cantons, on the one hand, must look down on this justice as something very relative, and on the other hand, get into the routine of just establishing himself according to the differences, as has actually happened, of estimations and preferences for one or the other Penitentiary determines the actions of the offender. In some cantons, there are offences that remain unpunished in others. One canton threatens a high minimum time in prison term, whereas in others it is only a few months' workhouse or prison; not to speak of the differences in the execution of sentences."

Preliminary drafts

The Swiss Prison Association was the first professional organisation to call for legal unity and in 1871 addressed a similar motion to the Federal Council. The Swiss Lawyers Association joined in this concern. In 1887, a large number of its members under the leadership of the Bernese criminal lawyer Carl Stooss (1849–1934) followed up on the request and issued a resolution to the Federal Council. In 1888, National Councillor Ludwig Forrer (1845–1921), together with other members of parliament, submitted a motion demanding that the legislation of the criminal law be transferred to the federal government. The Federal Council commissioned Carl Stooss. He followed the example of Eugen Huber and began with extensive scientific preparatory work, with which he obtained an overview of the cantonal laws ("The Swiss Criminal Codes compiled for comparison", 1890, "The Essentials of Swiss Criminal Law", 1892/93).

Carl Stooss (1849–1934). Stooss studied law in Berne, Leipzig, Heidelberg, and Paris and then worked as an advocate and court president. He first became a private lecturer at the University of Berne, then a Full Professor of Criminal Law for four years. In 1888, he left the chair because he had received the commission for the creation of a Swiss penal code. After completing this work in 1893 Stooss did not find any secure employment in Switzerland and therefore followed a call to Vienna in 1896. He was unable to implement his plan to renew Austrian criminal law. Picture: Staatsarchiv des Kantons Bern (State Archives of the Canton Berne), FN Jost P 613.

In 1893 Stooss presented a preliminary draft for a general part of a Swiss criminal code and already in 1894 a full draft.

The preliminary draft was internationally acclaimed. The dualistic sanction system with its combination of punishments and measures (*dualistic-vicarious system*) was a satisfactory balance between the demands of two combating criminal science schools at the end of the 19th century. While the classical school saw the main penal purpose in revenge, the modern school campaigned for a prevention-oriented sanctioning. With the dual nature of the sanction system, Stooss took into account the legitimate concerns of both schools. With the penalties and the penalty rule of Art. 63 StGB the principle of fault was maintained, but simultaneously prevention could be achieved by introducing measures. Also considered progressive were the special juvenile criminal laws of the preliminary draft and the conditional postponement of the execution of short prison sentences.

Constitutional basis

From 1893 to 1895, the first expert commission discussed the preliminary draft, but it ended in a clinch. The constitutional basis for the law was created at the same time as for civil law in 1898 by a referendum. The draft was accepted by a substantial majority but rejected by the cantons Uri, Schwyz, Ob- and Nidwalden, Freiburg, Appenzell Innerrhoden and Valais. In these rural and Catholic cantons, the federally motivated resistance to a legal unity was the strongest. In other words, legal integration in criminal and private law was achieved with the votes of the urban, industrialised and Protestant cantons.

Priority issue

Since the federal competence had been created at the same time, the question arose whether the civil or the criminal code had to be issued first. First, it seemed that the criminal law was given priority, but the federal authorities decided shortly after the referendum on the priority issue against the Criminal Code (StGB). Not least thanks to successful "lobbying" by Eugen Huber. The Federal Councillor Ernst Brenner, who from 1897 was the head of the Federal Department of Justice, supported the Civil Code (ZGB) project to the best of his ability. In 1901, the National Councillor Virgile Rossel, also a friend of Huber, submitted a motion calling for the Federal Council to implement the Civil Code as a matter of priority. This was probably also motivated by the fact that the political resistance to the criminal code seemed stronger than to private law. After the members of the first commission of experts had expressed their differences in opinion in the media, this legislative project eluded any "good press".

The resistance of the federalists and the supporters of the death penalty also stirred against the draft. The death penalty had been abolished with the constitutional revision of 1874 but had been reintroduced in 1879, as the crime rate had increased sharply in the wake of a major economic crisis. Because the preliminary draft did not provide for this punishment, the draft as a whole was rejected. After the appointment of Stooss to the University of Vienna in 1896, the local project lacked an intellectual father and promoter. Stooss could only follow the development of his plan from a far. The fact that Eugen Huber, for whose appointment he had once worked as Dean of the Bernese Law Faculty, had become a competitor in the question "Which code first, civil or criminal code?" now seemed to him an irony of fate.

Emil Zürcher (1850–1926). Zürcher studied law in Zurich and Berlin. After completing his doctorate Zürcher worked as a lawyer, then he led a law practice together with Ludwig Forrer (National Councillor and Federal Councillor) and from 1881 to 1926, he was a judge. Zürcher initially made a name for himself with his draft for the Zurich Criminal Code of 1886. In his opinion, the purpose of the punishment was less in retaliation than in the improvement of the offender and the prevention of crime. In 1890, he became a professor at the University of Zurich. As the successor of Carl Stooss, Zürcher wrote the proclamation of the Federal Council from 1918 on the Criminal Code. As a representative of liberalism, Forrer spent 31 years in the Zurich Cantonal Council and 20 years in the National Council. After leaving the National Council, he worked as an expert on the Advisory Commission of the National Council. Picture: UZH Archives, Sig. AB.1.1180.

Eduard Müller (1848–1919). Müller's father was a Protestant pastor. That is why he probably first studied theology in Geneva before he changed subject and completed a law degree in Berne, Leipzig, Heidelberg, and Paris. After graduating, he first worked for a law firm, and then opened his own. His political career led him from the Bernese Grand Council on to the National Council and then the Federal Council, where he led three different departments between 1895 and 1919. As Minister of Justice, he pushed ahead with work on a national civil and criminal code. Müller received an honorary doctorate from the University of Zurich for his efforts. Müller's sympathy for Germany during the First World War brought him much criticism from French-speaking Switzerland and foiled his fourth election to the Federal Presidency. Picture: Staatsarchiv des Kantons Bern (State Archives of the Canton Berne), T.D. Personen 18.

Further delay

On the initiative of the Zurich criminal law professor Emil Zürcher (1850–1926), the Federal Council set up a second expert commission in 1901, which was to continue the preparatory work for the criminal code. However, their proposals got little resonance, unlike the recommendations of the Expert Commission for the Civil Code, which had been submitted at the same time. From 1903 to 1907, the work on the criminal code was suspended entirely. In 1908, a new commission of experts made a preliminary draft, which was delayed by the Federal

Council. It was not until 1911 that it was taken up again and discussed by the third commission of experts, which led to the draft of 1916. However, now, due to World War I, the revision of the Military Penal Code took precedence. After the war, the death of Federal Councillor Eduard Müller (1848–1919), who had been heavily involved in this project, as well as the flaring federal resistance led to further delays.

When parliamentary deliberations finally began in 1928, they dragged on until 1937. Moreover, because the referendum was called against the draft, the project had to be subjected to a plebiscite in 1938. The law was narrowly accepted and put into effect in 1942. As in 1898, the political divide between the urban, industrialised, Protestant and the rural, agrarian, Catholic cantons was evident in 1938. While in the canton of Zurich, 72 % of the population voted in favour of the law, 81 % were against it in Appenzell Innerrhoden.

The fifty years legislative history spent for the creation of the Criminal Code (StGB) shows even more precisely than with the Civil Code (ZGB) how difficult it was to establish a legal unity in Switzerland. Stooss and Zürcher did not live to see the enactment of "their" law.

* * * * *

Timeline on the origin of the federal criminal code

1848	Rejected motion of the canton of Solothurn for transfer of responsibility to the Confederation
1851	First Federal Military Penal Law
1853	Federal law on federal criminal law
1871	Entry of the Swiss Prison Association to the Federal Council
1887	Resolution of the Swiss Lawyers Association to the Federal Council
1888	Motion by Ludwig Forrer to standardise criminal law
1888	Federal Council commissions Carl Stooss for the creation of a federal criminal law
1890	Submission of the comparative illustration by Carl Stooss
1893	Submission of the General Section of the Criminal Code by Carl Stooss
1894	Submission of the draft of the criminal code by Carl Stooss
1893–1895	Deliberations of the first commission of experts
1898	Referendum and adoption of the constitutional basis
1901	Motion by Virgil Rossel for the preference of the Civil Code

1901–1903	Debates of the second expert commission chaired by Emil Zürcher. The proposals are not well received; the work on criminal law is suspended.
1911–1916	Deliberations of the third expert commission chaired by Emil Zürcher
1916	Submission of the preliminary draft of the third commission of experts
1916	Postponement of discussions in favour of the revision of the Swiss Military Penal Code (MStGB)
1928–1937	Parliamentary deliberations
1938	Referendum vote
1942	Entry into force of the Swiss Penal Code

* * * * *

10.4 The long road to federal procedural law

Enshrinement of cantonal autonomy

The national legal unity in core spheres of the civil and criminal law has been achieved only with delays and concessions. Compared to other European countries, it was realised very late. A concession to the opponents of legal unity was the continued existence of the cantonal autonomy in the procedural law. Whereas in other federal states of the 19th century the standardisation of civil and criminal procedure law was often an essential step towards national legal unity, in Switzerland it was achieved in neither the 19th nor the 20th century.

In the Helvetic Republic, projects for a civil procedural law and a general court organisation law were drafted, but they did not get beyond the draft stage. Even after the adoption of the Federal Constitution of 1848, the political will was just enough to regulate the proceedings in the newly created Federal Court by enacting a relevant law in 1850. In 1874, the Federal Supreme Court was reorganised with the adoption of the organisation law and provided with further powers. The procedural law for the trial before the lower courts remained in the hands of the cantons. Art. 64 of the aFC of 1874, the legal basis for the Swiss Code of Obligations, explicitly stated that the jurisdiction itself should remain with the cantons. Even more apparent was the Art. 64bis aFC, the constitutional basis for the ZGB and the StGB, which was introduced in 1898: "The organisation of the courts, the judicial procedure, and the jurisdiction remain, as hitherto, with the cantons."

The Swiss Lawyers Association, otherwise an engine of legal unification, only half-heartedly advocated this project. Although it was already on the agenda at the first preparatory conference in 1862, it was stated after extensive discussion, that the procedural law was always linked to the legal organisation, but since there were so many cantonal peculiarities, it would be difficult to reach an agreement. Neither the ZGB nor the StGB sparked a unification impulse for the procedural law. The Federalist concept, as the Bernese law professor Hans Merz (1907–1995) wrote in 1969, became dogmatic for this part of the legal system. The lack of vigour was also related to the fact that the lawyers' associations organised in cantonal associations had little interest in losing their "knowledge monopoly" concerning the peculiarities of the cantonal procedural law.

Background for the unification attempts

It was not until 1961 that the issue was revisited by the Swiss Lawyers Association. The Federal Court Judge Paul Schwartz (1905–1977) drafted a bill to adapt the cantonal civil procedure to the federal civil law on behalf of the association's executive committee. The cantons of French-speaking Switzerland and Ticino were reluctant, and the project was not pursued further. As in the last decades of the 20th-century issues of procedural law at the national and international level emerged, they were dealt with procedural regulations, which were governed by special laws of the Federal Government. Besides, the case law of the Federal Supreme Court developed "unwritten" civil and criminal procedural law on important issues. As a result, the procedural law was not only scattered, and it often remained unclear whether the cantonal law was applicable at all and to what scope. Therefore, the legal uncertainty increased, as did the difficulties in applying the law.

The many peculiarities of the cantonal trail laws turned out to be pitfalls in a trial for lawyers from outside the relevant cantons, and in complex cross-border criminal cases, they hindered efficient criminal prosecution. The latter was the case for new forms of crime (money laundering and other forms of economic crime, organised crime, cybercrime) in particular, with which Switzerland was confronted.

Federal Civil and Criminal Procedural Law

After several parliamentary initiatives in 1993 and 1994, the Federal Council set up expert commissions, which had the task of preparing relevant drafts. The *judiciary reform* approved in the referendum of 2000 introduced the federal competence for the standardisation of civil procedural law (Article 122 paragraph 1 FC) and the criminal procedural law (Article 123 paragraph 1 FC). At the beginning of 2011, the Swiss Code of Civil Procedure, the Swiss Code of Criminal Procedure, the Swiss Code of Juvenile Criminal Procedure and the Law on the Organisation of Criminal Procedure came into force. The Code of Civil Procedure did not introduce any fundamental changes to Swiss civil procedural law. In the sense of the "cantonal acquis", the existing provisions of the cantonal procedural rights, which had proved their worth, were to be adopted in the federal regulations. A high priority was given to the preliminary and extra-judicial settlement of disputes. From now on, the parties had to submit to arbitration or mediation before they could appeal to the sentencing court.

The national code of criminal procedure followed the prosecutor model, as it previously already existed in the canton of Zurich. Not only the indictment but already the preliminary investigation should now be carried out by the prosecutor and the examining magistrate. This caused organisational changes in some cantons. Essential innovations were the possibilities for an amicable understanding between offender and victim ("abbreviated procedure") and an agreement between the accused person and public prosecutor's office ("plea bargaining"). Also introduced was the right of the accused person to call in a defence lawyer at the first police interrogation. The juvenile criminal code was designed as a special law (lex specialis) to the Code of Criminal Procedure, and it contained only provisions that regulated the criminal procedure against juveniles. The court organisation remained with the cantons.

11 New Issues in Legal Policy and Legislation

In each epoch, new legal figures and new legal spheres emerge. This was also the case in the last two hundred years of Swiss legal history. Since the Helvetic Revolution Switzerland has an increasingly changing legal order. After the "Constitutional Revolution" during the turn of the 18th century followed the "Industrial Revolution". Both have significantly altered the living and working conditions of the people. Life moved from an agrarian-feudal world to cities and factories – and gradually toward democratic structures.

Labour and social rights were established to safeguard the material existence of people. In the wake of industrialisation and technological development, technology-, and environmental protection laws gradually developed. No less spectacular and meaningful is the development of legal equality of men and women.

11.1 Equality between men and women

The legal position of women in the second half of the 20th century experienced a significant transformation. If women were previously subordinated to the father, then to the husband who led the household, the difference in roles between the sexes led to gradual equality in the private as well as the public sphere. The effects of this change were reflected in the introduction of women's suffrage and voting rights in 1971, the inclusion of the gender equality article (Article 4(2) aFC) in the Federal Constitution 1981 and the revision of the marriage and inheritance rights in the Civil Code 1988. Even though legal equality between men and women may seem self-evident from today's point of view, this has historically been a (non-violent) revolution. During the major part of legal history, the woman did not exist as an acting subject. Consequently, she was excluded from all political offices and had in all legal exchange only limited competence. The transformation process to legal equality of women is similar to that of the gradual development of democratic structures and legal justice in the 19th century. However, it occurred with a significant delay. The democratic aspirations of the 19th century were directed at equality between men only and did not endeavour a shift in the legal position of the women.

The liberalism of the 19th century maintained, indeed even accentuated the previous patriarchal gender model. The federal state of 1848 was a male-dominated state, which granted political rights to men only. Women were denied a direct legal relationship with the state. For a long time, their relationship to the state was just indirect, mediated by men, of whom they were dependent by civil law. In international comparison, Switzerland granted "general" voting rights at an early stage, but only to men, whereas women's voting rights were admitted very late, practically as the last country in Europe.

The transformation in the late 20th century is even more evident in its significance when surveyed against the background of the legal position of the woman in the Ancien Régime and the 19th century.

Postcard from 1928. Swiss women with no political rights were depicted on postcards. The two letters ER on the right side of the picture represent the name of Elisa Reinert, who designed the card. Source: Swiss Social Archives, Sig. Sozarch_F_Fc-0010-49.

11.1.1 The legal position of women

Women subject to the domestic and protective authority

In the Ancien Régime, the woman was subjected to domestic and protective authority (*Haus- und Schirmgewalt*) of her father or her husband. The medieval concept granted the man a supervisory right over his wife in the same way as over his children and the servants living in the house. He could regulate her social contacts and discipline her for "transgressions" by exercising his right to corporal punishment. Daughters could not marry without his permission. The assets entrusted by the woman in the marriage were administered and used by him in a sort of trusteeship, and her use of them was subject to his consent. Her general legal ability to act was therefore restricted. In return, however, she had the same right as the children to be supported by the husband and to be represented by him in court. The head of the household was to a limited extent liable for the debts, damages, and crimes of his wife in the same way as for the other household members.

Increased importance of marriage

The institution of marriage was improved in the High Middle Ages by being made subject to ecclesiastical law and episcopal courts. According to church law, the marriage came about by the concurring declaration of intent of the marriage partners based on the principle *consensus facit nuptia* in Roman law. In contrast to the previous *Muntehe*, the bride could now express her will, which was decisive. In recourse to sacramental theology, the Church postulated the indissolubility of marriage since the 13th century, which restricted the arbitrariness of the husband toward his wife, because he could no longer just leave. In the fight against marriage between closely related kin, incest, and adultery, the Church also imposed restraints on unions and marriage bans. If one of the latter circumstances existed, a marriage could not be validated. Marriage impediments could be affirmed before the diocesan courts. Together with the institution of *separation of table and bed*, they therefore somewhat replaced the lack of a divorce option.

Marriage and Divorce

The Reformation introduced the secularisation of private marital law. The Reformers rejected the sacramental character of the marriage and assigned their judgment to newly created marital courts. That led to locally different arrangements for entering and dissolving a marriage. In the reformed and parity cantons of the Confederation, several grounds for divorce gradually evolved, such as adultery, deliberate abandonment of a marital union, incurable mental illness, and impotence. In the 17th and 18th century also general reasons for divorce evolved. The cantons started to allow a divorce due to "insurmountable aversion". However, marital courts only cautiously pronounced divorces. Similar to the reformed matrimonial law, the Catholic Church started to require marriage before the priest in the early modern age. In the fight against secretly closed unions, which often led to significant legal uncertainties, the Council of Trent decided in 1563 a mandatory form of marriage. From then on, only a marriage *(sponsalia de praesenti)*, which was entered in front of a priest and two witnesses, would be valid. This form was used until the end of the 16th century in the Catholic cantons of the Confederation and was reaffirmed with additional penal stipulations. Besides, a prior public proclamation of the marriage was now requested to be able to assert the previous existence of unions. Moreover, the registration of the wedding in a marital register became mandatory.

Matrimonial property and inheritance laws

The Land- and City Rights show multiple different systems of marital property and inheritance rights. For the marital property rights, the secular and not the ecclesiastical law was decisive. Some cantons applied the concept of property partition (Güterverbindung), in which each spouse retained the assets they brought to the marriage, but the husband, in addition to the management of the total matrimonial assets, also profited from the yields of the property brought in by the woman. In other cantons, the concept of asset-combination (Gütereinheit) dominated, where the woman retained no property but had the right to compensation of her assets. A third model was the concept of participation in acquired goods (Errungenschaftsbeteiligung), which was used to allocate the assets of the married couple acquired during the marriage to the total property. After separation, it was divided into two-thirds for the husband and one-third for the wife. Each canton had its peculiarities in the marital property laws. Besides, based on a marriage contract, the actual assets arrangements could be adapted to the needs of the married couple; wealthy married couples sometimes agreed on the separation of property. Marriage contracts were often used because the inheritance rights of the surviving spouse were usually limited to the utilisation of the property of the deceased husband only, based on the traditional notion that property was strictly bound to blood relations ("the good runs through the blood"). Influenced by the ideas of the Reception in the 13th and 14th century the legal figure of the bestowal (Gemächte) was introduced into local law, which eased the hereditary attachment of the property to the family. Together with a marriage contract, which needed to be concluded before the marriage, the bestowal allowed the possibility of mutual favour to one or the other of the married couple. The gradual emergence of an arbitrary succession next to the legal one demanded compensation of legally prescribed compulsory portions for the spouse.

Initially, there was no inheritance equality for the descendants. In succession, the sons were favoured, and the daughters inherited proportionally less from the estate of the parents. Sons were especially privileged in the transfer of real estate and agricultural property. To transfer the farm estate in its entirety to the next generation, it was assigned to one of the sons, either the oldest (Majorat), or more frequently, the youngest (Minorat). The other sons, as well as the daughters, received an indemnity in the form of a relatively small fortune (dowry) for their marriage. Daughters had a privilege in the distribution of the dresses and jewellery of the mother, sons in the distribution of the personal possessions of the father (clothes, weapons, horses). Since the 16th century, the Patriciate of some cantons developed specific legal figures following the customary law, for the transfer of properties and the provision of family members, such as the *Fideikommiss* in Lucerne and the family chests (*Familienkisten*) in Berne. Inheritance equality of daughters and sons was first attained in some City Rights of the late medieval period, while in the rural regions inequality lasted for a long time.

Gender Guardianship

In the rural areas as well as in the city women worked in a legally dependent position in the business of their father or husband. Based on the concept of the domestic and protective authority of the father or husband, he was entitled to gender tutelage of his wife and the single daughters living in the household. To be able to pursue an economically independent trade or profession, they needed his approval. This *cura sexus* was first relaxed in the City Rights for widows and single women who had left their father's household. In the textile industry, which was of great importance to many cities of the late-medieval Confederation, they worked as weavers, seamstresses, and furriers and freely disposed of their assets. The guilds did not allow a woman's membership. The widow's privilege (Witwenprivileg) allowed the married women to continue the business of a deceased husband, but this right was limited in time until they married again, or a son took over the enterprise. As a result, they were able to preserve the merchant's or craftsman's business for their livelihood and source of provision for the family left behind and ensured the inheritance of the profession and guild membership.

Exclusion from political rights

In the Ancien Régime, the limited maturity of women by civil law matched their complete exclusion from political institutions. As citizens of a town, they enjoyed military and police protection conferred to them by civil rights and they benefited from City Rights. However, they had no political rights and were excluded from the active and passive voting rights. They could not, therefore, be elected to the City Council and so did not have access to administrative and judicial authorities. In the provincial cantons, they were not allowed to participate in the provincial community assembly. They were also widely excluded from higher education. No women studied at the academies or schools of law. Legal practice and jurisprudence, like politics and administration, were complete men's domains. Even in the 19th century, this situation would not change much.

11.1.2 Beginnings of Gender Equality in the 19th Century

Initial efforts

The French Revolution eliminated social inequalities. The privileges of the nobility and the clergy, as well as the feudal rights, were abolished, and the land liberation introduced. However, the elimination of inequalities between men and women was not a concern for the most (male) revolutionaries. Only a few philosophers of the Enlightenment and politicians, such as Condorcet (1743–1794), Mirabeau (1749–1791), and Theodor Gottlieb von Hippel (1741–1796) proposed in their writings the legal emancipation of women. The English lady Mary Wollstonecraft (1759–1797) demanded rights for the woman, like the French autodidact Olympe de Gouges (1748–1793). Her *Déclaration des droits de la femme et de la citoyenne* of 1791 was set up in the same form as the *Déclaration des droits de l'homme et du citoyen* (1789). The writing did not bring her any recognition. Instead, she was executed on the scaffold for high treason in the show trials of 1793. The ideas, which she represented were lost in the revolutionary and post-revolutionary era and were not revived until the second half of the 19th century.

From the middle of the 19th century onwards, informal women's organisations were formed in Switzerland, initially at cantonal level. To improve their legal position under civil law, they intervened in the revisions of the cantonal and federal constitutional law and private law. The small gain of these efforts was a result of the dominant bourgeois way of life in the 19th century. The bourgeoisie regarded the family and kinship highly and emphasised the gender-specific distribution of roles. Women of the middle-class had to differentiate themselves from the socially lower classes, where women had to work in agriculture, do cottage work or labour in factories to secure the material existence of the family. The duties of women in a middle-class household were reduced to child rearing, doing the housekeeping and the (passive) cultivation of art, music, and literature. The man alone was responsible for the material existence of the family, and only he assumed office and therefore responsibility in the state, politics and the army. The gender-specific division of the working environment devaluated their domestic work. This perpetuation of the legal incapacity of the woman continued until the 20th century, especially for married women.

In the 19th century, the bourgeoisie fought against the feudal burdens and the Fideikommiss and started a de-feudalisation of land- and inheritance rights. To gain material possessions and political influence, it sought to break the supremacy of the old elites. In the matrimonial law, on the other hand, the status distinctions between men and women were prolonged. This "feudal remnant" in marital law is a characteristic feature of legal history not only in Switzerland, but it lasted longer than in other European countries.

Cantonal marriage and inheritance law

The cantonal civil codes reflect the bourgeois-patriarchal concept of marriage. In nearly identical words, the following principles were expressed:

- The husband is the head of the family and owes the wife and children protection and financial support; the woman attends to the household, and she owes, like the children, obedience to the man.
- The husband determines the place of residence of the family; the wife receives the (family) name and the civil rights of the man.
- The husband manages and uses the assets brought by the wife to the marriage. Without his consent and, if necessary, that of state authorities, the wife cannot do any significant legal transactions. She has only independent power over the household allowances paid to her by the husband to cover household expenses.

Partial lift of the gender guardianship

For *unmarried* women, gender guardianship was gradually abolished in the 19th century. In Geneva and Zurich, this had already been established in 1714 and 1715. The other cantons, however, often delayed the process of emancipation, since the property of single women would become an asset for the municipal authorities as a heritance. In the cantonal parliaments, the representatives of the municipalities, therefore, sought to prevent changes in this issue as much as possible. Thus, the cantonal civil codes enacted in the 1820s held on to this institution. The first canton, which renounced the guardianship of unmarried women in its Civil Code, was Freiburg (1834), followed by Ticino (1837) and Solothurn (1841). In the canton of Berne, the change took place for the cantonal part of Jura in 1839 and the rest of the canton through the emancipation law of 1847. This law was initiated through a petition signed by 138 women. For the first time, they made use of the right to petition laid down in the Bernese Regeneration Act (1831). By the 1870s in most of the other cantons, the guardianship of single women was abolished, be it by a particular law, or by the fact that newly enacted cantonal codifications did not mention women among persons to fall under guardianship.

The Federal Law on Personal Capacity to Act of 1881 lifted the guardianship of single women throughout Switzerland. Until then this legal institute was still in force in the cantons of St. Gallen, Appenzell, Uri, Grisons and the Valais. In the case of unmarried women, widowed women, and divorced women, the legal ability to act could only be withdrawn if they were considered as spendthrifts or if there was a possibility of a future emergency due to mental or physical afflictions. For married women, there was no change. The Federal Law of 1881 explicitly excluded them from this legal innovation. They continued to be subject to the marital guardianship. Some cantonal laws in the German-speaking part of Switzerland, however, granted the women the power to dispose of their separate property (Sondergut), while the laws in the French-speaking part of Switzerland followed the Civil Code and held on to the marital authority of the husband (autorité maritiale).

Secularisation of the Marriage Law

During the 19th century, marriage was performed before a priest in most of the cantons; the religious marriage was then also acknowledged by the state. However, in the cantons of Geneva, Neuchâtel, Ticino, and Basel-City, marriage had to be concluded before a registrar of the state. The constitutional revision of 1874 gave the Confederation the power to legislate on marital status and the right to marriage and placed the right to marry under the protection of the Confederation (Articles 53 and 54 aFC). Article 58 par. 2 aFC abolished the church jurisdiction. Thereby the federal authorities tried to solve a problem that had long been smouldering. The Catholic cantons had until 1848 forbidden confessional mixed marriages. Since the Federal Constitution ensured the freedom of establishment for all members of Christian confessions, one could no longer negate the fact of the increase in marriages between spouses of different faiths. A federal law of 1850 stated that confessional bans on unions were no longer admissible. The cantons were not anymore allowed to prohibit marriages between spouses of different confessions or to hinder them by disadvantages for the spouses and the children. To enable a divorce for these married couples, contrary to the church law, a supplementary law was passed in 1862 on the dissolution of mixed marriages. This law included a divorce before cantonal courts and, as a substitute, before the Federal Supreme Court. Because some Catholic cantons sought to undermine these provisions with prohibitively high economic requirements for the conclusion of the marriage, the federal authorities sought a further secularisation of the right of marriage. With the new constitutional provisions, a Federal Law on the Determination and Certification of Civil Status and Marriage (Civil Status Act) was issued in 1874. It introduced the marriage, concluded before civilian authorities as the only form of marriage allowed under state law (obligatory civilian marriage) and laid down standards for a divorce. In most Catholic cantons, this brought about a profound change of the legislative system, since there the individual right to marriage was still subject to canonical law. Representatives of Catholic cantons, therefore, rejected the Civil Law during the parliamentary deliberations but were overruled after fierce debates.

Abolition of marriage bans

Article 54 par. 2 aFC stipulated that the right to marriage "should not be restricted either by ecclesiastical or economic considerations or by past conduct or by other reasons given by the police." This right not only targeted confessional prohibitions on marriage but also aimed at the incapacity to marriage due to social welfare reasons. Since the municipalities were responsible for the provision of the poor, communities and cantons tried to impede marriages between the poor with marriage bans, to avoid having to support a whole family instead of just one person. In particular, in rural communities with a weak lower class of day labourers and small farmers, the provision for the poor was a heavy burden on the community budget, which they tried to avoid by granting a marriage permit only after proof of a minimum estate. For recipients of public social support, persons in need and people with a bad reputation the permission to marry was denied. For public authorities, the suspicion of future difficulties was often enough as a reason. The consequences of such refusals were lengthy legal disputes between the municipalities and the persons willing to marry.

The freedom of marriage was therefore heavily restricted until 1874 for the more impoverished population. These cantonal prohibitions on marriage led to many persons being involuntarily single, a high marital average age, and many extramarital born children. Thus, the rights on illegitimacy took up much space in the cantonal legal codes. The Federal Civil Law Act no longer stipulated any impediments based on religious, economic or police-related reasons against marriage.

11.1.3 The long road to equality and women's voting rights

Access to university studies

Since the 1840s, women started attending lectures at the universities as free listeners. In 1867, the University of Zurich was the first to open the regular study program to women. This step met considerable political and media polemic against women's studies: women belonged "into the house" and "to the hearth". As the first Swiss female student, Marie Vögtlin (1846–1916) completed her medical studies in 1872. The first female Swiss law student, Emilie Kempin-Spyri (1853–1901), graduated in 1887 with summa cum laude as Ph.D., but she was denied the admission to the bar. The Supreme Federal Court rejected her legal claim since the access to the bar was linked to active citizenship, which was only granted to men.

Marie Vögtlin (1845–1916). Vögtlin's father was a reformed priest, who supported his daughter fully on her way to becoming a physician. Without his influence, Marie would not have been able to enrol at university. At that time, a woman wanting to study was a scandal throughout Switzerland. After completing her medical studies in Zurich, Vögtlin completed further studies as a gynaecologist in Leipzig. In 1874, she opened her own doctor's practice in Zurich. A year later, she consented to a marriage with the proviso that she could retain her practice and continue her work. Vögtlin was a co-founder of the first women's hospital in Switzerland, which in 1901 opened in Zurich as the so-called "Pflegi" (Hospice). She worked on various women's projects. One of these was the admission of female doctors to advanced physician training, a goal which she could not achieve since her male colleagues were vehemently against it. Many of the later female Swiss medical doctors joined the "Medical Women's International Association". In 1922, they organised a congress in Switzerland and founded the "Vereinigung Schweizer Ärztinnen" (Association of Swiss Doctors). Picture: Swiss Social Archives, Sig. Sozarch_F_Ka-0002-143.

With the new educational possibilities emerged a class of educated women, who expressed their views on the problems of the time in lively publications, which covered prostitution, the poverty of factory workers and alcoholism, as well as the lack of professionalisation of "women's professions" and the lack of civil and political equality. The newly established National Women Associations further promoted these issues. Only a few male jurists supported the legal and political equality of women at the turn of the 20th century, such as the constitutional lawyers Carl Hilty (1833–1903), Max Huber (1874–1966) and Werner Kägi (1909–2005).

Patriarchal marriage law in the Civil Code

Eugen Huber registered the demands of the women associations carefully during the editorial phase of the Civil Code. In 1893, he explained to the Federal Council how he intended to deal with it during the preparation of the Civil Code. The Civil Code shall "shape the relationship between husband and wife in such a way that the responsibility of the husband as the family head is expressed more clearly than before, and that the freedom of the wife in the commercial life and her influence on the family and the home is legally recognised."

The Civil Code, however, held on to the current patriarchal understanding of the marriage. In its marriage law, the husband was proclaimed the head of the family who was to determine the matrimonial home and to take due care of the wife and child. The wife had to manage the household and assist the husband with advice and deed; she would receive the family name and the citizenship of the husband. The Civil Code largely conformed to the tradition of the cantonal laws of the 19th century. Although the marital guardianship was no longer used as a concept, in parts it continued to exist. The husband was still the representative of the marriage union; the wife represented the marital union only "in care for the current needs" of the household. If she abused this power of representation, the husband could withdraw it from her. A profession or occupation by the wife had to be expressly or implicitly approved by the husband.

Women's associations complained about the restrictions on the wife's ability to act during the consultation phase of the Civil Code draft. Despite the criticism, the draft was mostly kept unchanged on these issues.

However, the Civil Code removed the unequal treatment of children in the inheritance law; children inherited from then on "in equal parts". The transfer of agricultural estate on preferential conditions of the settlement was also opened to daughters, and the future establishment of Fideikommisse was prohibited.

Voting rights for women

By the turn of the twentieth century, Swiss women's associations intensified their efforts to obtain the right to vote and to be elected; the Social Democratic Party also took up this issue. In 1919, the Federal Parliament passed two postulates to the Federal Council, which however did not deal with them for several decades. The economic and political situation of the 20s and 30s in the 20th century were anything but favourable for this issue. The financial crisis - and the resulting strengthening of conservative and fascist currents (fronts) led to the favouring of the housewife marriage (Hausfrauenehe) model. After 1945, the Federal Council was repeatedly asked through parliamentary motions. In 1957, it presented the Parliament bill for the introduction of women's voting rights. Parliament adopted the proposal, however with the hope that it would not get a majority vote from the people.

Two-Thirds of male voters voted against it in 1959. Despite an economic upswing in the late 50s, the "Zeitgeist" could not yet tolerate participation of the "unpredictable" majority of women in politics. During the Cold War, the traditional role models of women and families were held high in Catholic as well as liberal circles as a progressive alternative to the collectivism of the communist world. Only the cantons of Geneva, the Vaud and Neuchâtel had approved the federal bill. In these cantons, women's right to vote was established by 1960 at the cantonal and communal levels. This dam burst, together with the protest movement of the youth in the late 60s, motivated the parliament and the Federal Council to prepare a second draft bill, which was adopted in 1971 with a two-thirds majority.

The considerable time lag of Switzerland compared with other European countries in the introduction of women's voting rights was due to the system of direct democracy and was only surpassed by the Principality of Liechtenstein, which followed in 1984. Most cantons introduced women's voting rights before or after 1971. Except for Appenzell Ausserrhoden, which followed in 1989, and Appenzell Innerhoden that had to be forced to introduce it by a decision of the Federal Court in 1990.

Billboard: Basel 1946, "Workers Party", Museum für Gestaltung (Museum of Design Zurich), Sig. 51-0808;

Billboard: 1920, principal unknown, Museum für Gestaltung (Museum of Design Zurich), Sig. 50-0079;

Constitutional equality

The number of women in municipal authorities and cantonal parliaments as well as in the Federal Assembly increased steadily. After 1971, women were also elected to courts, expert committees and parliamentary committees, which allowed them to influence legislation and jurisprudence. The people's initiative on "Equal Rights for Man and Woman" submitted in 1976 by a Women's Congress, led to an addition in the constitution: "Man and woman are entitled to equal rights. The law ensures their equality, especially in the family, education, and work. Man and woman are entitled to equal pay for equal work." As a result, wage lawsuits ensued, followed by the opening of equality offices on the federal and cantonal level, and then in 1996 a federal law on the equality of men and women was put into force. This law seeks to eliminate discrimination in the working world.

Revision of Marriage and Inheritance Law

With the revision of the marriage and inheritance law, which came into effect in 1988, the Civil Code dismissed the model of the housewife marriage. After that, the spouses were legally allowed to decide on marital task assignments. Most of the differences in the legal position of husband and wife were eliminated. The spouses now jointly define the marital home and, according to their strength, contribute to the support of the family (Art. 163 ZGB). Restrictions on the ability of the wife's capacity were abolished. Ordinary property regime is now the joint ownership of acquired goods. The spouse's inheritance right was enhanced at the expense of the children. Before that, the surviving spouse had to choose either a quarter of the inheritance of property or half the utilisation rights, but now the spouse receives half of the whole property. Therefore, the revision of 1988 has established, after nearly a hundred years, most of the women's associations demands, voiced at the end of the 19th century. The revision of the divorce and children laws in the year 2000, i.a. introduced the possibility of divorce based on agreement, the allocation of claims from occupational retirement provision and joint parental care for the children after marriage. These revisions were part of a comprehensive reform of the family law in the Civil Code, which had become a "large construction site". It consisted of new adoption laws (1972), children laws (1978), protective custody laws (1978), and included a new law on guardianship. In 2013, this part of the Civil Code, which had been mostly unchanged since 1912, enforced new regulations on child protection and adult protection, which should strengthen the right of self-determination of the affected, and professionalise the relevant authorities.

The Partnership Act, which entered into force in 2007, gave same-sex couples the right to register their partnership officially. As a result, they enjoy almost equal status to married couples in social insurance, inheritance and tax issues.

11.2 Formation and development of social legislation

From the night-watchman state to the welfare state

The current liberal understanding of the state in the middle of the 19th century did not emphasise economic and social concerns of the country for its citizens. Among the state objectives formulated in Article 2 of the Federal Constitution of 1848, the "promotion of the general welfare" was the last to be mentioned. After multiple military occupations of Switzerland by foreign troops, and after the Sonderbund War of 1847, the "assertion of the independence of the fatherland towards the exterior" and the "implementation of interior peace and order" had priority. Nonetheless, the social and economic development of the next 150 years has considerably altered the tasks and self-image of the state. The intensification of industrialisation, which took place simultaneously with the emergence of the Federal State, led to new and increasingly different work conditions in the factories. State intervention was required to protect workers. From the liberal "night-watchman" state, the welfare state emerged through the serial transfer of tasks to the state in the 20th century. In Article 2 (2) of the Federal Constitution of 1999, the promotion of "general welfare" is mentioned first, followed by the promotion of "internal cohesion" and "cultural diversity".

11.2.1 Labour law

11.2.1.1 Municipal and cantonal precursors

The social legislation started with the labour law. Before the Confederation set up a national regulation with the Factory Act in 1877, various cantons had already set up their own rules. Those cantonal labour laws had predecessors in the Ancien Régime.

Predecessors in the Ancien Régime

Labour regulations already existed in the Late Middle Ages. In medieval cities, the primary concern was the regulation of the working modalities (working hours and wages) between artisans, journeymen, and apprentices, whereas in the rural areas it was between peasants, farmhands, and maids. The city guilds introduced regulatory frameworks for its members. The early modern time mandate practice (Mandatspraxis) also led to first sovereign regulations, such as in the Bernese "Rules of services half-done" of 1530. The labour law provisions in the mandates were applied to the conclusion of a contract, the content and the termination of employment. Town councils also set up wage and tariff regulations for artisans and servants. Rules for the protection of servants have long been confined to the protection against physical violence from the employer. It was only in the 18th century that regulations, which postulated the employer's duty to provide care in case of illness or accident, were introduced.

The emergence of the watch and textile industry as part of the early industrialisation led to official wage stipulations. For example, in the Zurich Factory Regulation of 1717, which defined wages for wool-, silk-, cotton- and stockings-factories, in the Bernese Stocking-weaver-rules of 1703 and 1724, and in the Basel factory rules for the silk ribbon industry („Fabriqueordnung für die Seidenbandindustrie“) of 1738. *Fabrique* did not mean a machine-equipped company, as in the 19th century, in which many employees worked simultaneously according to standardised specifications, but the production of semi-finished and finished textile products. Based on the relocation system (Verlagssystem), an entrepreneur – often an urban merchant – placed the production equipment (i.e. the loom) and the textile raw materials at the disposal of rural outworkers and paid a salary for processing them.

First cantonal regulations

Factories in the modern sense emerged in the 19th century in the watch industry in Geneva, later in the textile industry of northeast Switzerland. These factories were often built along watercourses, to utilise hydroelectric power, and therefore decentralised. That prevented the emergence of industrial "conurbations" like Manchester or the German Ruhr region, followed by a sizeable social misery of workers. Nevertheless, the situation of the workers in Switzerland was also miserable. The profit-orientation of the entrepreneurs, the rapid wear and tear of the machines as well as the increasing international competition led to long working hours and, depending on the production branch, to meagre wages. Since a husband's income was not sufficient for the livelihood of a family, women and children were also forced to work in factories.

The small size of the political structures led rather early to state regulations in Switzerland, which sought to curb the intolerable effects of factory work. The first cantonal regulations dealt with child- and woman-labour and in general with working hours. Widespread child labour left efforts of cantonal authorities to introduce and enforce compulsory schooling in vain. Therefore, the Canton of Zurich issued an "Ordinance for Minors in Factories" in 1815. It prohibited child-labour under the age of nine and night-work and limited children's working hours to 12 to 14 hours. Similar regulations were subsequently issued in other cantons, usually integrated into a cantonal school law. They often had to be enforced against the resistance of the factory owners, but also against the parents who feared for this source of income. Extended unexcused absences from school were the result.

A 7-year-old girl at the winder. The spooling of the yarn on weft and warp spools was a preparatory work for weaving. The yarn is wound on the bobbins from a winder or a strand on a yarn bobbin. Among the homeworkers, women or children did this work; men worked on the loom. Picture: Canton Schwyz, around 1900–1910, Swiss Social Archives, Sig. Sozarch_F_Fb-0013-39.

Outworkers in the embroidery shop. The father is sitting on the pantograph of the hand embroidery machine. The pantograph is a device with which a small pattern can be scanned and transferred to the fabric. The embroidery machine embroiders this pattern on the fabric. The father handles the embroidery machine and guides the material. Embroidery is done with 200 or even more needles. The boy is standing at the threading device with which the stick needles were strung. Threading was the task of women or children. Picture: Photography around 1900–1915, presumably Appenzell, Swiss National Museum, Sig. LM-101938.225.

Glarus as a pioneer

In 1848, the provincial community assembly of Glarus approved for the first time a factory law, which stipulated maximum working hours for adult workers. The regulation was limited to cotton spinning, the most important industry at the time in Glarus. Glarus proved to be a pioneer throughout Europe with this step to a labour law for adults. That was also a consequence of the direct-democratic system, which enabled the workers to represent and implement their concerns at the provincial community assembly. It also favoured the adoption of a specific law for factory police in 1864, which provided for comprehensive labour protection for all trades. It stipulated in addition to maximum working hours of 12 hours, a ban on night work as well as the obligation to provide safety precautions in the factories. It also established a waiting period for women in childbed: Women should not work for a time of six weeks before and after birth. This regulation, like the one for child-labour, was initially not observed. Due to economic necessity women often worked until shortly before birth and soon afterwards, increased infant mortality was the result.

11.2.1.2 The stages of federal legislation

The following cantons, in which industrialisation had gained a foothold, had also been enacting factory laws since the middle of the 19th century: Zurich, St. Gallen, Berne, Basel-Land, Basel-City, Schaffhausen, Aargau, Ticino, and Schwyz. In most of these cantons, however, the protective regulations were limited to young workers. Other cantons drew up legislative proposals, which however failed. Their cantonal private law codes usually regulated employment contracts. Because these legal systems used the concept of freedom of contract based on Roman law, they included hardly any protective regulations.

Factory Law

A study carried out at the suggestion of the "Schweizerische Gemeinnützige Gesellschaft" revealed that there was a need for further action in the country. Since the 1850s, efforts to implement regulations by way of concordats had repeatedly failed. That is why as part of the constitutional revision in 1874 the Federal Government formulated a legal foundation. Article 34 par. 1 aFC reads as follows: "The Confederation is entitled to set uniform regulations on the use of children in factories and the duration of the work of adult persons in them. It is also entitled to enact rules for the protection of workers in a commercial operation which threatens their health and safety". The Implementation of this legislation followed as early as 1877 with the "Federal Law on Work in Factories" (Factory

Law). The fact that this constitutional mandate was completed so fast was due to the accelerating industrialisation of the time and the lack of cantonal regulations for the protection of adults. This federal factory law was partly based on the model of the Glarus factory law revised in 1872. In addition to technical work safety measures, it introduced a standard working day of eleven hours for adults, in principle a ban on the night- and Sunday-work as well as additional regulations for the protection of women and children. For children under the age of 14, a work ban was introduced. This law constituted a first, nation-wide intervention to the authority of the employers to regulate employment conditions. In the following democratic vote, it was highly controversial; not only the factory owners opposed it, but also many workers who feared a reduction in their earnings.

Liability arising from factory operations

In 1881, the "Federal Law Concerning Liability arising from Factory Operations" earmarked a liability for damages caused by accidents under the performance principle, which had already been introduced in 1875 for the construction and operation of railways. A factory was now liable even when it was no fault of its own when workers had had an accident in the facility. This system was abolished after the introduction of compulsory accident insurance in 1918.

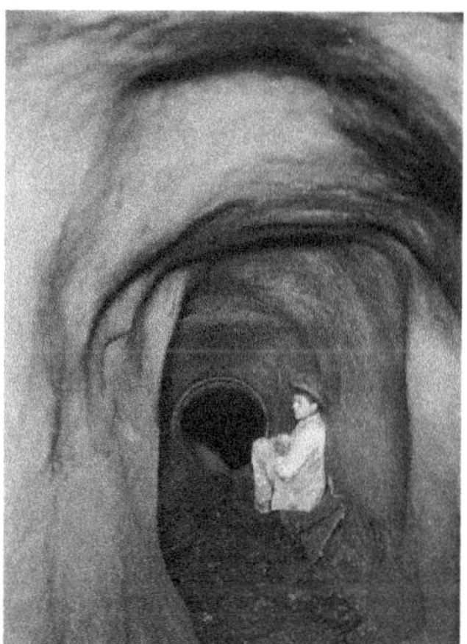

Miner's boy in a mountain tunnel. Until late into the 19th century, there were not only female miners but also children who had to work underground because they were able to penetrate small tunnel openings due to their small body size. It was only in 1935 that Article 2 of the International Labor Organisation (ILO) stipulated that women are not allowed to work underground. Picture: Photography around 1900, Swiss National Museum, Sig. LM-146345.

Labour Law

The cantonal legislation extended the regulations of the public employment safety law to other forms of employment. Initially, this was only limited to women and adolescents. Until the First World War, individual cantons followed with general working laws for men. Even after that, the public employment law was kept under the authority of the cantons. Several drafts of a general Federal Law on labour in trade and industry failed. Only the "Federal Law on Labour in Industry, Trade, and Commerce" in 1964 got a popular majority. It introduced the 46-hour week, as well as two paid holiday weeks and replaced the cantonal labour protection law.

The loss of jobs caused by the recession of the 1970s showed the limits of voluntary unemployment insurance. In 1976, the Article 34^{novies} aFC introduced the compulsory unemployment insurance for employees and was finally enacted under the 1982 Unemployment Insurance Law.

11.2.2 Social insurance law

Private Insurance

In the 19th century, industrialisation and railway construction increased the demand for capital and risk hedging. In the 1850's many banks (i.e., the Schweizerische Kreditanstalt (Credit Suisse) 1856, the Swiss Volksbank 1856, and the Basler Bankverein in 1869) and insurance companies (i.e., 1857 Rentenanstalt (Swiss Life), 1861 Helvetia, 1863 Schweizerische Rückversicherungsanstalt (Swiss Re), 1864 Basel, 1872 Zurich and 1875 Winterthur insurance) were established. The laws on liability from 1881 and 1887 led to a boom in private insurance. The insurance companies separated the workers' casualty insurance and occupational liability insurance into independent branches of businesses. In addition to the later established state insurance companies, private insurance companies played an essential role in the formation and development of the social security system.

German social security system

The Swiss social legislation was significantly affected by the enactment and conception of the German social security system developed by Otto von Bismarck (1815–1898). Bismarck, appointed Chancellor of the newly founded German Reich in the wake of the Franco-Prussian War of 1870–1871, initiated the German social insurance laws mainly for political reasons. After the economic crisis in 1873, the Social Democratic Party gained much influence. With the

Law on Socialists (Sozialistengesetz) 1878, all socialist groups in the Reich were banned. To appease the labourers, social insurance legislation was introduced in rapid succession. After the legislation on Health Insurance in 1883 followed that of Accident insurance in 1884 and 1889 the law on old age- and disability insurance. The fundamental concept chosen by Bismarck formed more or less the base of the Swiss social insurance legislation:

- The social risks should not be covered by a national insurance, but by several separate insurance institutions, which are not an integral part of the general public administration.
- The social insurance schemes should not be run by private insurance companies, but by public insurance companies, and should be based on a compulsory plan for employees. For self-employed persons, the agreement should be voluntary.
- The social insurance plans should be financed from three sources: employers' and employees' contributions, as well as government grants. A tobacco tax should be introduced for the latter.
- The contributions of employers and employees should be based on wage percentages.

KUVG

In close accordance with the legislation in Germany and Austria, the Federal Council prepared a bill in 1889. With Article 34bis aFC, the constitutional authority for national health- and accident-insurance should be established. An extension of the law to an invalidity- and old-age insurance was, according to the Federal Council, politically unenforceable and therefore premature. The new article was ratified in 1890 with a significant majority vote. However, the "Federal Law on Health and Accident Insurance including the Military Insurance" failed in 1900 because of the compulsory scheme that was envisioned for the health- and accident insurance. Opposition against the draft originated from the part of the current cantonal and private health insurances, which feared for their membership register. Only the final article on Military Insurance came into force in 1902.

The second bill prepared by the Federal Council, the "Federal Act on Health and Accident Insurance" (KUVG), renounced a general obligation for health insurance. Every Swiss should have the right, but not the obligation to conclude health insurance. Subsidies were foreseen for the existing health insurance funds as far as they guaranteed specific minimum benefits and provided equal opportunities for both sexes. The mandatory accident insurance was limited to industrial labourers but was also extended to non-occupational accidents. A public accident insurance institution (SUVA) should be established as the holder of this insurance. The document thus conceived, was adopted by the people in 1912 and entered into force as federal law on health- and accident-insurance in 1914/1918. In 1912, the Federal Department for Social Insurance was set up to supervise the health insurance funds and to direct the subsidies. In 1917, the Federal Insurance Court responsible for settling claims under the accident insurance was set up. Its authority was gradually extended to the entire social insurance legislation of the federal government. With the introduction of state accident insurance, some private insurance companies lost a valuable business. Factory liability laws were abolished after that.

Despite several attempts, the revision of the KUVG repeatedly failed in the course of the 20th century. In 1964 in a partial revision, the legally minimum benefits were increased, and the federal contributions to the health insurance fund raised. Mandatory accident insurance for all employees was established in 1981 with the "Federal Law on Accident Insurance". Employers and self-employed persons were given the opportunity to insure themselves under the same conditions as employees. Compulsory basic health insurance was introduced with the 1996 "Federal Law on Health Insurance" (KVG).

AHV

Efforts to introduce a federal old age- and invalidity-insurance system started after World War I. Until then, only a few cantons had provided proper insurance, with mostly voluntary admission or limited to civil servants. A membership offered by the Rentenanstalt (today Swiss Life) since 1894 in the "people's insurance" (Volksversicherung) was also voluntary. The post office through stamps initially handled the collection of premiums. At the end of the 19th century, company pension funds emerged, which were reserved for selected employee groups. For the majority of the population, old-age provision was, therefore, a private matter. With changes in the working world and the social structure of the family, the increase in mobility and the rising life expectancy, retirement provision became an almost unsolvable task for many people. In 1899, the provincial community assembly of Glarus approved a mandatory, cantonal old age- and invalidity-insurance system, which came into force in 1916. Appenzell Ausserrhoden and Basel-City followed in 1925.

The First World War also brought Switzerland food shortages, inflation, and unemployment, which led to significant social and political upheavals. When the national strike (Landesstreik) was declared in November 1918, a civil war could just barely be prevented. The political authorities were firmly in favour of the introduction of a 48-hour week and the expansion of the social security system, to overcome the socio-political tensions between the working class and the bourgeoisie. In 1919, the Federal Council presented to the Parliament a bill for a constitutional amendment, which should give the Federal Government the authority to introduce an old-age-, surviving dependents- and disability-insurance. The proposal was adopted in a popular vote in 1925 with a vast majority. A draft law was however rejected by the population in 1931. With its uniform premiums and minimum pension entitlements, it was not acceptable. In light of the global economic crisis, the financial viability of this social welfare act was also debated.

As in the case of the health- and accident insurance, the statutory regulation of the *AHV* failed in its first attempt. After a phase of stagnation, the project succeeded only after World War II. During the war years, the authorities and the population had been able to gain some experience with the "Wage compensation regulations for soldiers" introduced in 1939.

Billboard for Vote 1931. The bill was rejected by 60.3 % of the votes. A one-time pension of CHF 200.- per annum was foreseen, financed by wage contributions, alcohol- and tobacco taxes. A concurrent vote on tobacco taxes was narrowly rejected with 50.1 % No votes. Image: Poster design Karl Scherer, 1931, Swiss Social Archives, Sig. Sozarch_F_Pe-0246.

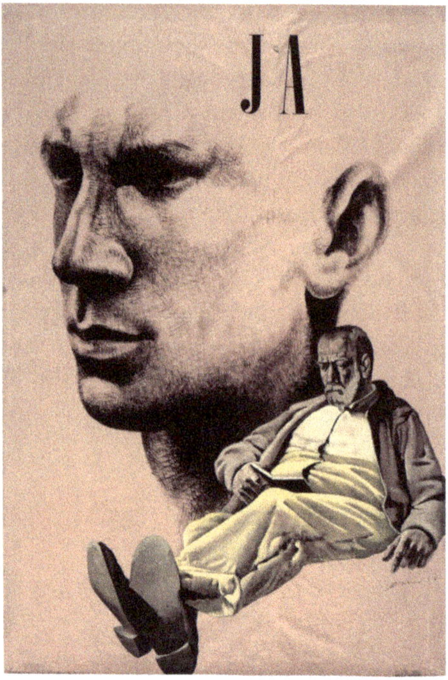

Billboard for Vote 1947. With an 80 % voter turnout, the bill was approved with 80 % Yes votes. The amount of the minimum pension was set at CHF 40.- and CHF 125.- for the maximum allowance. The premium rates have more than doubled since 1947. Image: Billboard design Hans Erni, 1947, Swiss Social Archives, Sig. Sozarch_F_Pe-0646.

This wage compensation plan was financed on the one hand by employers' and employees' contributions (2 % each) and on the other hand by subsidies from the Confederation, which had access to the finances of the cantons. The serving soldiers received the compensation through a cantonal or private compensation fund. A committee supported by trade unions and political parties submitted an initiative in 1942 with the aim of transferring this system into the AHV. An expert commission appointed by the Federal Council proposed the following points: progressive pensions, an obligatory pension scheme, a pension age of 65, funding by scaled salary percentage through an allocation process (Umlageverfahren), and the organisation by equalisation funds. Despite opposition from the entrepreneurs, the French-speaking federalists, and the Catholic conservatives, the plan was adopted in 1947 with an overwhelming majority and was put into force in 1948. In 1959, the "Federal Law on Invalidity Insurance" (IV) followed, which, in addition to pensions, also provided funds for the reintegration into the working world.

Until the end of the 20th century, the AHV and the IV were subject to numerous political initiatives and revisions, which addressed issues the pension age, the pension ceiling and their indexation, the premium rates and additional benefits. The social welfare system experienced rapid expansion, in particular through the efforts of Federal Councilor Hans Peter Tschudi (1913–2002, Member of the Federal Council from 1959–73).

The principle of three pillars

The eighth revision of the AHV in 1972 improved the position of married women in the AHV, and de facto secured the three-pillar principle in the revision of Article 34^{quater} FC. This concept built on a counterproposal by conservative politicians against an initiative of the left-wing parties, which wanted to introduce a people's pension based on the Scandinavian model. The three pillars of retirement and invalidity insurance should consist of the AHV (1st pillar), occupational retirement provisions (2nd pillar) and self-provision (3rd pillar). These three components should enable the elderly, disabled and surviving dependents to continue their usual lifestyle. The pension entitlements from the first and second pillar should correspond to 60 % of the last gross income for an unmarried person and 80 % for a married couple. In 1985, the second pillar became obligatory with the enactment of the "Federal Law on Occupational Pensions" (BVG). The 10th AHV revision of 1994 improved the position of the woman using rent splitting and by providing education and care credits. Self-sufficiency with the aid of the 3rd pillar has been favoured since 1985 by tax deductibility.

In a European comparison, the social insurance schemes in Switzerland were introduced quite late. However, this effect of referendum democracy on major national projects is not only detrimental. The slow build-up and diversification of the multi-financing system, together with the economic upturn, has led to a considerable improvement in the social welfare situation until the end of the 20th century, without the problem of uncontrollable dimensions of the sovereign debt, as in other countries.

* * * * *

Timeline of Legislation of Labour and social insurance law

1874	Constitutional basis for occupational health and safety protection
1877	Federal Act on Work in the Factories (Factory Law)
1881	Federal Act Concerning Liability arising from Factory Operations
1887	Extension of the Federal Act on Liability arising from Factory Operations
1890	Constitutional authority to create a health- and accident insurance
1900	Rejection of the first bill: Federal Act on health-and accident-insurance, including military insurance
1912	Adoption of the second proposal: Federal Act on Health-and Accident-Insurance (KUVG)
1913	The newly founded Federal Department of Social Insurance (BSV) starts its activities
1918	The KUVG is enacted
1918	The Swiss Accident Insurance Agency SUVA begins its operations
1925	Rejection of the Federal People's Initiative "For an old-age-, surviving dependents- and disability-insurance (AHV)"
1925	Adoption of the Federal Decree on Old Age, Surviving dependents ' and Disability Insurance
1993	Rejection of the Federal Act on Old Age and Surviving dependents' Insurance
1948	Federal Act on Old Age and Surviving dependents' Insurance (AHVG)
1959	Federal Act on Disability Insurance (IVG)
1976	Federal Decree on a New Approach to Unemployment Insurance
1983	Federal Act on Compulsory Unemployment Insurance and Insolvency Compensation
1985	Federal Act on Occupational Retirement Provision (BVG)
1996	Federal Law on Health Insurance (KVG)

* * * * *

11.3 Influence of the technological development on legislation

Impact on legal harmonisation

Industrialisation was the driving force in Switzerland for the initially cantonal and later national legal harmonisation in the core areas of private law. The improvement of the roads and the opening up of the country using railway lines enabled extended trade relations. The exchange of persons and goods accelerated and at the same time, costs were reduced. The fragmentation into cantonal legal spheres had increasingly retarding effects and hindered trade. The local commercial laws proved to be inefficient and inadequate in geographically extended trading areas. The need for consolidated national legislation in commercial law was immense.

Increase in regulatory tasks

The technological development starting with factory work and the railroad industry, not only shaped the form and content of the classical private law, but it also challenged the federal government and the cantons since the middle of the 19th century to take over new regulatory tasks. That resulted in an increasing level of government activity and a shift in the perception of the state. The Swiss state changed to a social welfare and regulatory state by the transfer of new authority and tasks. On the one hand, the state had to protect citizens from aberrations accompanying industrialisation and market economy, through work and factory legislation and the creation of social services and support for the provision for their lives. On the other hand, by creating the legal framework conditions, the state had to promote technical development and in the meantime mitigate its potential threats. The risks arising from railways, roads and hydropower plants demanded new norms in the penal code and liability laws. Besides, technical knowledge had to be protected by patent law from unauthorised access.

After World War II, the nation's widespread motorisation, public road construction, the boom in aviation, the construction of nuclear power plants and the introduction of electronic data processing and the Internet led to an accelerated standardisation activity by the Federal Government. Because of its complexity and its social significance, the regulation of these new technological advancements was considered as a primary federal task. The synchronised introduction of many new social services until the end of the 20th century led to an explosive expansion of federal law. To mitigate the negative aspects of technological development, environmental regulations, land use planning laws and data protection laws were developed, and the criminal code was supplemented with new sanctioning standards.

11.3.1 Railway legislation

The turmoil during the Sonderbund War delayed the construction of the first railway projects. Therefore, after 1847 railway lines were hurriedly erected in various parts of the country. In particular, the competition between the Swiss Central Railway (Centralbahn) and the Swiss North-East Railway (NOB), which was concentrated in eastern Switzerland, accelerated the railway construction. Until 1870, the main tracks were completed in central and western Switzerland. The alpine routes were also launched, and in 1882, the Gotthard railway was opened. By 1900, some 3,800 kilometres of railway lines were finished.

Framework of private railways

The construction and operation of the railroad tracks were initially in private hands. Therefore, individual lines were often planned and implemented without consultation, but rather in competition with each other. For the investors of private capital, considerations of return on investment were decisive. For this reason, lines with the possibility of high yields were first built, which were usually situated close to populated centres. The rural and alpine regions were neglected. Foreign investors initially funded most projects. The establishment of banks in Switzerland since the 1850s was motivated by the fact not to leave this business to international competition.

After the founding of the federal state, the parliament faced the issue of constructing a national railway network. In 1852, the National Council and the State Council voted against a Federal Railroad in favour of a structure for private railways. In the same year, the "Federal Law on the Construction and Operation of Railways in the Swiss Confederation" came into force. That left the cantons the right to issue a concession for the operation of railways but kept the supervisory power at the federal level using various methods.

Spanish Bread Railway, 1847. In 1847, the Swiss Nordbahn inaugurated the 25 km long railway line from Zurich to Baden, the first in Switzerland. By train, the journey took only 45 minutes. The train soon got the commonly known name Spanish-Bread-Railway. The "Spanish Bread" was a famous pastry made with much butter. The recipe originated in Northern Italy from the times when the Spaniards ruled. This delicacy was very popular with the Zurich upper class, but in the strictly protestant Zurich, it was not allowed to be made. It was only produced in Baden, the venue of the Tagsatzung, and since the train was used for the purchase of these pastries, it received this nickname. Image: Photography, Swiss Federal Institute of Technology, Bildarchiv, Sig. Ans_02230.

Therefore, the canton had to submit the concession to the Federal Government for approval, and the Federal Government was given the right to grant authorisation for tracks. The government was also responsible for defining the requirements on the technical standards. It could also require the concessionaires to cooperate in the planning of the tracks. As a further step, the government was conferred the right to essential services relating to the defence of the country. Thus, the concessionaires had to offer free of charge transport to the military post and militia personnel and to permit telegraph lines along the railway lines. The cantons were in charge of the details of the concessions. They granted temporary concessions with variable terms. To enable the concessionaires to acquire the land required for the construction of the tracks, they were given an expropriation right.

A distinctive feature of the Law of 1852 was the fact that it set the course toward a federal railway. Although it gave the cantons the responsibility for the railroads, it also reserved the right of repurchase of the installations by the Federal Government. After the expiry of fixed deadlines and against a fixed compensation to the investors, the government could take over the railway infrastructure.

Gotthard Railway, Express train, ca. 1910. The construction of the Gotthard railway line took from 1874 to 1882. With a length of 15 km, the tunnel was the longest in the world at the time. For the steam locomotives to be able to cope with the slope to the tunnel, the access ramps had to be built with many loops. In 1916, the Swiss Federal Railway's (SBB) Board of Directors decided to electrify the route to be less dependent on foreign coal supplies. The construction lasted until 1922. Because at the beginning not enough electric locomotives were available, they were only used for the mountain rides of passenger trains and were hooked-up in front of the steam locomotives. In 1960, SBB's last railway line was electrified. Image: After a postcard, Swiss Federal Institute of Technology, Sig. PK_004113.

The Franco-German War of 1870–71 revealed the shortcomings of the cantonal sovereignty on railroads: neither the economic supply of the country nor the redeployment of troops was guaranteed. Therefore, the second railway law of 1872 transferred the right to grant railway concessions from the cantons to the Federal Government. The government now controlled the concessionaires' planning and forced the obligation to transport private and public users. Thereby the lines between private and public law were blurred. Ironically, at the time of the enactment of this legislation, the Federal Government did not yet have any legislative power on railways; this was amended in 1874 with Article 26 aFC.

The railway crisis and Repurchase Law

At the end of the 1870s, railways in Switzerland tumbled into a severe crisis. Numerous railway companies were in financial difficulties, had to merge or went bankrupt. Since the Federal Government had a strategic interest in the construction of the Gotthard railway, it enabled the completion of this route with generous subsidies. Because of this precedent, the government also had to pay subsidies to the cantons in western and eastern Switzerland, so that they could construct their alpine routes at the Simplon and the Splügen. The Federal Government thus used the railway crisis to expand its influence in the railway sector. After having failed to get the main lines by initially acquiring them through free purchase, the Federal Council submitted a Repurchase law in 1897. The law authorised the Federal Council to repurchase the five most essential railway lines at the earliest date of repurchase, which amounted to nationalisation of those lines and its branch lines of totally 2,748 km of railway tracks. After a popular vote in 1898, the government acquired all five operating companies by 1909 and gradually transferred them to the Swiss Federal Railways (SBB), which had started operations in 1901. Until 1948, further railway companies were incorporated.

The railway crisis ended the phase of cautious restraint of the Federal Government on the issue of nationalisation of transport companies. From then on, a kind of automatism of the responsibility and the intervention of the central government developed, whenever the transport interests of the nation seemed to be at risk. With its first success in legal harmonisation, like the Labour Law of 1877, the Code of Obligations of 1881, and the Civil Code of 1912, the Federal Government had established a legitimate basis for the harmonisation or nationalisation of other fields of activity in the 20th century. At the same time, it was able to install itself as an institution that guaranteed a balance of interests in the federal system. By directing subsidies to railway companies in different regions of the country, it also accommodated regions, which initially had opposed the expansion of the central power.

The railway laws were a test and model case for the new, interventionist attitude of government by the federal bodies, and led to the transformation of existing and emerging new legal spheres.

Expropriation Law

The operating companies had to be allowed to expropriate private landowners, to ensure a favourable course of the railway tracks. Even the advance surveys of the terrain represented an interference with the title of the property. Since the 1830s, the admissibility and the form of the expropriation rights were addressed in the cantons, and first legal norms were established. The problem had initially arisen in road construction; in the canton of Zurich, the first Law of Cession (Abtretungsgesetz) of 1832 was an essential prerequisite to expedite road construction. The Federal Constitution of 1848 in Article 21 reserved the right of the Federal Government to establish public works or to support their establishment in the interests of the Swiss Confederation. For this purpose, it was authorised to assert the right of expropriation in return of full compensation. The property was therefore not protected in its existence, but only in its value. The constitutional regulations were confirmed in the Federal Expropriations Law of 1850, which also legitimised private persons to exercise the expropriation right. The law, which initially applied exclusively to railroad construction, quickly displaced cantonal expropriation rights in this field.

Right to concession

The right to concession, both the substantive principles and the procedure, was also exercised at the federal level in response to railway construction. Under the first Railway Law of 1852, the Federal Government only had the right to approval for cantonal concessions, and only with the second Railway Law, the authority of concessions was transferred to the central government in 1872. The concession had to strike a balance of the a priori not equal interests of the operating companies on the one hand with the interests of the public and the nation on the other.

Liability Law

Not only the construction and operation of the railways presented a potential hazard previously unknown, but also their use. Those who wanted to travel by rail had to "resign" and expose themselves to unfamiliar hazards. To protect the physical integrity of railroad users, liability rights, which until then had been based on Roman legal principles, needed to be reformed accordingly. The Federal Law on liability (1875) heavily influenced by the German Reichshaftpflichtgesetz (1871), extended the liability of the operating companies not only to their employees but to everybody involved in some sort. In case of personal injury and material damage, the operator could only be exonerated if he could prove force majeure or negligence on the part of the victim or a third party. The fault of the operating company was therefore assumed, and it had to absolve itself by a reversal of the burden of proof. The culpa liability (*Verschuldenshaftung*) was replaced by a hazard liability (*Gefährdungshaftung*). Hazard liability was applied in other areas as well, where the public was exposed to hazards arising from technology, such as in the Factory Law (1877), for the post office (Postal law 1905), for aviation (Aviation law 1948), for pipelines transporting gas and fuels (Pipeline law 1963) and nuclear power plants (Liability Law for Nuclear Power 1983). Since the end of the 19th century, the liability law developed in two ways: while the civil code kept the practice of culpa liability (Article 41 of the Code of Obligations), specific legislation introduced new liability principles to deal with the dangers of the technological development. To cope with the massive financial risks associated with these extensions of liability, operating companies insured themselves by concluding liability insurance after World War II; the risk was so passed on to insurance companies.

In railway law, several peculiarities of legal development in the technological context can be seen, some of which can also be found in the subsequent legal coverage of other technologies:

Absence of jurisprudence

The Railway Law was created in an interaction between politicians, economists, and technicians. For a long time, jurisprudence hardly dealt with this subject matter. Although the Railway Law developed simultaneously with the national codes of private law, university jurisprudence had only a minor share in its development. The academic guild devoted itself instead to the traditional, historically grown legal bodies of the civil and criminal law. Legal knowledge, therefore, became dependent on the technical expertise and international examples. *Technical-scientific experts* proclaimed regulations for this legal subject matter and not lawyers. The absence of jurisprudence still manifests itself today in the marginal presence of technology law in the area of legal academic education. It is also typical that research on the history of law has examined the history of the national codifications down to all its ramifications, but there exist only a few pioneering works on contemporary railway history.

Special Legislation

The new technological achievements and the related public works made new legal regulations necessary. These were primarily enacted as Special Legislation bypassing the comprehensive legal codes. This was not only the case for the railway but later also for electrical installations, road traffic and national roads, aviation and the use of the water and nuclear power. This ad-hoc approach was not only because of the lack of guidelines from the jurisprudence but also due to the singularity of the individual technical phenomena, their technical complexity, and their rapid development. Another reason was the fact that some technological achievements like nuclear power, were politically highly controversial, but at the same time of great economic importance. The regulations often had to be overhauled and enacted based on a superficial and rushed approval of international models. The time pressure to pass these rules meant that these legislative solutions could not be integrated into the traditional legal system and were not compatible with other legal fields. To harmonise the legal basis, at least an overall revision of the area of Liability Law was initiated in 1988.

International standardisation

To ensure that railway transport was connected beyond the borders of the country, it was essential to provide international standardisation, such as in the area of the track gauge or shipping laws. These were often specified at international congresses and conferences. In addition to railway conferences, there existed since the 1850s conferences on copyright law, patent law, postal and telegraph services and the electricity industry. Their resolutions were integrated into the national law. In the field of scientific law, the federal legal order was significantly influenced by international regulations. Bilateral and international agreements followed soon. Switzerland not only participated in the railway sector but also at an early stage in international agreements in the field of intellectual property law, postal-, telephone- and telegraph-services and provided the seat for global organisations.

11.3.2 Protection of intellectual property

Privilege System

With the industrialisation and mechanisation of the labour environment, the issue of the legal protection of inventions, brands, and models emerged. Given the increasing economic competition, the protection of intangible property became a critical competitive advantage. With the *privilege system*, specific legal protection existed already before the 19th century, just as with literary and artistic works. The printer or publisher (but not the author) of a book was granted a privilege by the decision of the local City Council or the Tagsatzung; the reprint of the work was therefore prohibited under penalty for third parties. In a mandate of 1531, the City Council of Basel already banned the book printers of the city from reprinting books from the competition. Several resolutions of the Tagsatzung dealt with privileges against the reproduction of musical compositions, psalms, and lexicons among others. Official brands, such as on textiles, regarding defined manufacturing rules were deemed as a seal of quality. St. Gallen and Appenzell disputed in the mid of the 16th century before the Tagsatzung on the use of the terms "cancer" and "scorpion" as a designation of origin on textiles. The inventor or manufacturer of a product was only granted a temporary monopoly position. There existed, however, no entitlement to obtain a privilege; this was an act of grace by the authority.

Helvetic Republic and cantonal law

During the Helvetic Republic, a patent law based on English and French standards was ratified in 1801. To improve the weak state finances, the administration was relying on the establishment of new companies and the promotion of modern technology. The textile industry, in particular, was confronted with stiff competition from England. After the Helvetic Republic, most cantons returned to the privilege system. Only a few cantons created regulations on copyright or designer protection. In 1835, Ticino enacted a law on the protection of copyright, the rules of which were applied in the same way as to the granting of patents. The Civil Code of Solothurn contained some brief regulations on "authors' rights", as well as on patents and trademark rights. Copyright regulations were also found in the Civil Codes of Grisons and Schaffhausen.

In the young federal state, trade relations intensified between the cantons and foreign countries. That led in 1856 to the establishment of an inter-cantonal "concordat on the protection of the literary and artistic property", in which initially only half of the cantons joined. The concordat was not encouraging: the level of protection provided was modest, and the regulations were ambiguous. In 1864, a copyright treaty was signed with France. Swiss producers pressed for an exclusion of the protection of inventions and models.

Further state treaties on copyright followed with Belgium (1867), Italy (1868), the North German Confederation and other German states (1869). This practice had disappointing results for Switzerland. The members of those cantons, which had not entered the concordat of 1856 were still not protected by copyright laws, in contrast to the foreigners living in Switzerland, who were protected by the bilateral state treaties. Representatives of interest groups - manufacturers, engineers, and publishers - were pushing for legislation on intellectual property for the whole of Switzerland, especially since they faced an increased American competition since the 1870s. They hoped for a substantial improvement of their competitiveness through a copyright law. Resistance against this plan emerged not only from the "usual" federalist forces, but also from several industry groups, which did not want to protect their production methods using public patents, but instead through factory secrecy. Liberals, in particular, opposed patent protection laws based on reasons of freedom of trade; for them, invention patents seemed to limit their free commercial activity unnecessarily.

First national laws

After two failed attempts in the years 1866 and 1872, the constitutional revision of 1874 passed the requirements for a federal copyright law. In 1887, the constitutional basis for the protection of patterns and models (both Art. 64 aFC) was established. A decisive factor for the approval in the first popular vote was the current, problematic situation of the Swiss industry during the economic crisis of 1873, and the second element was an effort to establish protection of inventions internationally. Swiss representatives had already participated in the patent congress in Vienna in 1873, which promulgated patent protection universally, and Switzerland was one of the first signatory states of the International Convention for the Protection of Industrial Property (1884, Paris Convention). The Federal Council wanted to reach agreements with the other European nations, which had issued similar laws. After the constitutional reforms, they swiftly took up the legislative work. In 1879, a Federal Law on the Protection of Factory Brands and Trade Marks was introduced, which envisioned trademark protection based on the Civil Code. The brand had to be registered with a public authority, which entered it into a directory and announced it officially. That meant that the legitimate applicant had the right to exclusive use. In contrast to the former privilege system, the Federal Law on the Copyright of Works of Literature and Art, which was ratified in 1883 following the German model, protected the author and the artist. Books and works of art were respected as their intellectual property. In 1888, a patent law and federal law on commercial patterns and models followed.

The Patent Law of 1888 only declared those inventions patentable, which could be exemplified by models. Chemical and pharmaceutical products, as well as foodstuff, were thereby excluded from patent protection, as a result of pressure from several interest groups. Representatives of foreign companies, on the other hand, protested, because Swiss firms could counterfeit their products without sanctions. In a constitutional revision (1905), Article 64 aFC was therefore amended; the requirement of the model illustration was abolished. The patent law was also revised in 1907 so that even chemical methods could now be patented.

Revisions

In the 20th century, patent protection frequently expanded. In 1954, it was extended to inventions for the production of foodstuffs and textile finishing, in 1978 to drugs and chemical substances. The second revision also amended the patent law to match the Patent Harmonisation Convention of 1963 and the European Patent Convention of 1973. In 1978, Switzerland joined the European Patent Office (based in Munich), since international patent protection became ever more critical. At the end of the 20th century given the development of gene technology, the question was raised as to whether seeds and genetically modified organisms should be patentable. To protect against the misuse of gene technology, a federal law on gene technology was issued in 2003. A change of the patent law in 2007 determined that the human body as such is not patentable. In 2010, the federal competence for the regulation of research on humans in the healthcare sector was confirmed, and in 2014, a Federal Law on Human Research came into force.

Other fields of the intellectual property law were also revised and developed in the 20th and early 21st century. In 1922, a new copyright law was issued which was wholly revamped in 1992 and has since been repeatedly amended. The Trademark law was recently changed by federal law on the protection of trademarks and origin (1992) and newly regulated by international conventions. Design rights were adjusted in 2001 by a design law. The protection is always limited in time and only applicable after entry into a corresponding directory.

11.3.3 The environmental protection legislation

Utilisation and pollution of nature

The Federal Constitution of 1848 did not identify any regulations on the protection of the environment since environmental pollution did not exist as a problem. The country was not yet densely populated, and technology and the railways just started. For lack of means of transportation, people's living and working places were not separated. Local regulations dealt with neighbouring rights, the fire police, and the waste and sewage systems. In agriculture, mainly human workforce was employed, and when available animals were used to pull heavy loads, non-farm animal feed and fertiliser were not known. As in the rural areas, cities were heated with wood and not yet with coal. Only after the construction of the railway network the import and distribution of black fuel started. By the end of the 19th century, coal had become the primary source of energy for individual heating, as well as for trade and industry, and consequently led to air pollution. From the 1880s onwards, electric power, which could be generated in the first hydroelectric power stations, was another source of energy. With the emerging motor vehicle traffic and aviation since the 1930's petroleum as the primary energy source gained in importance and with the commissioning of the first nuclear power station Beznau I in 1969 also nuclear power.

First federal legislation

The Federal Constitution of 1874 contained first, selective regulations for the conservation of nature. Article 24 (1) aFC assigned the superintendence of hydraulic engineering and forestry police in the high mountains to the Federal Government. This was exclusively for the sake of protecting humans against the natural forces and should be achieved by conserving the forestland. The implementation law of 1876 stipulated that forest owners be obliged to preserve the area of forestry and, in case of deforestation or natural forest damage, to reforest at the same location or to reforest the same amount of space elsewhere. In the constitutional revision of 1897, the restriction to the high mountains was omitted, and the Forestry Police Law of 1902 stipulated the preservation of forests for the whole of Switzerland. Art 25 aFC also authorised the Confederation to enact regulations on fishing and the protection of wildlife and birds. The "Federal Decree on the Participation of the Confederation in the Preservation and Acquisition of National Antiquities" in 1886 created the legal basis for activities of the Federal Government in the field of the preservation of monuments.

The expansion of hydropower energy production by public and private companies at the end of the 19th century led to an increased need for administrative regulation, which the Confederation satisfied with the Electricity Law of 1902 and the Water Economy Law of 1916. The latter required the operators of hydropower plants to preserve the "natural beauty" at the site.

Water Protection

The accelerated industrialisation and urbanisation in the first half of the 20th century led to massive pollution of the waters. Industrial and private sewage were channeled into the lakes and rivers. Due to high-yield production methods in agriculture, they were additionally polluted and over-fertilised. After initial cantonal efforts of protection, the Confederation was entrusted with the right to regulate the protection of water. However, the implementation of the measures envisioned in the Water Protection Law of 1957 was delayed as they were placed at the discretion of the cantons, which were often short of professional expertise and financial resources. Especially the construction of water treatment plants made only slow progress. To ensure that the law would not end a dead letter, a revision in 1971 set a deadline for the municipalities of ten years for the implementation of water purification measures, and subsidies were boosted. The economic boom in the 1970s promoted the generous subsidisation of sewage plant construction by federal and cantonal authorities. A second revision of the 1991 Water Protection Law further reinforced the importance of environmental protection in this area.

Increasing ecological impact

Since the middle of the 20th century, a gradually more compact set of regulations for the protection of the environment was enacted at the federal and cantonal level. Increasing prosperity created environmental problems, but it also facilitated the implementation of protective measures. Instead of merely sectorial protection against dangers to humans and nature, efforts were now being made to provide a more general precaution and planning. The Federal Government and the cantons responded to the fast-rising environmental impact of industry, as well as the effects of private and public transport. The motorisation of the population, a cyclical strong economic growth, and the lifestyle and leisure habits of the consumer society led to the destruction of the landscape by roads, residential and commercial buildings and soil and air pollution, soaring energy consumption, and excessive noise pollution. The remaining agricultural land was subjected to a highly intensive farming utilisation. The broad population was focused on environmental protection through apparent signs of the disruption of the natural habitat (dying fish, dying forest and ozone exposure).

Land use planning right

Various cantons had been enacting laws for the construction of streets and residential quarters in urban settlements since the second half of the 19th century, and these rules also contained rudimentary planning regulations. The Building Regulations of Basel-City (1918) left an inner city zone and divided the remaining urban area into three residential zones and one industrial zone. In rural areas, however, private construction activity took place for a long time without public planning. The cantons issued more comprehensive planning and construction laws in the 1960s, to curb the fast increasing urban sprawl of the landscape. With these laws, municipalities were forced to define specific zones for building activity. However, the separation in construction and non-construction zones was not strictly designated, and in many places, non-agricultural buildings could be constructed outside the planned construction zones.

Several cantonal and federal people's initiatives had attempted to curb land speculation. Although they were rejected, they helped to accelerate the legislative efforts at the federal level. The *National Road Article* (Article 36bis aFC), adopted in 1958, forced the Federal Government and the cantons to protect the economically usable land during the construction of highways "as much as possible". The *Nature and Cultural Heritage Protection* Article of 1962 (article $24^{sexties}$ aFC) prompted the Confederation "to preserve the native land- and townscape, historical sites and natural and artistic monuments for the sake of public interest". The protection of natural and cultural heritage sites was kept under cantonal authority. The *Land Rights Article* (Articles 22ter and 22^{quater} aFC), adopted in 1969, handed the federal government the authority to approve property restrictions within its constitutional powers and to issue general principles for the cantonal planning of land use. In 1972, a federal act forced the cantons to define zones for protected scenery and recreation. The Land Use Planning Law of 1979 confirmed the separation of zones for construction and non-construction, already designated for in the revised Water Protection Law of 1971. In agricultural zones, only buildings could be erected for the agricultural use of the land or housing needs of the peasant population. The scattered construction method (Streubauweise) should be prevented from spreading in the hope of stopping the urban sprawl of the rural areas. Due to the obligation to draw up master plans, the cantons were encouraged to coordinate "spatially relevant activities" with the stakeholders involved and to define their interpretations on the spatial development of the cantonal area. Cantonal utilisation plans should specify the permissible use of the land. However, the population pressure still led to strong growth of the settlement areas, despite the land use planning laws. To limit this development, the citizens' initiative "Stop to the endless construction of second homes" was adopted in 2005. In 2013, the population also agreed to an amendment to the land use planning law, that should promote the so-called "dense construction", and cantons with over-dimensioned construction zones were forced to repeal zoning areas.

Environmental Protection Law

Shortly after the land-use planning article, the environmental clause (Article $24^{septies}$ aFC) was also ratified in 1971. That authorised the Federal Government to declare by public law, regulations on the protection of humans and their environment against harmful or annoying impacts. Combating *air pollution* and *noise* was the primary focus, but measures against radiation, odours, and vibrations were also implemented. The constitutional article also stated the authority of the Confederation to enact the implementation of the legislation. In contrast to the land use planning law, it was not only authorised to legislate in principle but was also able to regulate the details needed to fulfil the constitutional mandate.

The implementation of the measures should be divided between the Federal Government and the cantons, depending on the actual matter.

The approval of the implementation legislation was again delayed. The oil crisis of 1973 led to an economic downturn; the following recession pushed the environmental protection ideas into the background. Similarly, environmental protection as "cross-sector competences" did not appear to be easy to implement within the framework of the increasing legal and administrative structures. The Environmental Protection Law, adopted in 1983, covered noise protection, air pollution control, radiation protection, waste, soil protection and an environmental impact assessment for polluting plants and installations. Based on this law, which was revised and improved in 1995, some more sensible regulations (including the Ordinance on Air Pollution Control 1985, Noise Protection Ordinance 1986, Ordinance on the Environmental Impact Assessment 1988, Radiation Protection Ordinance 1994) were adopted. Since the 1990s, various other environmental legislation has also been revised. With the Forest Law of 1993, the old Forestry Police Law of 1902 was adjusted to the newly developed environmental protection laws. At the same time, Switzerland's cooperation to solve environmental problems intensified on an international level.

11.3.4 Computer science and data protection law

Computer Science

Computers had been used in Switzerland from the beginning of the 1960s, initially in companies that needed to process a significant amount of data, such as in banks and insurance companies, at the post office and Swiss Railways (SBB). They soon made their way nationwide into enterprises and the public administration and contributed actively to improve efficiency. In the 1980s, the Personal Computer (PC) replaced the electronic typewriter. What initially seemed to be a toy for technology enthusiasts was soon to become a standard commodity in the broad population. The Internet boom reached Switzerland in 1995. The Internet enabled not only private and professional communication via PC, but also a cost-effective and straightforward acquisition of information. A few years later the mobile phone made communication and information gathering from anywhere possible. After the engines, railways, and cars, Switzerland experienced another technological revolution around the turn of the 21st century. That changed not only the working environment and the recreational activities of the people but also their relationship to the state and their position as consumers.

Information Technology Legislation

Numerous new legal questions have arisen and still arise concerning information technology: How can a contract be concluded and a service paid on the Internet? What kind of liability is asked for if false information is given on a homepage? How do electronically gathered data need to be archived? To what extent does copyright exist for texts, images, films and music downloaded from the Internet? How to design licenses for commercial software? How can individuals defend themselves against infringement of personality rights on the Internet? Similar to the case of railway laws in the nineteenth century, a qualified answer to these legal questions requires a more in-depth knowledge of the technical subject matter. As a young branch on the tree of jurisprudence, information technology law is an expert matter and occupies a marginal position in legal education. Likewise, as with other legal spheres arising in the wake of technological development, it is a cross-sectional discipline that involves different established legal subject matters. Some of the new legal questions can be addressed with existing legal norms, such as private or public law. For other issues, existing statutes had to be supplemented (revision of the copyright law in 2007 or the introduction of facts of the case of computer delinquency in the penal code in 1995). In some areas, new regulations were necessary (the Federal Law on certification services for electronic signatures of 2003 or the control on electronic authentication in 2011). Finally, international law has usually a considerable influence. Various guidelines of the European Union are relevant, but also the International Agreement on Cyber Criminality ratified by Switzerland in 2001.

Right to privacy and protection of data

The development of information technology facilitates not only communication and information between citizens but also the corporate world and the state. Despite the advantages, there likewise exist massive dangers. Companies are trying to improve their marketing activities by using data of individual Internet users to snoop out their consumer habits. As the global surveillance scandal of the year 2013 brought to light, states such as the USA, Great Britain, and China as well as France and Germany spy unscrupulously on their own and foreign citizens. Such actions are justified with reference to the fight against terrorism and other crimes, and sometimes to raise tax morale. Through the – in theory - voluntary, but merely unavoidable use of the Internet, a private person becomes a "transparent citizen". The new technologies allow the State to access the data of citizens, as has never been the case in history before.

Thanks to federalism and the traditionally high status of privacy in Switzerland, the surveillance state is still less thriving than in other countries. The Federal Supreme Court recognised the right to privacy in 1976 as part of the then yet unwritten fundamental right to personal liberty. With the revision of the Federal Constitution, it was adopted separately in Article 13 FC and therefore enhanced in value as an independent fundamental right. According to Article 13 par. 2 FC, each person has the right to protection against abusive data processing. Articles 27 et seq. of the Civil Code form the basis for the protection of the personality under civil law. The protection of the personality has been substantiated by the Federal Law on Data Protection adopted in 1992, both by constitutional law as well as by civil law. The preliminary preparations on this bill began already in the mid-1970s. The political authorities and the population were frightened at the time by the scandal surrounding the private databank, which Ernst Cincera (1928–2004), the "hunter of subversives" and later National Councillor of Zurich had created on "left-wing" politicians and private individuals. In 1989 it became also publicly known that the Swiss agency for state protection had created 900,000 observation cards on individuals without a legal basis; this "Fishenäffare" became the critical incident in the history of Swiss data protection.

Regarding its content, the Data Protection Law was influenced by the Data Protection Law of the German Federal State Hessen adopted in 1970, which was the first data protection law in the world, but also by the Data Protection Convention 1981 of the European Council. The Data Protection Law protects data relating to individuals or identifiable persons. It applies to the processing of data by private persons and by federal bodies. The latter have to provide information about collected data not only on demand but also need to inform the affected persons on their own. Moreover, cantonal data protection laws regulate data processing by cantonal authorities. The 2008 data protection law was supplemented by substantial special legislation and by standards of data protection at the European and international level. In 2016, the people adopted a revision of the Federal Law on the Intelligence Service, in which the Data Protection Law - with strict conditions - was slightly relaxed. With the review, the Federal Intelligence Service received information acquisition and monitoring rights as well as monitoring tools in order to combat terrorism.

However, the best data protection law is of no avail if the users of the modern means of communication ignore recommended protective measures. Many people are very lax in dealing with the Internet and provide more or less intended information about them. Especially for young people, the permanently available entertainment of PCs and smartphones may just be too tempting.

* * * * *

Federal legislation relating to technological development

1852	Railways Law I, Federal authorisation requirement for Cantonal Railway Concessions
1872	Railways Law II, Transfer of authority for railway concessions to the Confederation
1875	Liability Law, Culpa Liability of operators of concessionary enterprises of the Confederation
1876	Federal Law on the Protection of the Forest Inventory, Implementation Law of Art. 24 (1) aFC
1877	Factory Law, Protection of the public from hazards due to the operation of factories
1879	Factory and trademark protection Law, Protection of private trademarks
1883	Federal Law on copyright protection of works of literature and art, Protection of the intellectual property of authors and artists
1888	Patent Law, Protection of Technical Inventions
1888	Federal Law on the protection of industrial designs, Protection of patterns and models
1902	Forestry Police Law, Statute of the forest conservation requirement for the whole of Switzerland
1902	Electricity Law, Regulating energy generation by hydropower
1905	Postal Law, Protection of the public from hazards by the post office
1916	Water management Law, Use of hydropower
1948	Aviation Law, Airspace, aircraft and personnel as well as legal relationships arising from operations in aviation
1957	Water Protection Law, a comprehensive legal basis for measures against water pollution
1963	Pipeline Law, Construction, and maintenance of pipelines
1979	Land Use Planning Law, Economic use of the land and coordination of relevant activities in land utilisation
1983	Nuclear Energy Liability Law, Liability for nuclear hazards in nuclear installations or through the transport of nuclear materials
1983	Environmental Protection Law, Protecting animals and plants, their communities and habitats against damaging impacts
1993	Forest law, Protection of forest inventory

* * * * *

Bibliography

Monographs

AUBERT JEAN FRANÇOIS, Petite histoire constitutionelle de la Suisse, 3. ed. Berne 1979

BEER ELLEN J. et al. (ed.), Berns grosse Zeit. Das 15. Jahrhundert neu entdeckt, Berne 1999

BISCHOFBERGER HERMANN, Rechtsarchäologie und Rechtliche Volkskunde des eidgenössischen Standes Appenzell Innerrhoden, vols. I und II, Appenzell 1999

BLUMER JOHANN JAKOB, Staats- und Rechtsgeschichte der schweizerischen Demokratien, vols. I und II, St. Gallen 1850–1858

BLUNTSCHLI JOHANN CASPAR, Staats- und Rechtsgeschichte der Stadt und Landschaft Zürich, 2. ed. Zurich 1856

CARLEN LOUIS, Rechtsgeschichte der Schweiz. Eine Einführung, 3. ed. Berne 1988

CARONI PIO, „Privatrecht". Eine sozialhistorische Einführung, Basel/Frankfurt on the Main 1988

COING HELMUT (ed.), Handbuch der Quellen und Literatur der neueren europäischen Privatrechtsgeschichte, vols. I–III/5, Munich 1973–1988

CONRAD HERMANN, Deutsche Rechtsgeschichte, vols. I und II, 2. ed. Karlsruhe 1962–1966

ELSENER FERDINAND, Die Schweizer Rechtsschulen vom 16. bis 19. Jh., Zurich 1975

FASEL URS, Bahnbrecher Munzinger, Gesetzgeber und Führer der katholischen Reformbewegung (1830–1873), Berne 2003

FASEL URS, Eugen Hubers Vorlesungen, Berne 2014

FELLER RICHARD, Geschichte Berns, vols. I–IV, Berne 1946–1960

GSCHWEND LUKAS/KRAMER GEORG, Gerichtshoheit und Landesherrschaft. Die Entwicklung der Gerichtshoheit in Churrätien unter besonderer Berücksichtigung der Verhältnisse in der Grafschaft Werdenberg, in: Werdenberger Jahrbuch 19 (2006), pp. 9–28

HAGEMANN HANS-RUDOLF, Basler Rechtsleben im Mittelalter, Basel/ Frankfurt on the Main 1981–1987

HELBLING HANNO et al. (ed.), Handbuch der Schweizer Geschichte, vols. I und II, 2. ed. Zurich 1980

Heusler Andreas, Schweizerische Verfassungsgeschichte, Basel 1920

His Eduard, Geschichte des neueren schweizerischen Staatsrechts, vols. I–III, Basel 1920–1938

Historischer Verein der fünf Orte (ed.), Innerschweiz und frühe Eidgenossenschaft, vols. I und II, Olten 1990

Holenstein André (ed.), Berns mächtige Zeit. Das 16. und 17. Jahrhundert neu entdeckt, Berne 2006

Huber Eugen, System und Geschichte des schweizerischen Privatrechts, vols. I–IV, Basel 1886–1893

Im Hof Ulrich et al. (ed.), Geschichte der Schweiz und der Schweizer, 3. ed. Basel 2004

Kley Andreas, Verfassungsgeschichte der Neuzeit. Grossbritannien, die USA, Frankreich und die Schweiz, Berne 2004

Kölz Alfred, Neuere schweizerische Verfassungsgeschichte, vols. I und II, Zurich 1992–2004; idem, Quellenbuch zur neueren schweizerischen Verfassungsgeschichte, vols. I und II, Zurich 1992–1996

Kraus Dieter, Schweizerisches Staatskirchenrecht, Tübingen 1993

Landolt Niklaus, Untertanenrevolten und Widerstand auf der Basler Landschaft im 16. und 17. Jahrhundert, Liestal 1996

Meder Stefan, Rechtsgeschichte. Eine Einführung, 2. ed. Cologne/Weimar/Vienna 2005

Pahud de Mortanges René/Prêtre Alain, Anwaltsgeschichte der Schweiz, Zurich 1998

Peyer Hans Conrad, Verfassungsgeschichte der alten Schweiz, Zurich 1978

Pfenniger Heinrich, Das Strafrecht der Schweiz, Berlin 1890

Pfister Rudolf, Kirchengeschichte der Schweiz, vols. I–III, Zurich 1964 -1984

Pieth Friedrich, Bündnergeschichte, Chur 1945

Poudret Jean-François, Coutumes et coutumiers, vols. I-VI, Zurich 1998–2006

Rappard William E., Die Bundesverfassung der schweizerischen Eidgenossenschaft 1848–1948, Zurich 1948

Rennefahrt Hermann, Grundzüge der bernischen Rechtsgeschichte; vols.I-IV, Berne 1928–1936

Schlosser, Hans, Grundzüge der Neueren Privatrechtsgeschichte, 10. ed. Heidelberg 2005

Schmidt, Eberhardt, Einführung in die Geschichte der deutschen Strafrechtspflege, 3. ed. Göttingen 1995

SCHOTT CLAUSDIETER, Trauung und Jawort. Von der Brautübergabe zur Ziviltrauung, 2. ed. Frankfurt on the Main 1992

SCHWINGES RAINER C. (ed.), Berns mutige Zeit. Das 13. und 14. Jahrhundert neu entdeckt, Berne 2003

SEGESSER VON PHILIPP ANTON, Rechtsgeschichte der Stadt und Republik Luzern, vols. I-IV, Lucerne 1850–1858

SENN MARCEL, Rechtsgeschichte - ein kulturhistorischer Grundriss, 3. ed. Zurich 2003

SENN MARCEL/GSCHWEND LUKAS, Rechtsgeschichte II – Juristische Zeitgeschichte, 2.ed. Zurich 2004

SENN MARCEL/GSCHWEND LUKAS/PAHUD DE MORTANGES RENÉ, Rechtsgeschichte auf kulturgeschichtlicher Grundlage, 2. ed. Zurich 2007

SIFFERT, RINO, Verlobung und Trauung. Die geschichtliche Entwicklung des schweizerischen Eheschliessungsrechts, Zurich 2004

STETTLER BERNHARD, Die Eidgenossenschaft im 15. Jahrhundert, Zurich 2004

STOOSS CARL, Die Grundzüge des schweizerischen Strafrechts im Auftrage des Bundesrates vergleichend dargestellt, vols. I und II, Basel/Geneva 1892–1893

THORMANN PHILIPP/VON OVERBECK ALFRED, Das schweizerische Strafgesetzbuch, vols. I–III, Zurich 1940–1943

VISCHER LUKAS/SCHENKER LUKAS/DELLSPERGER RUDOLF (ed.), Ökumenische Kirchengeschichte der Schweiz, Freiburg/Basel 1994

WESEL UWE, Geschichte des Rechts. Von den Frühformen bis zum Vertrag von Maastricht, 3. ed. Munich 2006

WIEACKER FRANZ, Privatrechtsgeschichte der Neuzeit, 2. ed. Göttingen 1967

Reference works

STIFTUNG HISTORISCHES LEXIKON DER SCHWEIZ (ed.), Historisches Lexikon der Schweiz (HLS), Basel 2002 ff.

ERLER ADALBERT/KAUFMANN EKKEHARD (ed.), Handwörterbuch zur Deutschen Rechtsgeschichte (HRG), 5 vols. Berlin 1971–1988

CORDES ALBRECHT/LÜCK HEINER/WERKMÜLLER DIETER (ed.), Handwörterbuch zur Deutschen Rechtsgeschichte (HRG), vol. 1 ff., 2. ed. Berlin 2004 ff.

www.ingramcontent.com/pod-product-compliance
Ingram Content Group UK Ltd.
Pitfield, Milton Keynes, MK11 3LW, UK
UKHW021829100926
8556IPUK00004B/234

9 783631 792094